St Michael®

Exploring the
British Countryside

David Bellamy

St Michael®

Exploring the British Countryside

David Bellamy

ACKNOWLEDGEMENTS

Photographs
All photographs other than those listed below: Peter
Loughran – Newnes Books.
Page 11 Judy Todd; 44 Wildlife Studies Ltd; 47
Robin Fletcher – Bob Gibbons Photography; 68
Owen Newman – Nature Photographers; 79 top
Frank V. Blackburn – Nature Photographers; 90
Roger Tidman – Nature Photographers; 109 Frank
V. Blackburn – Nature Photographers; 173 Wildlife
Studios Ltd; 186–187 Nigel Holmes; 202 Richard
Mearns – Nature Photographers;

Artwork
Pages 32 Roger Gorringe – R. P. Gossop; 36 Martin
Camm – Linden Artists; 37 John Michael Davis; 59,
63, 66 Ian Garrard; 76 Roger Gorringe; 87, 99
Charles Stitt; 138 Arthur Singer; 140 Ken Oliver;
156–157, 163 John Michael Davis; 172 Keith Linsell;
211 John Michael Davis; 221, 222, 223 James
Nicholls; 231 Tudor Art

Map on page 9 by Clyde Surveys Limited,
Maidenhead

Map on page 10 reproduced from the 1983 Ordnance Survey
1:50,000 Lake District Tourist Map with the permission
of the Controller of Her Majesty's Stationery Office,
Crown copyright reserved.

Published in 1985 for
Marks and Spencer p.l.c., Baker Street,
London
by Newnes Books,
a Division of The Hamlyn Publishing
Group Limited
84–88 The Centre, Feltham, Middlesex.

Some of the sections were originally published in
Discovering the Countryside with David Bellamy.

ISBN 0 600 35869 0

Printed in Italy

Introduction

I AM OFTEN ASKED, 'Which is my favourite country?' and the answer is always the same, an emphatic, 'Britain!'

The reasons I give are three. One, it is one of the most diverse places on earth. Oh, I know it isn't very big and I know it has a very limited flora and fauna, but a short journey can take you across a fascinating range of geology, vegetation and land-use history, and all that makes for diversity. Two, it is a country well supplied with maps, roads, tracks, hotels, youth hostels and caravan and camping sites, so it is easy to get to any location. Three, it has and has had more -ologists (geologists, biologists, entomologists, ornithologists, ecologists, etc. etc.) per acre than any other place on earth, and so a lot is known about our countryside.

I must also confess that it has more than its fair share of floras, faunas and field guides, so you might ask, 'Why another?' Well, most of them deal with single groups of plants and animals or single special localities full of rarities of one sort and another. This book deals with the whole cross-section from the soil to the tree tops and beyond. What is more, it deals with the common abundant things, the things you can see on an ordinary afternoon's walk, in an ordinary bit of countryside not too far from your home.

I bet that as you read it you will be amazed at all you have missed or have taken for granted in the past without giving them a second thought. There is no getting away from the fact that the best way of finding out 'about' the countryside is to take a walk with the local expert. So that is exactly what we have done; taken experts on their own favourite walks and let them share their secrets and tricks of the natural history trade with a cameraman and you.

Did you know that chopping the tops of certain types of trees at intervals of between 10 and 20 years can extend their natural lifespan many fold? What is more, such coppice management helps provide one of the most exciting habitats for our wildlife.

Did you know that Six-spot Burnet Moths fly by day and that Bumble Bees can carry more than 60 per cent of their own weight of pollen; that Police-man's Helmets were introduced from the Himalayas and now grow in profusion by some of our rivers; or that Small Copper butterflies like to have their lunch in sunny hollows in sand dunes? There they feed on Ragwort and can, in a good summer, produce three generations of adult butterflies.

Did you know how to tell whether a Hazel nut has been eaten by a Wood Mouse, a Bank Vole or a Grey Squirrel; how to identify the Blue Moor Grass, or an oligotrophic lake; the difference between a ripple and a riffle by its Ranunculus; or distinguish between the four species of Limpet which make their homes on our sea shores?

If you don't know the answers, then read on, find out, and then put your new found knowledge to good use on your local woodland, grassland, waterside or seaside walk. Use the list of locations to plan special walks at weekends and on your holidays, and as you walk through this fabulous countryside of ours, think on these things.

Since the last war the British Isles has lost 95 per cent of its old meadows rich in flowers, insects and grasses; 80 per cent of its chalk grassland; 50 per cent of its woodland; and 50 per cent of its lowland heath, all important habitats for wild flowers and wildlife. These are not pie in the sky statistics but facts and figures from the Nature Conservancy Council itself.

Something must be done now to turn this tide of destruction and to put our countryside back into good heart. The best way to accomplish this is to have a large body of informed people tramping our highways and byways with their eyes and their minds open and active. Yes, you are the eyes and the ears of conservation, and you are the only voices that can speak up on behalf of both the plants and animals.

If you have read this far and you are not already a member of your County Conservation Trust, you should be ashamed of yourself. If you are young and active, then, of course, you will be a member of WATCH and the British Trust for Conservation Volunteers. Bird lovers have the R.S.P.B., and Wildfowl Trust; woodland walkers, the Woodland Trust and Forestry Commission; seaside walkers, the Marine Conservation Society; countryside walkers, the National Trust, the Council for the Protection of Rural England or Wales, the Countryside Commission and many, many more.

Please don't shirk your responsibility. If you want any more information, send a stamped addressed envelope to The Conservation Foundation, 11A West Halkin Street, London SW1X 8JL stating your interests and queries and I will do my best to help.

Thank you for caring, and carry on walking with an ever open mind.

Out for the day

A WALK IN THE COUNTRYSIDE is recognised as one of the most popular weekend and holiday pursuits in Britain. But whether you are an enthusiastic walker or are simply looking for a pleasant stretch of country to take the family for a picnic, there is always the same tantalising question: where shall we go? The choice would appear to be greater than it has ever been with quick and easy access to large areas of Britain but in reality the situation is more complex. Most of the countryside is privately owned which means that public access is limited. A farmer would no more appreciate you picnicking in one of his carefully nurtured fields than you would if a stranger suddenly turned up and set up camp in your front garden. Fortunately, rural Britain is criss-crossed by an intricate network of public footpaths and rights of way which enable walkers to explore most of the countryside to the full. It has been estimated that the footpaths in England and Wales add up to a total length of more than 120,000 miles. In Scotland the situation is slightly different but in practice access is even greater. In addition to

these rights of way there are areas of the countryside where the public has more general access. For example, country parks established by county councils, as well as many National Trust properties and Forestry Commission parks.

How do you find out where these rights of way are? For somebody who is likely to go walking more than once or twice a year an Ordnance Survey map is an essential companion to any walk. These maps will show you all you need to know. The most popular walkers maps are the Landranger Series (1:50,000) with a scale of mapping which represents approximately $1\frac{1}{4}$ inches (3 cm) to every mile (1.5 km). These show public footpaths as single red dotted lines and bridle ways as single red broken lines. The more detailed Pathfinder Series (1:25,000) has a scale of approximately $2\frac{1}{2}$ inches (6 cm) to every mile (1.5 km) and includes more information such as woodland types and field boundaries.

Any member of the public can walk along a public footpath and dogs can be taken if they are

NATIONAL PARKS

Some of the most popular areas for walking in Britain are the ten national parks. These are areas which have special planning controls covering all types of development. They are parks as such but the administrations which govern them are advised by the Countryside Commission and, therefore,

recreational land use is given a higher priority than in some other regions. Because of the scenic beauty of many of the parks, large areas are often owned by bodies such as the National Trust. However, normal farming practices are generally carried out in these areas and walkers should respect the rights of the farmers and other landowners.

Brecon Beacons (Parc Cenedlaethol Bannau Brycheinog)
It is an upland area of flat-topped mountains, lush valleys and moorland covering 1344 square kilometres of South Wales. The majority of the upland is grazed by sheep and in some areas herds of wild ponies may be seen. Information centres include: Abergavenny, Brecon and Llandovery.

Dartmoor
This last great wilderness of Southern Britain covers 945 square kilometres of Devon. Within its boundaries lie three national nature reserves and two forest nature reserves. The best-known and most interesting forest reserve is Wistman's Wood. The park is very wild in places and has many quaking mires and tussock bogs. The northern part is a military training area. Information centres include: Exeter, Newton Abbot, Okehampton and Plymouth.

Exmoor
Exmoor is England's smallest National Park at 686 square kilometres comprising mostly high heather moorland cut by deep combes. Its northern boundary is the coastal cliffs which face the Bristol Channel. The moorland supports herds of red deer. Information centres include: Minehead, Lynmouth, Lynton and Combe Martin.

Lake District
The largest (2248 square kilometres) and most famous of our National Parks. Its habitats range from coastal sand dunes, and upland moor to England's highest mountains and largest natural lakes. On the fells are found red deer and rare mountain plants such as alpine lady's mantle and alpine saxifrage. The forest museum at Grizedale introduces the visitor to the area's woodland wildlife. Information centres include: Ambleside, Keswick and Broughton in Furness.

North York Moors
Encloses an area of 1432 square kilometres. At its heart is the largest area of heather moor in the country. Around this are rolling limestone dales noted for their rich flora and fauna. Along the North Sea coast runs the Cleveland Way which takes in the whole of the park's coastline. Information centres include: Middlesborough, Northallerton, Saltburn and Whitby.

Northumberland
The Northumberland National Park covers the bleak open country of the Cheviot Hills in the north, the heathland at the Simonside Hills and the valleys ofRedesdale and North Tyne in the South. Its single nature reserve contains one of Britain's best examples of blanket bog. The whole area is being rapidly afforested with conifers. Information centres include: Newcastle-upon-Tyne, Otterburn, Rothbury and Hexham.

Peak District
Covers an area of 1400 square kilometres of pastured hills, broad valleys, moorland and wooded dales. The southern limestone region is known as the 'White Peak', the northern Gritstone region the 'Dark Peak'. It is the most visited of our National Parks and most densely populated. Information centres include: Bakewell, Buxton, Ashbourne, Manchester and Sheffield.

Pembrokeshire Coast (Parc Cenedlaethol Penfro)
The smallest of all our National Parks at 583 square kilometres. Its primary asset is the 272 km cliff line some of the finest in Europe. Here lies the nature reserve of Skomer Island supporting puffins, razorbills, and manx shearwaters. On Romsey Island is a breeding colony of grey seals, and Grassholm Island is a RSPB reserve. Information centres include: Pembroke, Fishguard, Tenby, St. David's and Milford Haven.

Snowdonia (Parc Cenedlaethol Eryri)
Encloses 2171 square kilometres of North Wales. Habitats range from sand dunes and marsh on the coast to moorland and mountains inland. In its several upland nature reserves arctic and alpine plants can be found including the early-flowering purple saxifrage. Fine examples of native ash and oak woods are found at Coed Camlyn and the Vale of Ffestiniog among others. Information centres include: Bangor, Machynlleth, Caernarvon and Conway.

Yorkshire Dales
Comprises 1761 square kilometres of high fells, moorland and lush green dales. The moorland varies from thin vegetation in the south to tussocky highland in the central and northern area of the park. There are two nature reserves at Ling Gill and Colt Park and the famous limestone pavement above Malham Cove. Information centres include: Harrogate, Ilkley, Skipton and Richmond.

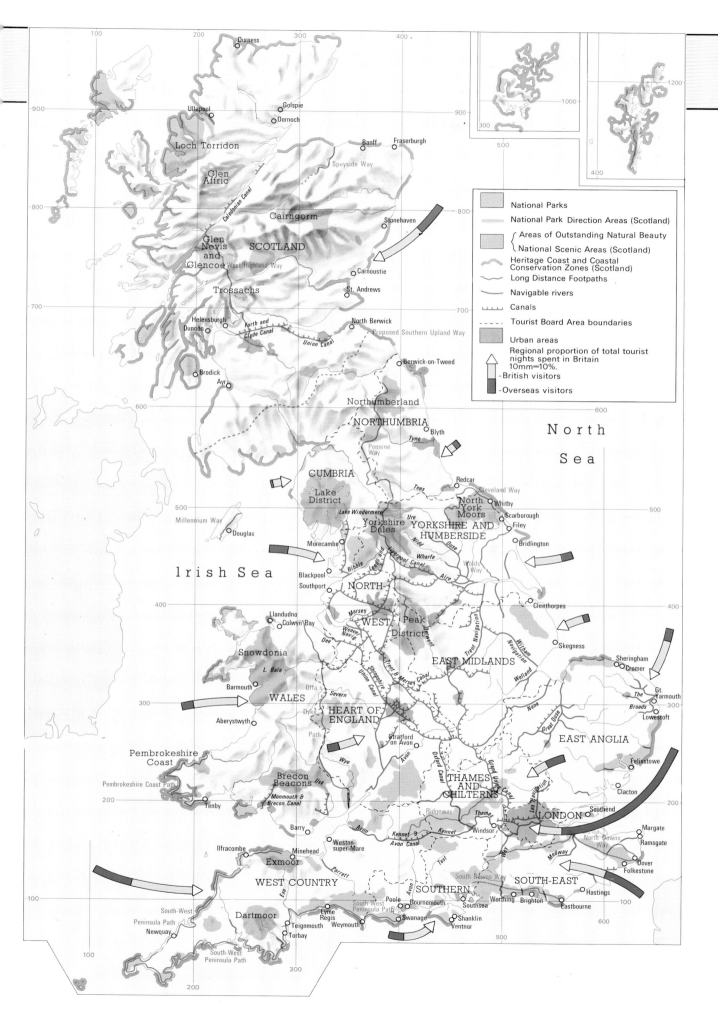

Durness

Ullapool

Golspie
Dornoch

Loch Torridon

Banff   Fraserburgh

Glen
Affric   Speyside Way

Cairngorm

Glen
Nevis
and   SCOTLAND
Glencoe   West Highland Way   Stonehaven

Carnoustie

Trossachs   St. Andrews

Helensburgh   Forth and   North Berwick
Dunoon   Clyde Canal
                  Union Canal   Proposed Southern Upland Way

Brodick   Berwick-on-Tweed
   Ayr
                                     Northumberland

                                   NORTHUMBRIA
                                                    Blyth
                                          Tyne
                                    Pennine
                      CUMBRIA   Way
                       Lake   Redcar
                      District   Tees   Cleveland Way
                                                      North   Whitby
Millennium Way   York   Scarborough
                                      Lake Windermere   Moors   Filey
   Douglas   Yorkshire   Ure YORKSHIRE AND
                                       Dales   HUMBERSIDE
                                               Nidd   Bridlington
                       Morecambe   Wharfe
Irish Sea   Leeds and Liverpool Canal Ouse
                                   Ribble   Wolds
                      Blackpool   Aire   Way
                      Southport   NORTH-
                                                            Cleethorpes
                   Llandudno   WEST   Peak
                      Colwyn Bay   District
                                     Mersey   Derwent   Skegness
                   Snowdonia   Weaver Navig.   Trent Navigation
                                    Dee   Witham
                        L. Bala   Trent & Mersey Canal Navigation
                                         Shropshire   EAST MIDLANDS Sheringham
                   Barmouth   Offa's Union Canal   Cromer
                               Severn Canal   Gt.
WALES   Dyke   Yarmouth
   Aberystwyth   HEART OF   Nene   The
                    ENGLAND   Broads Lowestoft
                                     Stratford
                                     on Avon   EAST ANGLIA
                             Wye   Avon   Felixstowe
Pembrokeshire   Brecon   Oxford Canal
   Coast   Beacons   Ust   Clacton
Pembrokeshire Coast Path   Monmouth &   Grand Union Canal
                                Brecon Canal THAMES AND
   Tenby   CHILTERNS   Southend
                          Barry   Avon   Ridgeway   London
                                           Kennet &   Kennet Windsor   Margate
   Ilfracombe   Minehead   Weston-   Avon Canal   North Downs Way Ramsgate
                super-Mare   Parrett   Test   Dover
       Exmoor   South Downs Way SOUTH-EAST Folkestone
WEST COUNTRY   SOUTHERN   Hastings
                           Avon   Worthing Brighton Eastbourne
                     Exe   South West   Poole Bournemouth Southsea
   South-West   Peninsula Path Lyme   Weymouth Swanage Shanklin
   Peninsula Path   Dartmoor Regis   Ventnor
   Newquay   Teignmouth
                   Torbay
South-West
Peninsula Path

North

Sea

Legend:
National Parks
National Park Direction Areas (Scotland)
Areas of Outstanding Natural Beauty
National Scenic Areas (Scotland)
Heritage Coast and Coastal Conservation Zones (Scotland)
Long Distance Footpaths
Navigable rivers
Canals
Tourist Board Area boundaries
Urban areas
Regional proportion of total tourist nights spent in Britain 10mm=10%.
-British visitors
-Overseas visitors

Caledonian Canal

9

A selection of features shown on Ordnance Survey Landranger Series maps

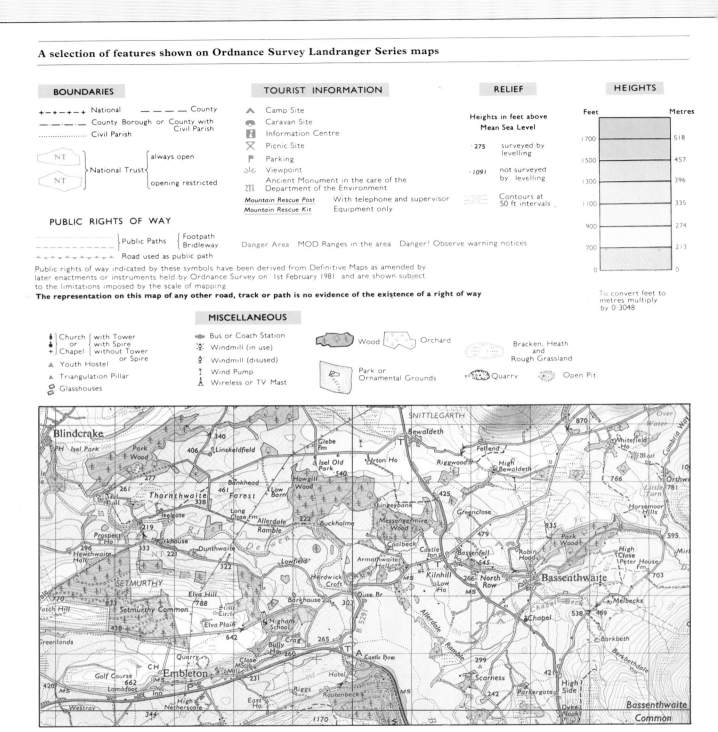

BOUNDARIES

+−+−+−+ National − − − − County
−.−.−.− County Borough or County with
.... Civil Parish
Civil Parish

NT / NT — National Trust { always open / opening restricted

PUBLIC RIGHTS OF WAY

.... } Public Paths { Footpath
− − − − − − − }   { Bridleway
ʈ ʈ ʈ ʈ ʈ ʈ ʈ — Road used as public path

Public rights of way indicated by these symbols have been derived from Definitive Maps as amended by later enactments or instruments held by Ordnance Survey on 1st February 1981 and are shown subject to the limitations imposed by the scale of mapping

The representation on this map of any other road, track or path is no evidence of the existence of a right of way

TOURIST INFORMATION

▲ Camp Site
⌂ Caravan Site
🛈 Information Centre
✕ Picnic Site
P Parking
☀ Viewpoint
ℳ Ancient Monument in the care of the Department of the Environment
Mountain Rescue Post — With telephone and supervisor
Mountain Rescue Kit — Equipment only

Danger Area   MOD Ranges in the area   Danger! Observe warning notices

MISCELLANEOUS

Church { with Tower
or { with Spire
Chapel { without Tower or Spire
▲ Youth Hostel
▲ Triangulation Pillar
▨ Glasshouses

🚐 Bus or Coach Station
Windmill (in use)
Windmill (disused)
Wind Pump
Wireless or TV Mast

Wood   Orchard

Park or Ornamental Grounds   Quarry

Bracken, Heath and Rough Grassland

Open Pit

RELIEF

Heights in feet above Mean Sea Level

·275   surveyed by levelling
·1091   not surveyed by levelling
— 250 —   Contours at 50 ft intervals

HEIGHTS

Feet	Metres
1700	518
1500	457
1300	396
1100	335
900	274
700	213
0	0

To convert feet to metres multiply by 0·3048

kept to the path. Horses and pedal bikes as well as people can use bridle ways but you cannot take a motor vehicle onto either of these unless you have the permission of the landowner. Remember that although there is no statutory footpath width an estimate of two people walking side-by-side is regarded as an acceptable guide. The owner of the land through which the footpath runs is responsible for the upkeep of the gates and styles. Also remember that if the footpath crosses a ploughed field or one with growing crops you should follow the direction of the footpath and not attempt to skirt around the edge of the field where you could be accused of trespassing.

Having established where you can go, the next stage is to decide what type of countryside you would like to explore. Perhaps a gentle stroll along the rolling Downs or something more invigorating such as a walk along a coastal cliff-top path? Most people will have noticed, even from a casual glance from a train window, that large parts of the countryside today are dominated by intensively farmed arable and grazing land where the more traditional landscape of winding hedges and flower-filled meadows and woods has been superseded by uniformly featureless fields. A landscape such as this is not much fun to walk through and furthermore you will probably find more wildlife in comparatively suburban areas. So how do you find the best bits of the countryside? The walks and section introductions in this book will give you plenty of ideas but a good start is to study your Ordnance Survey map. Look out for a mixture of different features. For example, places with open water are always good for wildlife. So, perhaps, a river bordered by a wood may be an interesting area to explore, particularly if the river has lots of meanders which may indicate a variety of slow and fast waters with different types of water and bankside vegetation. Learn to read the contour lines which indicate the relief of an area. A general rule of thumb is that if the lines are closely spaced then expect steep slopes but if they are wide apart the land will be generally more gentle.

When looking out for an interesting woodland to walk through pay particular attention to features such as the type of trees. The Ordnance Survey Pathfinder and older Landranger series maps indicate whether a wood has broad-leaved or coniferous trees (usually a sign of a modern plantation). Look also at the shape of the wood. If it has a long sinuous edge, perhaps following a parish boundary the chances are that it is an old wood and may well have a wealth of animal and plant life. If, on the other hand, it has a uniform rectangular shape it is more likely to be a recently planted wood or windbreak. However, it could be that it is the remains of a larger wood that has been grubbed up over the years by successive farmers.

Similarly, if you are looking for an interesting downland walk look for those footpaths that lead to old hill forts or burial mounds. These were often placed in positions which commanded spectacular, and at one time, strategically important, views. Open land owned by the National Trust or county councils will also be worth a visit as they have probably been acquired because of their scenic value.

A walk in the country can be as demanding as you like. For some a gentle stroll amongst the intimate wooded scenery of lowland Britain is ideal. Look for landscapes with plenty of variety as shown in this photograph near Corfe Castle, which has a new vista around every corner to delight the eye. For those who like a more strenuous day out, the National Parks and uplands have some envigorating walks providing a complete escape from the pressures of town life, like this walk across the Forest of Bowland in the Lancashire Pennines. Make sure you are well prepared before tackling such a walk.

Woodland walks

British woodlands

THE NATURAL VEGETATION cover of the bulk of Britain is woodland. If you don't believe me, just stop cultivating your garden for the next fifty years or so and see what happens. Your choice blooms and well-kept lawn will soon disappear amongst a sea of scrub as nature re-asserts its hold on your real estate.

The exact make-up of this 'new forest' will be the only point in question. Will it be the same as that which covered the area before man dominated the land with his secateurs, mowing machines and all the other paraphernalia that allows the modern Joneses to keep up with the Capabilities of the Browns of the past?

When agricultural man first arrived in Britain, the scene was sylvan in the extreme: 95 per cent plus of these islands were covered with woodland. The lowlands of the north, the midlands and the south were dominated by oak, elm, Hazel and Alder, while in the highlands, especially in Scotland, the dominant trees were Scots Pine and birches.

The forest had already provided nomadic hunters with a surfeit of game: deer, boar, wild cattle, bison, wolf and even bears. In addition, they would have gathered edible roots, fruits and seeds to supplement their diets, and cut wood for their fires and the construction of their camps and habitations. However, these people had little or no effect on the forest itself – they lived much like the other forest inhabitants, as part of the balanced living system.

Neolithic man arrived on the scene around 5 000 years ago, bringing with him knowledge of the husbandry of animals, the cultivation of crops and the technology of flint implements. Axes were used to cut down the trees, elm leaves were used as fodder, and pastures were created in the cleared areas where crops were also grown. When the soil nutrients were depleted the new farmers simply moved on, clearing new forest and leaving the old to regenerate as best it could. About 500 BC, the climate took a distinct change for the worse as wetter and colder conditions prevailed. It thus became more difficult for the warmth-demanding trees to grow, especially at high altitudes and latitudes. So man, with the help of the deteriorating climate, pushed the forest back, replacing it with other living communities. Some, like the blanket bogs of the uplands and the wetter west, were natural. Others, like the fields, villages and townships, were man-made

and man-maintained. Yet others, best called semi-natural, were areas usually unwanted by man at that particular time, and were left to nature's own healing devices.

The dual economies of farmer and hunter up to the Middle Ages and beyond, kept the woodlands as an important part of any landscape, at least for the landed gentry. Coppicing and pollarding, which probably developed by accident during the period of flint-axe technology, became methods for the maintained productivity of managed forests. Those forest that remained were still a focal point for an ever expanding population and were of importance to an Iron Age people right up to the Industrial Revolution when coal and the harnessed power of steam pushed the population of Britain towards ever increasing limits.

Our native woodlands, whether natural or coppiced, fell into disuse as man's endeavours turned in other directions. Frequently, they were replaced by plantations often of a single and usually exotic species introduced from other lands, each monoculture managing to produce good straight timber as fast and as economically as possible.

It was this de-forested landscape that the conservation movement inherited earlier this century, disjunct scraps of woodland, at best linked by old hedgerows. Already many of the most important sites are in the care of the nation, either through the auspices of the Nature Conservancy Council or the National Trust. The County Conservation Trusts, under the umbrella of the Royal Society for Nature Conservation, are tending and restoring other woodland sites by lease or purchase. Modern economic forestry, led by the Forestry Commission, already considers amenity and wildlife concerns as an important part of the productive whole and Britain's plantations look to a brighter and more diverse future.

A WOOD IN SPRING carpeted with a shimmering sea of bluebells must be one of the most cherished sights in rural Britain. This is doubly appropriate as not only is the British Isles the best place in the world to see bluebells but these delightful flowers are often an indication of a diversity of other plants and animals.

Despite the fact that less than ten per cent of our land is still woodland and even less is ancient, we still have a rich heritage which can be traced back to the days of the pre-historic 'wildwood' after the last ice age when most of Britain was covered in a green mantle of forest. The

fragmented remains of this ancient landscape together with many more recent woodlands make up today's copses, spinneys, plantations and other woods. Yet there is still a tremendous variety of types of woodland – experts have identified twelve distinct forms of wood with many more further categories within these. Each of these woodlands has its own special characteristics ranging from the majestic relics of the primeval Caledonian pine forests in the Highlands to the intricate patchwork of oak-ash-hazel woods in Lowland England. Added to this, each wood has been managed over the

centuries subtley altering its structure and affecting its wildlife.

WOODLAND TYPES

Mixed oak woods   The Oak woodlands as described on pages 56–73 are our most typical woods. Often the oaks are interspersed with a shrubby coppice of hazel or birch and there is a rich ground covering of bluebells and honeysuckle on lighter soils, with bracken dominating in late summer, or a green sward of dog's mercury or even ramsons on heavy clayey soils. There are two distinct types of oak woodlands. Those on the poor hillsides of the west and north are usually dominated by sessile oaks and are often rich in ferns and mosses. Woodland birds such as pied flycatchers, redstarts and wood warblers are frequent summer visitors. On the heavy lowland soils the pedunculate oak predominates and if the understorey of hazel is regularly cut, birds such as nightingales and blackcaps can be heard.

Mixed ash woods These woods can be found throughout Lowland England sometimes growing with field maple and oak in more fertile soils. But the most fascinating ash woods are to be found on the limestone hills of the west and north. These woods, because of the dappled shade cast by the open canopy, contain a rich understorey of shrubs and many woodland flowers such as wood anemone, lily-of-the-valley and solomon's seal.

Beech woods It is said that gothic cathedral architecture was inspired by the cavernous vaulted appearance of these woods with their high dense canopy, sparse understorey and tall sinewy trunks. The beech was one of the last trees to colonize the British Isles before it was cut off from the continent and may be only native up as far as Derbyshire. The famous Chiltern beechwoods are largely recently planted woodlands which were created to provide wood for the local furniture-making industry. Despite the thick layer of leaf litter and shade cast by these magnificent trees some plants have adapted to live under them. Look out for the unusual honey-coloured birds-nest orchid which amazingly has no green leaves but obtains its nourishment through a fungus which is able to break down the nutrients in the leaf litter. In winter large flocks of finches are attracted to these woods to feed on the beech mast.

Alder woods These contrast dramatically with the open feel of the beech woods. They are usually found in valley bottoms and along spring lines and consequently are marshy places often with awkward clumps of tussock grasses and sedges amongst the rotting branches. They are probably our nearest equivalent to a tropical rainforest in appearance, as the branches are festooned with mosses and ferns and hung with straggling plants such as bindweed and bittersweet. Look out for bright yellow patches of marsh marigolds or kingcups in spring. The alder trees are often visited by flocks of siskins and redpolls in winter which feed on the seeds of the ripe fruits.

Pine woods and plantations The most dramatic change in our woodlands this century has been the planting of vast numbers of foreign conifers for timber. Many old broad-leaved woods have been felled and replaced with uniform ranks of spruces, larches and pines. While in the hills of the north and west the open moorland landscape has been transformed as huge blocks of land have been covered with these trees. Unfortunately, because they are not native, these woods do not support the range or numbers of wildlife that you can expect to see in a native wood. All is not bad,

Two contrasting types of British woodland: real Scots pine (*Pinus sylvestris* **var** *scotica*) **growing as nature planted them; a tumble of shapes and sizes amidst a glorious Scottish landscape (above).**

Epping Forest in the autumn – a rich mixture of wildlife and colour only eighteen stops on the Central Line from Oxford Circus (below).

however, as in their early stages these plantations can support a variety of birdlife and the wide rides needed for timber extraction can often be pleasant places for walking. But when the dense canopy of needles closes over, most wildlife disappears. The Scots pine is native to the Highlands of Scotland where you can still visit relics of the once mighty Caledonian forests. These remains are rich in plant life with a shrubby understorey of heathers and juniper and many interesting birds to see including the crossbill which specialises in extracting the seeds from pine cones.

Blowing its own trumpet of beauty – a patch of Bugle (*Ajuga reptans*) enjoying the spring sunshine between the coppiced stools.

has been planted on a cleared site. The long term relationship that develops between the plants and trees in an ancient wood cannot be replaced simply by planting similar species. It is therefore extremely important that our remaining primary woodlands are protected from destruction and, wherever possible, coppiced in the traditional manner.

Peter led us up a rather muddy path to an area that had been recently coppiced. The first thing that caught the eye, unlike so many woods, was the profusion of flowers. We picked our way carefully between the coppiced stools while Peter pointed out some of the species – Sweet Violets and Bugle, some of the last of this spring's Wood Anemones, nodding Water Avens and Primroses, Dog's Mercury and, in the far corner, a swath of Bluebells. By the side of one stool was a stand of tall green Wood Spurge, a relative of the familiar Sun Spurge which can be found along our hedgerows and at the edges of fields, with its bright green flowers and leaves which completely encircle the stem.

This first area had been cut two winters ago and was showing the results of one year's full growth. Already the different rate of growth of the various trees was quite marked. The Sallow shoots were two and a half metres high while the Ash poles were still comparatively short, bending and twisting like some medusa. This apparently bizarre growth is the result of the genetic make-up of the tree, each individual showing a different pattern of growth. The Hazel shoots were also lagging behind the Sallow and were mostly two metres tall. The main standard trees in this area were Silver Birches which, together with the Bluebells indicated that the soil in this part of the wood was essentially acidic. Despite the rapid regeneration of the coppiced trees, the site was essentially open and the flowers were obviously enjoying this state. On our walk around the wood, we were to see the influence of the various degrees of tree cover on the plant life.

From this first area, we returned to the main path which was deeply rutted and wet – an indication of the poor drainage which was probably a critical factor in the wood remaining intact for so many years. The bird song was all around us as the spring sun was producing the very best from Bradfield's warblers. Willow Warblers, in particular, could be heard singing, it seemed, from almost every thicket and their cascading song was underlined by the rich tones of

unseen Nightingales. This backdrop of song remained with us for nearly the entire walk. We rounded a corner which brought us in front of what looked like a devastated area. However, Peter was quick to point out what was going on.

'Here we have an area which has been coppiced this winter and most of the wood has been sorted and moved out. So unlike the first area which had one year's growth this one, apart from the stools, has only what has grown in the last few weeks.'

The floor was carpeted with a green mantle of Dog's Mercury which was broken

by the short stumps of the coppiced trees and a few Oak standards. Some of the larger stools were Ash – these stood out from the smaller Hazel and Sallow. We had a closer look at one which had a thick covering of mosses and lichens.

'This clump, which looks like a collection of individual trees, is actually part of the same tree. As the Ash becomes older, the centre seems to divide and rot away whilst the outer layers of the tree remain vigorous. This tree here is roughly two metres in diameter and will soon have new shoots growing from the outer stumps.'

Not the kind of Ash one usually finds drawn in a reference book. Considering the great antiquity of the wood, I asked Peter how old it might be.

'This could be three hundred years old – the coppicing actually seems to extend the life of these trees, as a good age for an Ash would normally be 150 to 200 years. We have one stool here which is over six metres across and it has been estimated that it could be a thousand years old, perhaps the oldest living thing in Britain, *and* still producing a good crop of poles!'

In the centre of the clearing was an Oak

A coppiced Ash stool amongst Sallows and birch standards. These ancient stools still produce a healthy crop of poles. Notice how the Sallow poles are already much higher than the slower growing Ash, after only one year's full growth.

43

The Nightingale (*Luscinia megarhynchos*) is a typical bird of our traditional coppiced woods. The distribution in Britain is mainly south of a line from the Humber to the Severn. Interestingly this coincides with the area where intensive coppice-with-standards woodland management was most prevalent. They feed on the woodland floor and breed in dense thickets – a combination which suits the patchwork of recently cut woodland and impenetrable stands of poles that are found in coppiced woodland. The decline in the numbers of Nightingales in Britain over recent decades has been partly attributed to the decrease in traditional woodland management.

standard with bundles of cut wood leaning against it. These clearly showed the different rates of growth of the various wood. The Hazel was about half the height of the Sallow poles. They were all the same age as all the stools had previously been coppiced ten years ago. I asked Peter what these would be used for.

'These bundles will be used in thatching: the shorter ones will be used as thatching pins, called broaches, while the longer rods will be used to keep the thatch down, and are called spars.'

By the path was a group of Sallow poles which had been 'stripped-barked'. This was to help the wood to dry out evenly, preventing it from splitting. They had been carefully picked out for eventual use as traditional scythe handles. When I picked one up, I could feel the slight bend in the wood which gives it its distinctive action.

Each of the different coppiced trees had their own uses. The Hazel is very versatile and has a long history of use as a fencing material, for example in Hazel wattles. The larger Ash poles are used here for rake heads and teeth as well as firewood. Some of the birch is used for scythe nibs. Wood that is not used for a specific purpose is logged and sold as firewood; a product which is increasingly in demand with the recent increase in the price of oil and coal and the popularity of wood-burning stoves. The tops of the trees, which used to be sold as faggots for burning in the old kitchen stoves, are now burnt on site and the ash is sold as an excellent pottery glaze. So nothing is wasted. Burning on site can harm the ground flora, so special areas are set aside for this. Across the woodland ride was another area of coppiced woodland that looked consider-

ably different to the first two areas we had looked at. The wood was quite high and thick with straight poles. This was approximately seven years' growth. I asked Peter if this meant that it would be cut in three years' time.

'Probably, but it depends if it is mostly Hazel. If there is more Ash we would leave that for as long as 25 years, possibly for use as firewood. You have to imagine that you are looking back to medieval times here because this is the same practice as then. The main difference is that then there would probably have been twenty people working on a wood of this size, whereas now there is just myself and our woodman, Joe Bennett. However, we have a lot of voluntary help, particularly with things such as the clearing of the dead underwood before cutting. This form of woodland management is very labour intensive and we would be unable to carry it out without the help of volunteers. You cannot bring great machines into the felled areas as this would destroy not only some of the stools, which are obviously the renewable resource, but also the ground flora, which is extremely important.'

Sobered by this thought, we had a closer look at the carpets of flowers on the newly cleared site. Although we had walked no more than a hundred metres from the first area, the types of trees and flowers were already showing that we had now moved onto a more neutral soil. Here was mostly the Dog's Mercury, which seemed to be the predominant plant of the wood. The fresh green shoots of Meadowsweet, which were obviously enjoying the damp conditions, could be seen starting to rise over the Dog's Mercury. Water Avens with its shy-looking pink and orange flowers could be found in

Opposite **A newly cut area, with Ash and Hazel stools in the foreground and a standard oak in the centre of the photograph. The poles stacked against the tree will be selected for use as thatching spars and broaches.**

The distinctive four-leaved Herb Paris (*Paris quadrifolia*) **amongst Water Avens** (*Geum rivale*) **and Dog's Mercury** (*Mercurialis perennis*).

little clumps – again the dampness was the key to its presence. Peter was intent on showing me one of the specialities of the wood, and in true botanist's fashion, eyes to the ground, treading carefully, he made his way over a cleared area. After a short search, he stopped to show me what I thought at first to be another clump of Dog's Mercury. However, closer inspection revealed a delicate little green plant with four leaves surrounding a strange looking flower with greenish sepals and straggling yellow petals. This was Herb Paris, *Paris quadrifolia*. I asked Peter why such a strange looking and elusive plant should have such a name.

'If you look closely at this plant you will see that it is made up of groups of four parts. You can see that there are four main leaves in a circle around the stem, then four sepals and in between these are four thin green petals.

Now, it is said that this symmetrical arrangement resembled a traditional love knot and from this it got the name *herba paris*, which means herb of a pair. Its other common name is herb true-love, again referring back to its resemblance to a love knot. Later in the year it produces a dark berry which is poisonous but was at one time used to treat inflammation of the eyes.'

Since we were down on the floor we had a look for some more flowers and it was not long before we came upon the showy flowers of an Early Purple Orchid. This, like the Herb Paris, is an indicator of ancient woodland and is also a lime-loving plant (a calcicole). It is interesting to reflect that one of the reasons why we can use these plants as guides to the origin of a woodland is perhaps because the plants evolved in a situation where the forest cover was more or less

continuous over large areas and that there-fore they did not need the ability to colonise fragmented areas. So now where secondary woodland has been planted, perhaps only a short distance from ancient primary wood-land, its flowers are unable to colonise these new sites. However, it is dangerous to generalise as plants behave differently in different areas. For example, here at Brad-field Woods the Bluebell is found only on the more acidic parts of the wood, whereas in western Britain its distribution is more general.

Before continuing our walk around the wood we stopped to look at the stump of an old Oak. A casual visitor might not give it a second glance but Peter knew that, like so many facets of the wood, if you knew what to look for, it had a story to tell.

'This was felled during what was prob-

ably the last major clearance of the timber trees. It was brought down during the 1930's using an axe and cross cut saw. Quite often animals use these old stumps as look-out posts or feeding tables.'

The large number of rabbit droppings clearly confirmed this. There were also some broken Hazel nut shells on the surface and I asked Peter what would have left them there.

'Yes, these are very interesting. There is a clean split down the centre of the shell which means, if we can find the other half of the shell, it could be squirrel.'

We searched around and sure enough found the other half making an almost perfect match.

'The squirrel that is found here is the Grey one and you can usually tell which nuts they have eaten because they gnaw a

A wattle hurdle being constructed. These were originally used for penning sheep on the Downs but are sometimes used today as garden fencing. They are made from hazel rods. Notice how the rods at the bottom of the wattle are not 'riven' or 'split' – this is done in order to give greater strength to the structure.

47

Two butterflies sunning themselves in the open areas and rides of the wood.
Bottom **An Orange-tip** (*Anthocharis cardamines*) **on Lady's Smock** (*Cardamine pratensis*).
Opposite bottom **A Peacock** (*Nymphalis io*).

small hole and then split the nut open with their bottom teeth, making a clean break along the line of its weakest point. Nuts that have small neat holes gnawed in them are usually the result of the work of small voles and mice and even, in woods like this, dormice.'

Suddenly the sound of birdsong was broken by a harsh bark. I turned around expecting to see somebody out walking their dog. But Peter immediately said that it sounded more like the sharp bark of a Roe Deer. Unfortunately, the deer did not show itself and we moved on deeper into the wood.

We had now come to a long straight ride with a fine springy turf. It was a lot drier than the main path and had a ditch running along each side. These had probably been dug during the Seventeenth and Eighteenth Centuries but some may be medieval. They

keep the ride dry in order to help with the timber extraction. Although the main feature of the woods was obviously the trees, these ancient rides were very important in themselves and, perhaps, are the vestiges of a prehistoric grassland, older than the wood itself. Bugle was growing in patches and some Lesser Celandine, that harbinger of spring, was still in flower in some of the more sheltered places. Peter pointed out the gradation from short grass in the centre of the ride to the taller herbs on either side before the coppiced wood. The rides support a tremendous variety of flowers, which in turn help support the woodland insect population. This includes several species of butterfly, for example the Brimstone, Peacock and White Admiral. Despite the inclement spring, some butterflies were around; in particular, we came across a

Three Hazel nuts which have been broken into by three different types of mammal. (A) Has been gnawed into by a Wood Mouse (notice the outer ring of teeth marks which it makes); (B) has been gnawed into by a Bank Vole (notice the cleaner edge); (C) has been split open by a Grey Squirrel (notice the groove that it has made, it then inserts its incisors in the hole and splits open the shell).

A B C

Peacock butterfly with rather shredded wings. Peter suggested that it had probably been attacked by birds. The gaudy wings with their striking eye spots would attract the birds away from the vulnerable body and so the butterfly is able to escape to see another day, although not looking at his Sunday best.

On the edge of the ride was a yellow flower looking rather like an overgrown Primrose. This was an Oxlip, a speciality of the ancient woodlands of the area. For many years it was thought to be a hybrid between the Primrose and the Cowslip, but is now recognised as a species in its own right. It has a very limited distribution in England, only being found in primary woodland on the heavy boulder clays of central East Anglia and west Cambridgeshire: yet another indication that we were in a special place.

Above **Traditional woodland harmony. Early Purple Orchid** (*Orchis mascula*) **and Dog's Mercury at the base of a three hundred year old coppiced Ash stool.**

Above left **Oxlip** (*Primula elatior*), **a speciality of the ancient woods of the boulder clays of central East Anglia and west Cambridgeshire.**

A large area which has been coppiced during the winter. The only trees still standing are the standard oaks; notice the distinctive shape of the crowns of these trees, produced by the dense under-wood. The piles of logs will be sold as fire-wood.

At the end of the ride which skirted the edge of the reserve we could see through the woodland edge and onto the intensively farmed Suffolk landscape. Between these arable fields with their absence of wildlife and the wood was a huge ditch with a noticeable mound on the woodland side. This was not the work of one man and his 'JCB' but rather the work of gangs of labourers under the supervision of medieval monks, as Peter pointed out.

'This is a medieval boundary bank which was constructed mainly to stop the neigh-bouring livestock straying into the woods and browsing off the new shoots from the coppice stools. These banks are character-istic of old coppiced woodlands and can often tell you a lot about the original boundaries or divisions within the wood. Most of them have the earth bank on the woodland side of the ditch, as here at Bradfield. At points along the bank are also old pollarded Oaks and Ash, which again clearly mark the boundary of the woodland, particularly where the coppicing goes right to the edge of the bank. Pollarding a tree means that they have been regularly cut back, not at ground level as with a coppiced tree, but at a height somewhere between two and three metres above ground to prevent livestock from reaching the new shoots. These pollarded Oaks, like the coppiced trees, can reach a great age, even though the main trunk can have rotted away, leaving holes for insects and birds.

We moved on along another muddy path. The growth alongside us, to my eye, all looked of the same age and I put it to Peter that a large part of the wood must have been cleared fairly recently.

aroma – it made walking quite a hungry business. Further on, we came to a patch that had not been coppiced for thirty years and the ground flora was noticeably different from the rich mixture of flowers that we had found on some of the more recently cut sections. Virtually the only plant that still seemed to be able to take advantage of the situation was the ubiquitous Dog's Mercury. It is probably because of the early flowering nature of the plant that it can survive under the dense cover of these older sections. However, if the wood was left to grow much longer it would itself start to deteriorate.

'If the coppice was left over forty years the Hazel, which is now overshadowed by the faster growing trees such as the Ash, would start to become shaded out and would not survive. To an extent, the fact that the Hazel comes into leaf a good deal earlier than its neighbours, like the Ash and the Oak, works to its advantage but eventually it will start to die off.'

I asked Peter if the old adage: 'The Oak before the Ash, we're in for a splash. The Ash before the Oak, we're in for a soak', had any grounding. Unfortunately he thought not, and proceeded to point out that in the woods there are individual groups of trees that regularly seem to come into leaf before others and that the timing was dependent largely on the genetic make-up of the individual trees and not the vagaries of the British climate.

We then came upon a clearing which must have been all of eight acres in extent. Peter and his woodman, with the help of teams of volunteers, had cleared it last winter and all

The boundary bank showing the steep bank on the woodland side and the open arable land beyond. In the foreground is a pollarded oak marking out the boundary of the wood.

'No. It has been coppiced on a fairly regular cycle, depending upon demand. We have between one and thirty-five years' growth in the wood, although we are attempting to bring some of the older areas back into the shorter cycle coppicing which is typical of the wood. Sometimes, with the older parts of the wood, as here, it can be difficult to tell the difference in age between one section and another. This is why it is helpful to coppice in one area and then move far away when you coppice the next winter so that the heights of the different parts are clearly defined.'

As we walked along between a section of 'twenty-year old' coppice, the air suddenly filled with the smell of fresh garlic. Peter pointed out a patch of Ramsons or Wild Garlic by the side of the ride. Our walk was to be continually punctuated by this glorious

Spring beauty in a coppice wood. A carpet of Ramsons or Wild Garlic (*Allium ursinum*).

that remained save the stools were the standard trees. The first clearing we had come to had mostly Silver Birch standards; here, however, the predominate tree was Oak. Great piles of cut wood lay in between these isolated Oaks. A lot of cut Ash poles would be going off to the local factory to be turned into rake heads and teeth. In front of us, were some huge Elm stools; these were larger than the Ash as they are a faster growing tree. The Oak standards were interesting as they ranged in age from comparative youngsters of thirty-five years (when the area was last cut) to about 100

years. So here a continual supply of Oak timber of a wide range of ages was clearly in evidence, demonstrating why the coppicing-with-standards form of woodland management had been so successful for so many centuries.

From this large area of recently cut woodland, we crossed over a footbridge which straddled the end of an intriguing pond. This was apparently dug at the same time as the great boundary banks. Although it is called the 'fish pond', there is currently little aquatic life in it, as it has dried out during the summer months in recent years. A new

caps were also singing and the beautiful mellow song of the Nightingale, which we first heard at the entrance to the wood, was still with us. Peter pointed out that Redstarts would soon be around, and in the evening Tawny Owls could be heard. It was pleasant to reflect that hundreds of years previously the labourers must have worked here and stopped to listen to the same sounds as we were hearing. The sense of continuity was marvellous. Practically the only difference was that, instead of simple but effective bill hooks and horses, Peter was using chain saws and tractors to cut and remove the wood.

From the pond, we moved into Monks's Park Wood, a deer park maintained by the monks. This part had been coppiced three winters previously and the ground flora was different again from the other sites we had looked at. Here there were tall woodland grasses growing up between the stools; walking was much more difficult as brambles were also covering the ground in places. However, as the trees continue to grow and start to shade out more and more of the

sluice has been installed which, it is hoped, will improve the situation. It is a haven for frogs and it is not unusual to come across them on some of the wetter parts of the woods. In fact, there are small natural pools throughout the woods which have formed in depressions which, it has been suggested, have remained the same since post-glacial times.

Whilst we were looking down at the pond, the sound of bird song was all around us. A Whitethroat was singing from a nearby thicket, rising into a brief song flight before disappearing into the trees. Black-

plants beneath them, the less shade tolerant flowers and grasses die back. So the balance is restored and the trees' growth does not suffer from this constantly changing pattern of plants around them. Peter pointed out an area in front of us, which had a thick cover of trees, as a piece of secondary woodland called 'Hewitt's Meadow'. It had a boundary ditch around it and was traditionally an area kept aside for deer and was still open until 1900 when it was allowed to become overgrown. These meadows were used as deer parks and are typical of medieval woodland. They were also called launds.

An area of two years' growth showing the increasing presence of grasses around an Ash stool.

53

The Rake Factory at Welnetham, Suffolk. The continued presence of this small factory producing scythe-handles, rakes and mallets has provided an example of the traditional symbiotic relationship between woodland management and local rural industry.

Below An Ash pole being turned down by hand to produce a scythe handle.

We then threaded our way through the cut stools to an adjoining area. Walking between the stools was not easy. There were two reasons for this: firstly, they were not in the neat regimented rows that we associate with modern coniferous plantations; secondly, all the newly cut stools had nasty sharp edges. Peter told me that this was intentional, as it was important that the poles were cut off at an acute angle so the rainwater could run off them easily. If they were cut level, the stool would soon become rotten. Eventually we came out into a fell that had been cut that winter, and I asked Peter how they moved the timber out as it was obviously so difficult to maneouver around in the wood.

'In the old times, the cut wood had to be moved out to the main rides by hand; this was usually done by bundling it up and carrying it out on the backs of the woodmen, which meant that it was hard and time consuming work. It was then loaded onto a horse-drawn cart. Today, we make racks into the fell and take out the wood with a tractor and trailer.'

As we walked along, we picked out the different species of tree that we passed – there were Ash and Hazel, Birch and Sallow mostly in the coppiced areas with the larger standard Oaks. There were coppiced Alder in the wetter patches and Peter told me that there were Small-leaved Limes in another part of the wood. Old Wild Cherries were growing along the uncut edges of the fells, together with Hawthorns. We came upon a Field Maple which was chiefly recognisable by its corky bark and hawthorn-like leaves. I put it to Peter that this diversity was surely exceptional, as most people consider coppiced woodland to be rather poor in tree species.

'In parts of the Midlands and East Anglia, these old coppiced woodlands are still surviving and generally have a good variety of species. In some areas, there are large woods which consist of coppiced Sweet Chestnut. These woods were introduced mostly after the Fifteenth Century, and can be found particularly in east Essex, Kent and Sussex. Sweet Chestnut is still used in these areas for fencing posts and hop poles.

Walking back through the wood with its sudden changes of view from dense thickets to open fells carpeted with spring flowers, Peter and I talked about the importance of maintaining the tradition of these woods which were sadly now an oasis for wildlife amidst a vast monolithic arable landscape. And yet the wood is not a museum piece. It is a working vital place which still caters for the needs of some of the local industries. Before we left, I helped Peter load up some Ash poles for the roof of a mock Saxon village house which was being constructed nearby. It would be nice to think that poles would have been cut from the same site for actual Saxon huts all those centuries ago, and that the unbroken continuity of use will carry on for as long again into the future.

An Oak Wood in Summer

The oak, be it Pedunculate or Sessile or even some intermediate between the two, is the stout heart of the British woodlands. It has so many places in our history, and fortunately is still not uncommon in our landscapes either as a dominant or co-dominant tree in mixed woodland, as standards in old coppice, or as single trees in farmland. I say 'fortunately', because of all our trees, the oak provides both food and a home for the greatest variety of insects and other invertebrates. Likewise, its rough fissured bark offers safe anchorage for an immense range of epiphytic lichens.

David Streeter is a natural historian par excellence, *a teacher in the grandest manner and a stalwart of nature conservation and especially of the Sussex Trust for Nature Conservation.*

Put the two together, Quercus *and Streeter, in the Sussex scene and you have got hours of fascination.*

A Wealden oak wood in high summer.

An Oak Wood in Summer
with
David Streeter

The leaves and acorns of a Sessile Oak (*Quercus petraea*). **Note, however, that although the acorns are sessile, the leaves have auricles at the base which is a character of the Pedunculate Oak** (*Quercus robur*).

A wood dominated by oak trees epitomises the traditional idea of an English woodland. This association is no accident as the predominance of oak over large areas of lowland Britain can be traced back to the climax forests of approximately 7000 years ago. Although in the intervening period man has radically altered the landscape, the ancestors of these oak woodlands still remain in places and these mighty trees have certainly not lost their ability to capture our imagination. To learn more about these fascinating woods and their associated animals and plants we made a journey to the heart of the Sussex Weald to visit an area of mixed oak woodland. Our guide for the day was David Streeter, Reader in Ecology at Sussex University and a well-known writer and broadcaster on our countryside.

We met next to the roar of August traffic rushing south to the Sussex coast, but before long we were heading off into the pleasant summer shade of the woodland. The urgency of the birdsong earlier in the year had died down and the quiet of the wood was only periodically broken by the high-pitched calls of tits, which were already moving around in small flocks, and by the busy humming of clusters of hoverflies and bees searching for nectar amongst the glades and sun-dappled branches. As we wound our way down into the heart of the wood David told us of the background to the area.

'The wood we are in today is part of the most wooded region in the whole of the British Isles. Sussex, in fact, is the most heavily wooded county in almost the least wooded country in Europe. Something like 15 per cent of the land here is woodland, whereas the national average is about 8 per cent. Therefore from the point of view of woodland conservation, this is a most important area, certainly in England.

'We are in the middle of the natural region known as the Weald, which is generally taken as being the area enclosed within the encircling rim of the chalk of the North and South Downs and the eastern edge of the Hampshire Downs in the west. It is a very ancient wooded area. The term "weald" itself comes from the Old English, "wald", meaning a forest, and in Anglo Saxon times it was known as "Andredes weald" which is a reference to "Anderida", which was the Roman port of Pevensey and one of the most important coastal forts in this part of the country. The Weald is mentioned in the Anglo Saxon Chronicle for AD 893 and is described as an area of about 120 miles long and 30 miles wide from north to south. The Venerable Bede described it as the haunt of large herds of swine and deer. It was clearly largely an impenetrable area, although modern archaeological and place-names research is showing us that certainly by the latter part of the Saxon period considerable areas had been cleared, largely for swine pastures.

'The central Weald is a very complex area geologically but to put it simply, it consists of an alternating series of sandstones and clays. The Ashdown Sand is the oldest and Ashdown Forest itself occupies the central area of the Weald. This is then followed by the Wadhurst Clay and then the Tunbridge Wells Sand, which is what we are on at the moment. The Tunbridge Wells Sand at this point forms a fairly coarse-grained sandstone and also outcrops as sand-rock. If we were to dig down just here we would come to this solid sand-rock which is only about 30 centimetres beneath the surface. At the moment we are at the highest part of the wood, about 170 metres (550 feet) above sea level, and we shall be walking down the valley onto the Wadhurst Clay with its rather heavier loamy soils. So here we are on sandy acid soils.

'The popular conception of the history of woodlands in this part of the world was that at one time it was one vast expanse of oak forest. I think we have to modify that picture today because research has shown that oak was not the dominant tree over all areas of lowland Britain. But certainly, I suspect this particular area is one where it may well have been. The wood is, in fact, a nature reserve of about 45 hectares (110 acres), managed by the Sussex Trust for Nature Conservation and owned by the National Trust. It has not been actively managed as far as we know for forty or fifty years, although there are small areas of coppiced woodland within it. Most of it, however, consists of old oak standards.'

Although still near the top of the ridge, we had by now made our way into an area dominated by mature oaks. David suggested that we should stop and have a closer look at the trees themselves. We gathered a few leaves and sitting by the side of the path we talked about these stately trees.

'Arguably the oak is the most important plant in Britain because it is the dominant plant of the country's natural climax vegetation. This means, not surprisingly, that it has more species of insect associated with it than any other plant in Britain – well over 300 species are dependent directly on the oak. And that figure only includes those that feed on the leaves and takes no account of the wood boring insects and those that feed on decaying wood. Ecologically speaking therefore it is obviously a very important tree.

'The first thing we have to say is that we have two species of native oak in Britain. Unfortunately they can be rather difficult to distinguish apart. In this wood we have both species and I have collected some examples of each and if we look at the leaves and acorns we should be able to tell the difference between the two. The Common or Pedunculate Oak, *Quercus robur*, has acorns with long stalks or peduncles, hence the name. The leaves of the Pendunculate Oak have no stalks or very short ones and the bases of the leaves have two very small

lobes which stand out at the junction of the leaf and the leaf blade. Also if you turn over the leaf you will see that its underside is completely devoid of hairs. The other species of oak, the Sessile or Durmast Oak, *Quercus petraea*, has acorns which have no peduncles, that is to say they are sessile, again hence the name. The leaves, on the other hand do have stalks, which can be up to one centimetre or more in length, and the base of the leaf blade typically tapers into the leaf stalk. Furthermore, if you look at the undersurface of the leaf you will find that the veins are minutely downy or hairy.

'This all sounds very nice and straightforward but the problem is that when you find an oak you often discover that it is very difficult to decide which species you are looking at. Although the books are very clear on the differences it is not the same at all when you come to look at the trees in the field. The reason for this is argued about,

Sessile or Durmast Oak (*Quercus petraea*) **a habit; b leaf; c acorn. Common or Pedunculate Oak** (*Quercus robor*) **d habit; e bark; f leaf; g acorn.**

59

but I suppose the obvious conclusion that one comes to is that the two species hybridise. Actually it is very difficult to get oaks to hybridise artificially and it is likely that they only hybridise naturally in the field rather infrequently. The other theory is that the two species are taxonomically very closely related and have separated fairly recently in geological times. The concensus view today, however, is that the explanation for this variability lies in the fact that sometime in the past and, perhaps, to some extent continuing today, the oaks have undergone a special type of hybridisation which is known as 'introgression'. This occurs when the individuals hybridise infrequently and the offspring of the hybrids backcross with the parents. So what results are populations of one or other of the species into which have been incorporated characters of the other species. You therefore tend to get populations where individuals show intermediate characters. But having said that, it is still generally true that over north and west Britain the Sessile Oak is the commoner species, whilst over much of lowland Britain, the Pedunculate Oak is the common one.

'An important ecological principle is that normally speaking where you have two species of organisms which are closely related, they should occupy slightly different habitats, or put another way, very closely related species very rarely have identical ecologies. Yet here we have in this wood the two oaks growing side by side apparently contradicting this – one of the important "dogmas" of ecological theory. This either means that the theory is wrong or alternatively that the oaks are separated ecologically in a way that is not immediately obvious. Let us assume for the moment that the theory is right and look for some differences in the natural history of the two oak species. First one has to point out that their geographical distribution is almost identical – the Pedunculate Oak extends marginally further north and south in Europe than the Sessile. For example, the Pedunculate Oak is found in Sardinia whilst the Sessile Oak reaches as far south as Corsica; they are that close. So to all intents and purposes they have identical geographical distributions. But what about their detailed ecology. The one thing that one can say fairly definitely is that the Pedunculate Oak will tolerate heavier clay soils to a much greater extent than the Sessile Oak. So over much of lowland and midland Britain where you have heavy clay soils the dominant oak is the Pedunculate. Now, on the other hand, where you have well-drained soils on sandstones you can find both species, but the factor which seems to separate them under those conditions is the general level of soil fertility. Where the soil is more fertile it seems that the Pedunculate has the edge over the Sessile Oak. Conversely, the less fertile the soil, the more likely it is that the Sessile will be the commoner of the two. But the pattern is far from clear. The problem becomes more acute where you get the picture complicated by the appearance of the Beech, *Fagus sylvatica*, which is our other major forest tree, certainly in southern Britain. This tree has an ecology that is similar to the Sessile Oak in that it likes a well-drained soil. It is certainly not confined to limestone and chalk, as some of the books suggest; the Beech simply likes a well-drained soil and so you will find it mixed on soils like the one we are now on, with the two oaks. Areas like the New Forest have almost equal proportions of the two oaks and Beech. However, like the Sessile Oak it will not grow on heavy water-logged soils.

'One factor which has complicated our understanding of the ecology of the two oaks is that they have been of prime importance to man for timber and so he has artificially changed their apparent ecology by hundreds of years of planting and felling. So it may no longer be possible wholly to interpret their ecologies properly, simply because we are looking at an artificial distribution.

'As far as the uses of oak are concerned, the Pedunculate Oak has always been the most favoured for timber. Paradoxically, one reason for this is that it has the most crooked branches and thus the most crooked timber of the two! One of the prime uses in the past for oak timber has been in the building both of houses and ships, and one of the things that the medieval builders needed were those lovely right-angled bends for supplying the "knees" and "crutches" for supporting roof timbers and so on. If you look at this oak in front of us you can see that the branches are full of these right-angled bends, whereas the typical branches of the Sessile Oak tend to be straighter.

'As far as planting is concerned, from a pure husbandry point of view the Pedunculate Oak is again preferred as its acorns store better. The trees that you often see growing by themselves in the open are usually

Pedunculate Oaks. Incidentally, as they are not hemmed in by other trees, the crowns of these hedgerow or parkland trees tend to be more open. Indeed, one thing you can do when you go into a woodland, which you think might be ancient woodland or one that has been there a long time, is to look at the crowns of the trees, if they are narrow then you can be fairly sure that they have grown up in competition with other individuals.

'If you want to see the finest oak woods in Europe then unfortunately you have to look outside Britain as we do not have any wholly untouched oak woods. The best woodlands of Pedunculate Oak are probably in some of the river valleys of Yugoslavia, while the best Sessile Oak woods are probably in parts of eastern France.

'We are here in late August and if you look at the oak at this time of year the one thing that strikes you more than anything else is that a lot of the leaves have virtually nothing left of them. It so happens that this year it looks as if between 10 and 15 per cent of the leaves have been eaten – some years you can get a devastating defoliation. This is simply a feature of the fact that the oak is palatable to an enormous array of herbivorous insects, particularly their larvae. By this time of the year most of these insects have matured and the predation pressure is off. Therefore what we can see is probably the maximum amount of defoliation for this year. Interestingly, if you look carefully at the oaks you will find that there are some leaves which have been hardly eaten at all. This is because in July many of the oaks produce a second crop of leaves on non-woody shoots. This is called lammas-growth, after Lammastide, one of the old country festivals, which occurs on the 1st of August. The distinction between the first spring leaves and this lammas-growth can be very dramatic; it is best seen in July. This means that even if the oak tree was severely defoliated in the spring, if it produced this second crop of leaves, it would not wholly lose its year's production. However, it would actually be wrong to argue that the oak, and, indeed, other trees that produce this growth, actually evolved this as a mechanism to overcome the effects of heavy predation loss early in the year. However, there is little doubt that the effect is to provide the tree with a "second string" to its annual "photosynthesis" bow!

'Whilst we are looking at the leaves there are two other features which can be very noticeable at this time of the year. One of them is the large number of different galls that you find. Perhaps the commonest gall on mature oaks is the spangle gall which you find on the undersurface of the leaf. These are little circular pustules which vary in diameter from two millimetres up to about five millimetres. Like a lot of galls on the oak, they are caused by a gall wasp belonging to the family Cynipidae. There are more species of gall wasp on oak than I know of on any other plant in Britain – around thirty species. Galls are not animal tissue but are the result of the plant's response to the invasion of gall-causing organisms, in this case, a wasp. They are a form of controlled cancer, if you like. An abnormal growth within which the larva of the gall wasp develops. This particular one that we can see here – the spangle gall – is the result of eggs that would have been laid by the female wasp in July and there is one caterpillar per spangle. These will continue to grow throughout the late summer, until the autumn when they will fall off – they usually fall off before the leaf itself – and the larva continues its life cycle still within the protection of the spangle but now within the added safety of the leaf litter. Over winter it pupates, hatching out in the spring as an adult, but all those emerging then will be female wasps. These female wasps will then fly up to the young flower buds of the oak and lay their eggs. These produce little round galls in the male catkins that look like currants. So next April you should have a look at the male catkins and you might find these reddish-yellow currant-sized galls. The larvae pupate inside the galls and eventually hatch out in early summer producing both males and females. The females, after they have been fertilized, will lay their eggs on the undersurface of the leaf, producing these spangle galls. Therefore you have two alternating generations – one that produces males and females in mid-summer and another in early spring that produces females only that lay eggs without fertilization.

'There are several species of these spangle gall wasp, three of which are quite common. This one is caused by a little beast called *Neuroterus quercusbaccarum*, which nicely obeys the rule that the smaller the animal, the longer the name! We were talking about the ecological theory that says that closely related species do not compete with each

other and here we have the possibility of three species of *Neuroterus* making spangles on the same oak! However, if you study them carefully you find that one species is commoner at the top of the crown, another around the edge and the third in the middle. Occasionally you will even find more than one species on the same leaf, in which case the different species partition up the leaf between them so that one species is commoner up the middle of the leaf, another produces spangles round the edge and a third, perhaps, at the tip.

'Other familiar galls that you can find are the oak apple gall, which does look, in fact, like an apple, and the "hop" or "artichoke" gall.

'Another feature which may be noticeable at this time of year is mildew on the leaves. This is a fungus disease (*Microsphaera alphitoides*) which is often common on the lammas growth and on oak coppice. Some years are worse than others and this year happens to be fairly bad.

'Let us follow the food chain through for a little while. What exactly is it that defoliates the trees so heavily? Well, I have already said that it was estimated some years ago, that well over 300 species of insect feed on oaks but again, it is an important ecological principle that you only normally have a small number of common species and a very large number of rarer species. A good example of that are the oak tree herbivores, as 90 per cent of damage that we can see here has been caused by only two species of moth. Therefore out of this great array of 300 or so species of beetles, bugs and moths, nearly all the defoliation has been caused by two species: the Winter Moth, *Operophtera brummata*, which will feed on a whole range of trees including fruit trees where it can be a pest; and the Green Oak Moth, *Tortrix viridana*, which only feeds on the oak. The Winter Moth has a very interesting life history – it seems to have the rather un-intelligent habit of emerging in the middle of November. The females are wingless, just to make the whole thing more bizarre, but the males are winged. The females emerge from their pupae in the ground during the winter and then climb the trunk of the tree where they mate with the males at night. They then climb further up, laying their eggs towards the tips of the branches or in crevices in the bark. The caterpillars emerge in the spring just as the leaves are breaking.

'The Green Oak Moth, on the other hand,

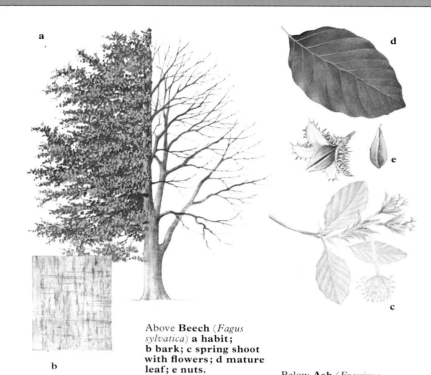

Above **Beech** (*Fagus sylvatica*) **a habit; b bark; c spring shoot with flowers; d mature leaf; e nuts.**

Below **Ash** (*Fraxinus excelsior*) **a habit; b bark; c flowering twig; d male flower; e leaf; f fruits.**

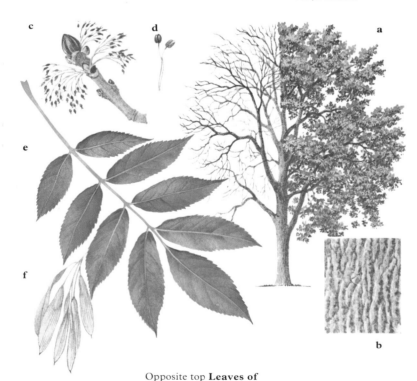

Opposite top **Leaves of Pedunculate Oak after a season's pre-dation. Over 300 species of insect are dependent directly on oaks, but most of the defoliation is carried out by the larvae of just two species: the Green Oak Moth and the Winter Moth.**

Opposite bottom **Spangle galls on the underside of an oak leaf. These are caused by a minute gall wasp,** *Neuroterus.*

has a more conventional life history. The caterpillars hatch just as the leaves unfold in early spring after overwintering as eggs. The adult moths appear in July and are quite small but do have forewings that are a most glorious emerald green colour.

'By May there is this enormous population of caterpillars feeding in the canopy. I can remember walking in the wood earlier in the year and it sounded as though it was raining. In fact, what I could hear was the caterpillar "frass" falling out of the trees and beating the vegetation beneath. When I looked at some of the leaves close to the ground, they were absolutely black with these caterpillar droppings. Following the food-chain through, this huge population is itself food for the woodland insect-eating birds particularly the tits and warblers. Interestingly, it is possible to estimate the size of this vast population of caterpillars.

'First, you have to calculate how much a single caterpillar eats. This you can do by taking some home and keeping them in tubes and measuring the amount of "frass" produced by each caterpillar in a 24 hour period. You then go back to the wood and lay a sheet beneath a tree and 24 hours later return and sweep up all the frass. This heap of caterpillar droppings is then weighed and if this is divided by the weight produced by one caterpillar, you have an estimate of the number of caterpillars in the tree above the sheet. People who spend their lives carrying out this kind of research are called "production ecologists".

'There is a link here with one of the major problems of oakwood ecology – the apparent lack of young trees. All the trees around here are roughly between 100 and 200 years old and there is very little apparent regeneration. This is something which worries foresters enormously and it is worth examining the possible reasons for this.

'All sorts of suggestions to explain this lack of regeneration have been put forward by ecologists but it is now generally agreed that the main cause is one which intriguingly links up the history of the management of these oak woods with their own internal natural history. One of the things you come across is that oak seedlings appear to occur virtually anywhere except an oak wood – you find them in your garden, on heathland, by roadsides and so on. It is much less frequent to find them under a dense woodland canopy. The reason for this is partly to do with the caterpillar story, as any seedling that comes

up and produces half a dozen luscious young leaves is going to be literally fallen upon in May by the hoard of caterpillars that have come adrift from the canopy above. So there is a reason why we cannot see many seedlings under an oak tree – they simply would not survive the predation. The question that then follows quite naturally is, has not that always been the case, so what circumstances make it so critical now? Well, under natural forest conditions you would have a completely mixed age-distribution of trees giving everything from saplings and young trees to mature trees and great gaps in the canopy caused by fallen trees. Where there are these natural gaps and clearings regeneration is able to take place. Now, an oak tree will live up to 350 years under normal conditions, and you would not expect natural gaps in the canopy to appear until the trees were at least that age. Now, most of our woods have been cut in the past and have generally regenerated from some fixed date in the past. This wood, for instance, we have looked at carefully and know that most of the trees are between 50 and 170 years old, making them middle-aged from the point of view of an oak tree. But more importantly, because they are all broadly the same age you do not have any natural gaps in the canopy and therefore there is little regeneration.

'It has been argued that a contributing factor is that the acorn crop is failing. However, if that is so, it must be largely for climatic reasons. Therefore, one is saying that the dominant plant of Britain's climatic climax is failing to regenerate itself because the climate is wrong. This is obviously not a tenable argument and although the crop does vary from year to year it is perfectly adequate.

'Another factor which affects the success of the acorn crop is that they are fed on by birds and mammals. One bird in particular does have an influence on the acorn crop and that is the Woodpigeon. This bird is primarily a forest species and unlike a lot of our native birds it is a true herbivore and has a crop like a pheasant or a partridge. It is therefore a grazing animal and under natural forest conditions it feeds on the ground in woodland clearings, and come the autumn it has a craving for a feast of acorns to liven its diet. But, of course, you again will ask if it has always done this in the past, why should it have such an effect now? Well, if one wanted to encapsulate in one sentence what man has done to the English landscape one could say that he has turned it from a forest with small areas of woodland clearing into a vast great woodland clearing with small areas of forest! Therefore any animal which is able to take advantage of these clearings has been enormously favoured by this change, and the Woodpigeon is a good example. What is more, man has improved the quality of the food grown in this big "woodland clearing" and pigeons take full advantage of this, as anyone with a cabbage patch will know to their cost. The Woodpigeon, then has increased its population dramatically as a result of man's activities and now, a far bigger population than the forest would naturally have been able to support still comes swooping in during the autumn for its annual feast of acorns. So here is a subtle and indirect way in which man has, perhaps, influenced the regeneration of the oak woods.

'Another feature which has changed over the years is the influence of large mammals on the forest. Most of our woods no longer have the great populations of Red Deer described by Bede. Nor do we have any Wild Boar left and they would have had an influence on the germination of the acorns. For, as well as eating them, they also churned up the forest floor while they rooted around, providing ideal conditions for germination. Many woods of the high Weald were used as swine pastures by the coastal manors and we know, for example, from studying Saxon documents and other evidence, that they were used primarily as pasture up until the Seventh Century.

'I suppose the pay off to all this is that in order to perpetuate the forest all that needs to be ensured is that each oak produces one offspring that will survive to maturity during its life. Try and imagine the number of acorns that one mature tree produces throughout its life – it is absolutely vast. It has been calculated that for each tree to produce one acorn to maturity the probability of acorn survival need be only something of the order of 1 in 18 million. So perhaps, if you don't see too many seedlings developing it is not quite as much a problem as some of the foresters believe. Also it is important to consider that naturally an oak takes 350 years to mature rather than 100–150 years, which is when the forester would regard a tree to be old.

A Speckled Wood sunning itself in a woodland glade. This woodland butterfly is common over much of southern England but is much more local over the rest of Britain.

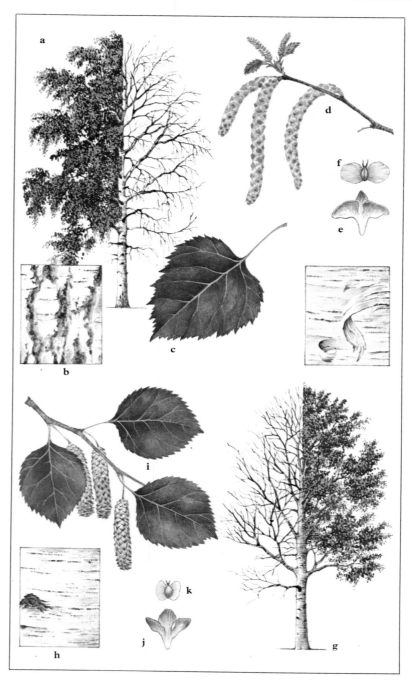

Silver Birch (*Betula pendula*) **a habit; b bark; c leaf; d flowering twig with male and female catkins; e scale; f nutlet. Downy Birch** (*Betula pubescens*) **g habit; h bark; i leafy twig with fruiting catkins; j scale; k nutlet.**

trees around here you can see that they have many dead branches on them, which would be anathema to a forester. But they are important to a large number of our rarest invertebrates, particularly beetles, some of which are specific to this habitat of dead wood on standing trees. So ironically, it is best to act in a positively negative way if you want to achieve this type of mature wood-land.'

Having had a good look at the trees we then moved off further into the wood and as we walked down David told us about the ground flora.

'One feature about woodlands that can tell us a great deal about the soil on which they are growing as well as the ecology generally, is the ground vegetation. And in these sandstone woods of the central Weald there are four plants which dominate the ground flora. Unfortunately, at this time of year, all we can see is the one, as we are surrounded by shoulder high Bracken. But if you were to come earlier in the year you would see three other species as well – Bluebells, Bramble and surprisingly enough, Honeysuckle. Four species which are all common British woodland plants. Totally unremarkable one might think, but if you told, say, a Japanese ecologist, that you had just come from an area with these four species he would say that you must have been in an oak woodland somewhere in Europe west of the Black Forest, south of Denmark and north of Spain. What's more he would have told you what type of soil you had been on. The reason that he could be so precise is the presence of the Bluebell, which although common here is globally an extremely restricted species. You do not find it outside the broad boundaries I have just mentioned and in Britain we are at the heart of its distribution range. The Honeysuckle is almost as restricted, but it goes a little further east and south. The Bracken, on the other hand, is one of the most widespread plants in the world but it is a useful indicator of acid, well-drained soils. It can be a very dominant plant, as it is here. It was probably originally a woodland glade species but as the woods became opened out it has been able to become even more dominant. It does not rely on sexual reproduction like most of the other ferns, but almost always spreads by underground rhizomes.

'The other interesting fact about Bracken is that, unlike the leaves of oak, it looks as if nothing eats it at all. It is said that it is a very

If you are managing an area of woodland as natural high forest the management prescription, interestingly, is to do nothing – one of the few occasions where this is true. This is to enable the older trees to fully mature and eventually die, opening out the canopy and providing dead and decaying wood. The importance of this dead wood in natural history terms is enormous. I believe it has been estimated that as much as 25 per cent of the British fauna, which it must be remembered is primarily forest dwelling, is in some way dependent on this dead or decaying wood. If you look at some of the dull plant from an entomologist's point of view, but this is only partly true. You don't have many insects feeding on it early in the year because the Bracken contains a lot of poisonous substances, including cyanides. But the cyanide content of the leaves declines as the season progresses so more animals feed on the Bracken later in the year, which is the opposite of the oak. The poisonous tannins in the oak build up as the season progresses so most of its predation occurs at the beginning of the season. If you look carefully at the Bracken fronds you will find that there are quite a few caterpillars feeding on them. These are mostly the larvae of sawflies, the preponderance of which is a peculiar feature of Bracken. Also at this time of the year you can find the tips

The stream at the bottom of the wood cuts its way through the porous sandstone under a dense woodland canopy which has enabled this humid micro-habitat to retain its links with a climatic period that was prevalent over much of Britain 5 000 years ago.

The Badger is one of our most popular woodland animals. Badgers will often have their sets at the edges of woods particularly on well-drained sloping ground. They forage at night around the fringes of the wood and the surrounding fields where earthworms are one of their main foods but their diet can vary enormously from season to season. These two Badgers are probably rooting around for insect grubs.

of the fronds curled up in a ball. This is a gall caused by a fly related to the house fly called *Chirosia parvicornis*. The other thing to look out for in late summer are little black cigar-shaped galls which can be found on the undersurface at the tips. This is another gall caused by a gall midge which is more or less specific to Bracken, called *Dasyneura filicina*.

'Here we are in a more open part of the wood and one of the things that you would expect to see in the clearings, is tree regeneration. In normal forest conditions you will find a sequence of tree species coming into the gap in the canopy leading up to the final re-establishment of oak or Beech, or whatever the dominant tree happens to be. The tree on this soil which functions as a "nurse crop" for the oak is the birch. Birches grow well on these infertile, rather well-drained soils. If this were a more fertile loamy soil the Ash would have been the first to colonise the clearing. Now, one of the things about the birch, which in a way is similar to the oak, is that we have two rather similar species – the Silver Birch, *Betula pendula*, and the Downy Birch, *Betula pubescens*. Here I have a shoot of each and if we look at the

young twigs, those of the Downy Birch, as the name suggests, are dull in colour because they are covered with a soft down. The twigs of the Silver Birch, on the other hand are a dark brown polished colour and are covered with little warts. Also, the shapes of the leaves are quite distinct, as the leaf tips of the Silver Birch are far more attenuated than those of the Downy Birch. Also the toothing on the margin of the Silver Birch leaf is much coarser and more irregular than that of the Downy Birch.

'Unfortunately, again like the oaks, you do find intermediates between the two. However, the reason for this is a little more clear than in the oaks. It seems that the Downy Birch arose as a result of a cross between the Silver Birch and an east European species, which is not found in Britain called *Betula humilis*. Now most hybrids are infertile but they can produce a fertile offspring if they undergo a doubling in the chromosome number. This is probably what happened and in effect a new species was formed – the Downy Birch. It is what the geneticists would call an allotetraploid and being a tetraploid species with a larger chromosome number they tend to be more variable than the "parent" diploid species. So the trick is – if in doubt, call it a Downy Birch. One word of caution, however, although the Silver Birch is generally a larger tree and is usually the one with pendulous branches, both the Silver and the Downy Birch can have the beautiful silver bark. The Silver Birch has a more continental distribution than the Downy and in this country you find that the Downy is quite often the commoner one on wet organic soils of the north and west. Where you have birch growing on chalk it will almost always be the Silver Birch.

'Both birches produce an enormous number of seeds each year and these germinate very readily, so it is quick to take advantage of any clearings. It does not form a very dense canopy and lets in enough light to allow young oak or Beech seedlings to develop yet, on the other hand, it makes enough shade to keep the ground flora from swamping the young seedlings.

'Birches have a large number of insects associated with them but not as many as the oaks. Generally speaking, the more common the tree and the longer its ecological history in an area, the larger will be the number of species that feed on it. There are two families of trees which are an exception to this and which have a larger number of insect species than you would expect, and those are the Rosaceae, which includes hawthorns, crab apples, Sloe and so on, and the other is the willow family – Salicaceae, which includes the willows, poplars and sallows. The converse to the general hypothesis is certainly true – that trees which have only recently been introduced have very few, if any, insects associated with them. Examples of this are the Sycamore and the Sweet Chestnut. A lot of evergreens also have few insects, for example, the Holly and the Yew. But this is not always the case as Scots Pine has a very large number of insects dependent on it.

'I should say at this point that relatively few insect groups have actually evolved the ability to eat leaves. We tend to think of one or two garden pests and imagine the world to be populated by a vast variety of insects feeding on leaves but if you look at all the thirty or so orders of insects, very few have evolved efficient means of feeding on leaves. The caterpillars of butterflies and moths, the larvae and adults of some beetles, gall wasps and sawflies and the bugs, have all exploited this food source. But that is only four orders. If you think about it, it is a very

hazardous existence as you have to be able to hang on to a pretty precarious perch in all kinds of adverse conditions. Not only that but you have to be able to eat through a leaf that is covered with a waxy waterproof layer which can be pretty tough. Add to all this the fact that the plants themselves have developed all sorts of mechanisms to combat insect predation, such as poisons, thick cuticles and all manner of thorns, spines and prickles, and you can see why so few insects have evolved to exploit them.'

We were now down at the bottom of the slope and were in a very different landscape. The old track way we had followed was now no longer open but surrounded by steep sided banks. The air had become more humid and noticeably cooler but the exciting thing was that the ground vegetation had gradually been changing and the dominance of the Bracken in the higher reaches had been slowly replaced by an increasing variety of different ferns. A stream was winding its way along the valley bottom and we sat beside this while David told us something of the history of this landscape.

'We have come down to the bottom of the valley and are now beside a stream which is running between great outcrops of the sandstone, which is producing some very steep sides, and the stream itself is full of sandstone boulders. The one thing that strikes you is that the whole atmosphere has changed, it feels cooler and damper. In other words it feels a bit like the climate you might find in a Welsh oak wood rather than one in Sussex. This is because of a special feature of these central Weald woodlands which sets them apart from most other woods in lowland Britain. The extraordinary thing is that there are a large number of plants and animals here which occur normally only in the extreme west of the British Isles. All this obviously requires some sort of explanation.

'The story seems to be that at one time somewhere between 5 000 BC and 3 000 BC, the whole of Britain and western Europe experienced a climate that was a great deal wetter than at present. This is called the Atlantic Period. In other words, the whole of western Europe was experiencing a climate similar to that which Ireland experiences today. Not only was it wetter but it was also warmer. At that time, then, species that are now restricted to the extreme western seaboard had a much wider distribution. Since then the climate

Idealised tracks of three of our larger mammals that might be encountered on a woodland walk. (A) Badger, with its broad hind pad and parallel row of toe pads; (B) Fox, with its closely spaced pads, notice the hair traces between the toes; (C) Domestic dog with its three-lobed hind pad and splayed toe pads (After Lawrence and Brown, 1967).

A

B

C

has become less oceanic and many species have become more restricted in their distribution but here in this one part of lowland Britain some of the species have persisted. Why is this? The answer seems to be in the very peculiar topography that we see here. These very steep narrow stream ravines faced with this very porous sandstone rock, which functions like a sponge, means that it is permanently wet and the atmosphere is constantly humid. Not only that, but this area has a rather peculiar ecological history in that until relatively recently this was still predominantly forest. Large areas were cleared probably around the Fourteenth Century, much later than the rest of lowland Britain, and even then it still remained one of the most heavily wooded parts of Britain. So these deep ravines have been permanently covered over in summer with a dense woodland canopy resulting in a micro-climate similar to that of western Britain.

'On this bank here we have the best example amongst the plants, of this particular phenomenon – the Hay-scented

Hay-scented Fern (*Dryopteris aemula*); a classic example of a plant with a disjunct 'oceanic' distribution, surviving as a relict in the Wealden oak woods.

Fern, *Dryopteris aemula*. It has lovely crisp fronds that look like big parsley-shaped leaves. It is one of Europe's rarest ferns and has a very "oceanic" distribution, being found in south-west Ireland, south-west England, the western edge of Scotland, western Spain, the mountains of the Azores and Madeira and here, in the Weald. It has this extraordinary "disjunct" distribution. It is doing very well this year but interestingly it is only growing on the north-facing side of the valley, so it is very selective even in this, its chosen niche. The humid atmosphere is supporting a superb variety of ferns. Below us are Hard Ferns and some Polypody. The Polypody is interesting because it is almost the only British plant, other than some mosses, which is habitually epiphytic. There are Male Ferns and Broad and Narrow Buckler Ferns as well as Borrer's Male Ferns and the delicate Lady Fern. We have even some Mountain Fern which is more characteristic of the fern meadows of the western Highlands!'

'So here we have a combination of ecology, archaeology, historical geography,

Hard Fern (*Blechnum spicant*); **a woodland fern of sandy soils. In the centre of the rosette of sterile fronds is an erect fertile frond.**

and pollen analysis all contributing information to explain this fascinating story. People keep turning up new things to strengthen the picture – a water beetle was found not far from here, about ten years ago, which was only previously known from Scotland and Scandinavia. It is flightless so it is unlikely to have arrived recently and is probably another example of a relict species.'

I must admit that I was rather amazed at the variety that was all around us but the dank atmosphere was beginning to creep through to our bones so we headed for a more open area nearby which, although it was wooded, was very different from the oak woods further up the slope. David explained.

'There are just one or two small areas of coppice in this wood and, here in the Weald, the most valuable and characteristic is Sweet Chestnut coppice. These are very different from the old primary woodland coppices of East Anglia where you have a mix of species. The ones here have been deliberately planted as a coppice crop. Sweet Chestnut is not a native to Britain as it was brought here by the Romans. I would suspect that they imported it not for its wood, but for the nuts, as in those days nuts were an important part of everyone's diet. However, since about the Seventeenth Century it has been extensively planted as a coppice species. Being southern European in origin it will only grow well in southern Britain and it also likes a well-drained soil. It is slower growing than Hazel and is cut on a 13–15 year rotation, forming beautiful long coppice poles. Today, it is the only hardwood coppice that is still really an economic proposition. It is used primarily for fencing and in this part of the country was also important in providing poles.

We made our way back through the wood past the ferns and the towering oaks until we came to an area where the trees looked rather small and stunted. It was obviously a different type of coppice to the vigorous Sweet Chestnuts in the valley bottom.

'This is an interesting feature. It is oak coppice which, in fact, is more characteristic of western Britain. One of the reasons that we have it here, is that we are now right on top of the ridge again and the sandstone is very close to the surface which limits the quality of the oak, which prefers a reasonable depth of soil. Oak is very deep rooting which is one of the reasons it does not do well on chalk which typically forms shallow soils. When the management of the wood was determined, it was obviously decided that because of this shallow soil, standard trees would not do well and so the oak was coppiced. If you look carefully you can see that the branches are coming up from old stools. It has not been coppiced now for some time and it is looking rather overgrown.

'What was it coppiced for? Well, the wood would have been used for all kinds of purposes but particularly it was used for charcoal. One of the things we must remember is that we are slap in the middle of what was the Wealden iron industry region. It is difficult to believe that 300 years ago this was the industrial heart of Britain, together with the Forest of Dean and the Lake District. The iron industry used an enormous amount of charcoal and to be of any use the oak had to be coppiced. It would have been cut on a twenty or thirty year rotation as it is slow growing.

'Another thing that it was grown for is its bark. Right up until the late Eighteenth Century leather was, after textiles, Britain's most important product in terms of value, and 90 per cent of the hides were tanned with oak bark. The amount that was used was phenomenal: for the period 1810 to 1815, England alone produced 90000 tons of oak bark for tanning. The tannin content of the bark declines with age so they did not

want anything too old and would therefore coppice the oak and strip the bark after, say, twenty years. This process of stripping the stems was called "flawing" and they used a special "flawing knife" for this. The bulk of the industry ceased in the 1830s when bark began to be imported from abroad, particularly from France after the Napoleonic wars. I can remember talking to the present Lord of the Manor's Reeve on Ashdown Forest about twenty years ago and he said he could remember his father, when he was a lad, talking about men going to the forest and flawing the oaks.'

Today the bark of the coppiced branches are covered with dense clusters of lichens and would now certainly be spared the flawing knife. We returned to the main path which had been worn down over the centuries by the comings and goings of countless generations of foresters and travellers. We had been the only people in the wood all afternoon, the birds were still foraging in the tree tops and as we approached the road the silence was quickly swamped by the familiar rush of cars. It had certainly been a fascinating walk, as David Streeter had clearly shown us that there was so much more to do than simply ambling along occasionally naming a plant or an animal here and there.

Opposite **On the well-drained soils of Southern England the Beech is an important forest tree. This photograph shows an old pollarded Beech. The branches would have traditionally been cut every fifteen years or so for firewood but judging from the size of the branches this individual has been left for at least a hundred years.**

The bark of this low coppiced oak is covered in a rich layer of lichens which testify to the humid atmosphere and the relatively unpolluted air.

73

Grassland walks

British grasslands and heaths

EVERY TIME YOU GET OUT the lawnmower you are conducting an ecological experiment, as you are not only doing battle with nature but are also aiding and abetting members of the most successful plant family in the world: the grasses. You don't believe me? Well, just stop mowing the lawn for a few years and see what happens. It will become more and more difficult to see anything in your garden as the lawn is taken over by shrubs, bushes and, eventually, turns into woodland.

Every year you put an enormous amount of energy into keeping your lawn nice and short by holding back the process of natural selection which, without you, would replace the open lawn with trees. In so doing, you are helping the grasses and certain other herbs to maintain their very successful stake in the environment. In the absence of people and mowers, grassland are maintained in their natural state by at least four other agencies: climate, soil, grazing animals and fire. Climate, especially too little rain, and soil, especially too much drainage, can so stunt and limit the growth of shrubs and trees that a natural grassland will develop. Fire and grazing can help in the maintenance of such grassland, prairie or savannah, in much the same way as

your lawn mower, by removing anything which is more substantial than a blade of grass. It is here that the grasses and grass-like plants, as well as certain other types of plants, come into their own as they are able to survive this constant grazing. They produce in effect, a self-generating cafeteria for a variety of grazing animals and an open plant community in which many other sun-loving plants can thrive.

The vast bulk of the British grasslands are not natural as they have been created and are maintained by man either with animal husbandry or more recently with leisure pastimes and sport, in mind. Nevertheless, many are very ancient and offer some of the most diverse and beautiful floras and faunas to be found anywhere in Britain. One of the most interesting questions is, where did all these beautiful grassland plants occur before man came on the densely wooded British scene? The answer is here amongst these grassland walks, which are often amongst the most rewarding of all. Grasslands are also nice places to take a picnic, but, when you do, be careful where you sit and always remember to take your rubbish home and leave all the grassland flowers for other walkers to enjoy.

THE WHALE-BACKED DOWNS of southern England and the picturesque Yorkshire Dales are both classic examples of walking country in Britain. These archetypal landscapes have a fascinating history of involvement with man which goes back to prehistoric times. The lowland valleys also contain a very different type of grassland, our ancient alluvial meadows – a rich habitat which is increasingly under threat both from changing agricultural practices and urban development.

CHALK AND LIMESTONE GRASSLANDS

The chalk and limestone grasslands of Britain, particularly the Downs of southern England are, perhaps, one of the most invigorating landscapes to explore for the walker. Their wide open vistas provide splendid views of the surrounding countryside and their gentle contours mean that they are easy on the feet. An added bonus is that these dry hills and coombes only really come to life during sunny summer days, so the nicer the weather during your walk, the more you are likely to see.

One of the chief attractions of these grassy swards is the profusion of wild flowers. Many of them are low growing, having adapted to the constant grazing of sheep. Look out for the tiny blue flowers of the milkworts and the yellow pea-like flowers of the vetches and trefoils. In autumn the hedges may be garlanded with travellers' joy or old man's beard – a sure sign that you are on chalky soils, as this climbing plant only grows on this type of soil. The real treasures to keep an eye out for, however, are the orchids. Some slopes may be covered in a delicate pink mass of pyramidal and fragrant orchids in mid-summer. But not all chalk grassland is so rich. A good indication that you are on a plant-rich sward is to look for features such as ant-hills. These take many years to form and would soon disappear if the land was ploughed. Signs of ancient settlements such as hill forts, lynches and ridge and furrow patterns may also indicate that the area has not been ploughed for a very long time. Even the colour of the grassland can help – the constant flowering and dying back of all the different plants throughout the year means that the sward may have a straw-coloured tinge to it, whilst a newly sown grassland which will be dominated by only a few grasses will probably appear a relatively bright green colour.

These grassland areas are particularly renowned for their butterflies and other insects. Look out for the blue butterflies on warm south-facing slopes and the marbled white butterfly where the grass is taller.

The northern limestone grasslands have their own specialities and the hard carboniferous limestones have produced some spectacular landscapes, such as at Ingleborough and Malham in Yorkshire, with their steep exposed cliff faces and rock strewn plateaux. On the wilder stretches of the dales and moors golden plover, curlews and wheatears can be seen in summer.

TRADITIONAL WATER MEADOWS AND HAY MEADOWS

Spring in the countryside should be a magical time. This is when even the most hardened city dwellers look to the budding trees and hedgerows and promise themselves that they must get out more often. Yet in these days of intensive arable farming they frequently find that the country is not as they remember it – the meadows with their carpets of spring flowers are difficult to find. Many of the old footpaths are still there but they flank great fields of winter wheat and barley where the only obvious signs of wildlife are the skylarks singing in the sky. There are still small areas which for various reasons have escaped improvement and can still boast a breath-taking display of colourful flowers. These plants have names that seem to echo their long history with man – dyer's greenweed, ragged robin, meadow saxifrage, common meadow-rue, lady's smock and ox-eye daisy.

In recent surveys patches of this type of meadow have been found in such diverse places as churchyards, pony paddocks and orchards. Certain plants such as the fritilliary, which is only found in these habitats, has dramatically decreased in numbers and is now found in only a few widely scattered sites such as in the *upper Thames valley* in Wiltshire where there are some fine series of water meadows. Other areas that have water meadows are the *Somerset Levels*, which cover a large area in central Somerset. These levels are flooded in winter providing good wintering conditions for water-fowl such as Bewick's swans and geese and breeding areas in the spring for snipe, redshank and lapwing. They have a rich grassland flora as well. The meadows in the flood plain of the River Arun at *Amberley* and *Waltham* and the River Cuckmere in Sussex are very good for both wintering wildfowl and summer meadow plants. The *Ouse Washes* in Cambridgeshire is justly famous for its wintering wildfowl, including large numbers of Bewick's swans and wigeon and also its nesting waders and ducks. It is also very good for wet pasture flowers. A particularly important stretch is owned as a reserve by the Cambridgeshire and Isle of Ely Naturalists' Trust at Manea.

LOWLAND HEATHS

The poor sandy soils that underly most of today's heathlands mean that they were relatively easy to clear of their thin forest cover when man first colonised these islands and these were consequently the first places to be farmed. For most of their history, however, these heaths have been treated as low quality land. This grazing has helped to create the open nature of the heaths with species of heathers and gorses and a few grasses dominating the scene. The poor soils mean that there are not the great variety of plants found on other soils but the dense cover provided by the shrubby nature of the heather means that there are many insects to see. Where there are clean boggy pools dragonflies can be found quartering along the water's edge and many species of beetles and wasps can be seen digging holes to lay their eggs in the friable soils. Because of the poor agricultural value of the land many of these heaths are owned by public authorities or used as training areas by the Ministry of Defence which allows limited public access. Perhaps the best time to see these heathlands is during August when the heather is in flower.

Above **In August the lowland heaths are a blaze of colour while the heather is in full bloom. The mixture of dense stands of mature heather and the more open young shoots provides a rich habitat for a host of invertebrates.**

Left **The towering limestone cliffs of Malham Cove, perhaps one of the most spectacular views along the Pennine Way.**

LOWLAND GRASSLANDS

1 North Downs Way Long-distance footpath forming part of the ancient Pilgrims' Way from Winchester to Canterbury and passing through some lovely chalk downland scenery.

2 South Downs Way This long distance foothpath from Beachy Head in East Sussex to the Hampshire border passes through some of the best areas of this splendid stretch of Downs.

3 Box Hill, Surrey. TQ 17 51 This beauty spot in the North Downs is a very popular area for weekend walking and despite its summer crowds of picnickers it still has a rich chalk flora and fauna which can be discovered by those prepared to explore. Juniper Hall Field Centre offers courses on the natural history of the area. National Trust.

4 Old Winchester Hill, Hampshire. SU 65 21 This chalk hill at the west end of the South Downs, is another popular weekend beauty spot. It has many interesting chalk plants including orchids and the round-headed rampion. National Nature Reserve.

5 Queen Elizabeth Country Park, Hampshire. SU 72 20 This park at the west end of the South Downs includes Butser hill which has steep grazed hillsides. An Iron Age demonstration farm is a feature of the park.

6 Danebury Hill, Hampshire. SU 33 37 A hill in the Hampshire Downs with a hill-fort dating back to the Bronze Age. Good chalk flora. Nature trail.

7 Kingley Vale, West Sussex. SU 82 11 This area of chalk downland and wood has some lovely open areas as well as an ancient yew forest. There is an Iron Age fort and tumuli. Nature trail. National Nature Reserve.

8 Ditchling Beacon, East Sussex. TQ 34 14 One of the higher parts of the South Downs with diverse scrub and chalk grassland flora and fauna. National Trust and Sussex Trust for Nature Conservation reserve.

9 Seven Sisters, East Sussex. TV 53 98 This famous beauty spot at the east end of the South Downs includes the chalk cliffs of Beachy Head. Country Park area including downland walks and meadowland in the Cuckmere Valley.

10 Wye and Crundale Downs, Kent. TR 07 45 One of the richest areas of the North Downs for chalk plants including many orchids and butterflies. Area includes a spectacular chalk coombe called the Devil's Kneading Trough. Nature trail. National Nature Reserve.

11 Queendown Warren, Kent. TQ 83 63 An area of old chalk downland with a rich flora and fauna, including orchids and butterflies. Leaflet. Reserve managed by the Kent Trust for Nature Conservation.

12 Dorset Coast Path. This is the Dorset section of the huge south-west Peninsula Coast Path. The section between Lulworth Cove and Ringstead Bay takes in some magnificent chalk cliffs and downs, including Durdle Door.

13 Hod and Hambledown Hill, Dorset. ST 85 12 A high chalk hill in the Dorset Downs crowned by an Iron Age hill fort. Excellent chalk flora and fauna.

14 Salisbury Plain, Wiltshire. SU 10 50 This area has some of the most extensive areas of chalk grassland in Britain. Unfortunately, a great deal is MoD land and access is limited to a few days in the year, such as Bank Holidays. Parton Down has excellent chalk flora.

15 Avebury, Wiltshire. SU 10 70 There are more prehistoric monuments in this area than anywhere else in Britain. The famous Avebury rings encompass the village. Nearby is West Kennet Long Barrow, a huge Neolithic burial mound. Also superb downland scenery.

16 Chiselbury, Wiltshire. SU 02 29 An ancient hill fort near Salisbury on an ancient routeway which now forms a 'green road' from Salisbury to near Shaftesbury.

17 Fyfield Down, Wiltshire. SU 15 69 Large area of chalk down with public access along footpaths. Good chalk flora and fauna. National Nature Reserve.

18 Brean Down, Somerset. ST 28 58 A narrow Carboniferous Limestone headland at the edge of the Mendips near Weston-super-Mare. Rich flora especially on the south-facing slopes.

19 Black Rock, Cheddar Gorge, Somerset. ST 47 54 A reserve including the steep valleys sides of the Gorge and some of the Mendip plateau. Good Carboniferous Limestone flora, including woolly thistle and many butterflies. Nature trail. Leased by the Somerset Trust for Nature Conservation.

20 Berry Head, Devon. SX 94 56 A Devonian Limestone headland in Torbay. Many rare and interesting plants. Nature trails and splendid views.

21 Gower Peninsula, West Glamorgan. SS 38 87 There are an excellent series of walks that can be taken from the village of Rhosili to explore the Carboniferous Limestone scenery of this beautiful peninsula. Best visited in spring for such flowers as spring cinquefoil and vernal squill.

22 Aston Rowant, Oxfordshire. SU 72 97 A large reserve on the Chiltern Scarp, split by the M40 motorway. Rich in chalk flowers and butterflies. Nature trail on Beacon Hill. National Nature Reserve.

23 Therfield Heath, Hertfordshire. TL 35 40 Despite its name this Chiltern reserve is outstanding for its chalk flora and fauna which includes the pasqueflower and the chalk-hill blue butterfly. Managed by the Herts. and Middlesex Trust for Nature Conservation.

24 Grangelands and Pulpit Hill, Buckinghamshire. SP 82 04 A chalk downland reserve in the heart of the Chilterns, including a fine range of chalk flowers and butterflies including the small blue and marbled white. Managed by the Berks, Bucks and Oxon Naturalists' Trust.

25 Dunstable Downs, Bedfordshire. SP 94 16 An area south west of Luton which is at the edge of the Chilterns. Ivinghoe Beacon (National Trust) is 244 metres high and provides good views of the Chilterns. Whipsnade Zoo is nearby. Totternhoe Knolls is a local reserve managed by the Beds and Hunts Naturalists' Trust.

26 Devils Ditch, Cambridgeshire. TL 60 63 A spectacular linear earthwork dating from about 500 AD stretching for over seven miles. The rich chalk grassland on the ditch is managed by the Cambridgeshire and Isle of Ely Naturalists' Trust.

27 Barnack Hills and Holes, Cambridgeshire. TF 97 04 A superb area of Oolitic Limestone grassland in the Soke of Peterborough, overlaying the remains of a medieval quarry. National Nature Reserve with smaller area managed by Northamptonshire Naturalists' Trust.

UPLAND GRASSLANDS

28 Upper Teesdale, Durham. NY 87 28 Visitor centre for area at Bowlees, Newbiggin. Outstanding region for upland flora with traditional haymeadows. Nature trails.

29 Humphrey Head, Lancashire. SD 39 73 A limestone headland in Morecambe Bay with a rich variety of flowers and splendid views across the bay.

30 Orton Meadows, Cumbria. NY 62 09 Hay meadows and grazed grassland on limestone soils. Rich in plant species such as bird's-eye primrose.

31 Hutton Roof, Cumbria. SD 55 78 A limestone pavement covering an extensive area with many characteristic species.

32 Ingleborough, Yorkshire. SD 75 75 A famous peak in the Pennine chain with spectacular limestone scenery including caves. There are large areas of limestone pavement including an RSNC reserve at Southerscales Scar, Chapel-le-Dale, which has good limestone grassland and typical pavement flora.

33 Malham, Yorkshire. SD 89 66 This popular area of the Yorkshire Dales has a wide range of Carboniferous Limestone features including scree slopes, limestone pavement and cliffs at Malham Cove.

34 Derbyshire Dales. SK 14 52 This area contains the southern-most limit for many of the northern plants such as the globe flower and melancholy thistle. There are many excellent walks using Matlock as a centre.

35 Great Ormes Head, Caernarvonshire. SH 75 82 A famous high limestone headland with a fascinating variety of maritime and limestone plants growing on its steep slopes, including many rare species.

LOWLAND HEATHS

36 Roydon Common, Norfolk, TF 68 22 An area of wet and dry heathland with many interesting heathland plants and insects including dragonflies. The wetter areas are dominated by cross-leaved heath and *Sphagnum* mosses. Partially managed by Norfolk Naturalists' Trust.

37 Breckland heaths, TL 80 80 An extensive area of dry heathland on sandy soils which overlay chalk, producing a distinctive landscape with many local plants and birds. Much of the area has been afforested but open areas still remain at various nature reserves such as Lakenheath Warren and Weeting Heath National Nature Reserves.

38 Chobham Common, Surrey. SU 97 65 Large area of heathland now bisected by motorway but with good areas of heather and wet heath still remaining. Very good for insects and other invertebrates.

39 South-west Surrey heathlands. SU 90 40 Very good dry and wet heathlands including Thursley Common National Nature Reserve, Frensham Common Country Park, Hankley and Witley Commons and Hindhead.

40 Ashdown Forest, Sussex. TQ 45 31. An area of heathland which was developed after the Wealden forest was cleared in the Middle Ages. Very good for heathland plants and insects.

41 New Forest, Hampshire. SU 28 06 An area of lowland heath of international importance containing extensive tracts of heather and valley bogs. Many local and unusual heathland plants and animals can be found including dragonflies, reptiles and warblers.

42 Purbeck Heaths, Dorset. SZ 00 83 Includes Studland Heath (national Nature Reserve) and Arne Heath (RSPB reserve). Very good area for heathland animals and plants including reptiles, birds such as the nightjar and Dartford warbler, and dragonflies.

43 Lizard Peninsula, Cornwall. SW 71 20 Unusual area of heath overlaying serpentine rock with many local and rare species of plant including Cornish heather.

Chalk
Chalk grassland
Limestone bedrock
Oolitic limestone

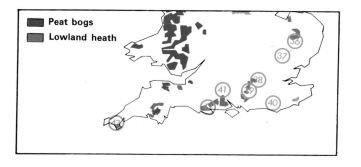

Peat bogs
Lowland heath

Bellamy's wild grass chase

Wherever you stand in the British Isles you are not too far away from grass. Yes, even in the middle of the vast acreages of moorland, there are grasses forming an important part of the living community. So, I thought I wouldn't move too far from my home, or off the tarmac and simply take a trip from the coast to the top of the Pennines and see what grasses I could find. The journey produced many kinds of grasslands, each one with its own old favourite species and each one with its surprises. What have sheep's fescue, common bent and daisies in common? Grazeability, and, from the look on the sheep's and cattle's faces, palatability! But they also have trample tolerance; a factor which is of immense importance when faced with a herd of hungry animals. The flowering heads of the grasses were there all the way along my journey, blowing in the breeze and repeatedly reminding me of their dominance in the landscape. I wonder what the same journey would have been like before man and his domestic animals nibbled their way onto the scene?

Here I am up in the Pennines amidst a glorious scene full of grasses (with a splash of colour from some knapweeds!) Over the wall is a small flock of sheep which work pretty hard at making sure it stays that way, for without their incessant grazing it would soon return to scrub and woodland.

Bellamy's wild grass chase

It is true to say that wherever you go in Britain you are never far away from that most important family of flowering plants – the grasses. To show you just how important grasslands are as part of the landscape I've decided to go on a series of walks today in the north-east of England, starting right down on the beach near Teeside and finishing up on the very tops of the Pennine hills.

So here I am with my feet almost in the sea and the very first plant that I have found growing on the beach is a grass – lyme grass, to be exact, *Elymus arenarius*. Now this is a nice, big grass, so it gives me an ideal opportunity to show you the very special features of grass plants. First of all, beneath the surface all the plants have a root system and this one is doing an important job binding the sand together. Then above the surface we have the stem or, to give it its correct botanical name, the culm. This stem is divided into a series of hollow sections called inter-nodes which are joined by nodes – the joints that stick out on your bamboo canes. The wierd thing about the stems of grasses is that you can't actually see them. This is because they are covered by a sheath of leaves. It is from the nodes that the leaves first arise; they then run up the stem enveloping it in a sheath until suddenly they turn away to form the leaf blade. On this lyme grass it is a beautiful blue-green colour. At the junction where it turns outwards, if you take a close look, you will see a thin membrane-like growth on the inside of the leaf called a ligule. In this grass it is just a tiny rim of tissue but in some other grasses it is much bigger. Also if you look carefully you can see two rather wierd lobes at the base of the leaf blade; these are called auricles. These features are always worth finding as they often help to identify the type of grass you have. If we continue to look up the stem we can see another node, another leaf sheath and blade, followed by another node and so on, until we see the culm sticking out of the top with a great mass of flowers on it.

Within this basic structure grasses have adapted to cope with a whole range of environmental problems. Here we are on a sandy beach which is a great place to visit on a sunny day but it is a pretty tough place for a plant to live. They can't make use of the seawater so they have to take advantage of any rainwater that falls. The rain then sinks away into the sand very quickly or is evaporated away by the salty winds. So our grass has to be able to hold on to what water it can

get. If you look at the leaf of the lyme grass and run your fingers across its surface you will notice that it is ridged and furrowed. Down in the deep furrows are the stomata pores from which water is lost and these are almost roofed over with a weft of microscopic hairs to cut back on the loss. If the going gets really tough the leaf will roll up into a tube and protect itself almost entirely. So that's our first grass – now let's start heading inland and see what we can find.

Behind us is a series of sand dunes which owe their existence almost entirely to the marvellous binding properties of the root systems of another grass – Marram grass, *Ammophila arenaria*. Beyond that is a low cliff where we should find more members of the grass family.

A short, sharp climb has taken us onto the edge of the cliff and here I am sitting looking out to sea from a nice patch of grassland sward. If I get down and have a closer look at it, the first thing that I can see is that the dominant plant is, you've guessed it, a grass. But what sort of grass? Well, here's the culm and there's a long, long leaf which is setaceous or hair-like. That tells me that I'm looking at red fescue, *Festuca rubra*. Really

Right Down at the seaside! Here is one of the first intrepid colonisers of the sands – *Elymus arenarius*, lyme grass. It has tough leaves that can roll up to stop it losing moisture and protect it from enthusiastic botanists.

Opposite Up on the cliff top there is already a dense covering of grasses. Here we have the fine leaves of red fescue, *Festuca rubra* and the striking flowers of the bloody crane's-bill, *Geranium sanguineum*, which is a good indication of rich limestone grassland. The name crane's-bill refers to the fruits which look like the beak of a miniature crane.

the only way for you to be sure which species of grass you have is to look very closely and make some drawings of the important parts like the leaf shape and the ligule and compare it with a good guide when you get home. A must for anyone keen to study grasses is a wonderful book with lots of clear drawings, called simply, *Grasses*, by Charles Hubbard. Once you know what to look for and are familiar with the common species it is not nearly so difficult as it first appears. Start by trying to identify some local grasses.

In amongst the red fescue are an awful lot of other plants and standing out above everything else are the striking deep red flowers of the bloody crane's-bill, *Geranium sanguineum*. Now, because it is a lime-loving plant that immediately tells me that the underlying rock here, as we are in the North East, is magnesium limestone. If we search around we should find some other plants that like a fairly basic soil. Yes, there is some lovely rock-rose, *Helianthemum chamaecistus*, with its yellow crinkly petals, and over here is some salad burnet, *Poterium sanguisorba*, both plants that you wouldn't be surprised to find along any stretch of the chalk slopes of the southern Downs. Here is something that tells me we are still close to the sea – sea plantain, *Plantago maritima*. The leaves of this plant grow in a typical plantain-like rosette, but are rather fleshy and channelled and every now and then, along the edge, there is a little glandular tooth which says that it is sea plantain rather than the much commoner long-leaved ribwort plantain, *P. lanceolata*. So we can see that a grassy sward can allow room for plenty of other plants to grow. However, normally if the grassland was left to its own devices it would eventually be taken over by coarser plants and scrub-up, climaxing as an area of woodland. In a way the grasses sign their own death warrants by producing such a super matrix for other plants to grow in. But this little scrap of grassland right on the coast is rather special in that the constant effects of high winds and salty sprays have kept the ranker plants at bay. Therefore this is an example of truly natural grassland and would have been the type of place where plants which now cover our open countryside first originated. Almost everywhere else that you see grassland it has been created and maintained directly or indirectly by man. Every time you get out your lawn mower and mow the lawn you are holding back the process of natural succession to woodland.

When man first arrived on the British scene he found that nearly all the landscape through which he had to travel was festooned, swathed and covered in forest. The only places where there were open habitats that could support grasses in any numbers were mountain tops, sand dunes, the edges of saltmarshes, maybe the occasional river cliff and sea cliffs like this. But why do the grasses appear to thrive under all this constant cutting and chewing to which man and beast subject it. Well, we can see the answer to this if we just look at the leaf of our red fescue. There's the leaf blade again and below it is the sheath and there right at the base is where the growth of the leaf actually occurs, from what is known as a meristem, where cells are actively dividing to provide new growth. So if I was a cow and came along chewing at these delicious grasses I could eat my fill and still leave the meristem right there at the bottom, so that the grass could still thrive. So where there is this grazing pressure only the plants that can do this or that have regenerative buds right down on the surface, or even underneath the ground, can survive. So the grasses are at an enormous advantage. Another way in which grasses are able to make full use of these open situations is that they can spread vegetatively, putting out numerous underground stems called rhizomes or surface ones called stolons which can soon make a dense green carpet of grasses, as anyone who has planted a lawn will know.

Talking of lawns, if we just clamber over this ridge we can have a quick look at some superbly kept areas of grassland. Here I am standing beside an immaculately maintained green on a golf course. We've just made sure that we aren't disturbing anyone, so if I get right down on my tummy I can have a close look at this mini-habitat. Absolutely perfect! This patch has been so beautifully tended and clipped that it is difficult to make out what type of grasses are growing. There appears to be three different sorts here and then nothing else at all, which just shows what man can do, for the patch we have just walked over from, not ten metres away, has been recently surveyed and contains over 100 species of flowering plant.

Now, as we go on our journey we are going to see how man has managed certain areas of the countryside, often with the result of creating large areas of grassland. So if we head for the car we will drive along and see what we can find.

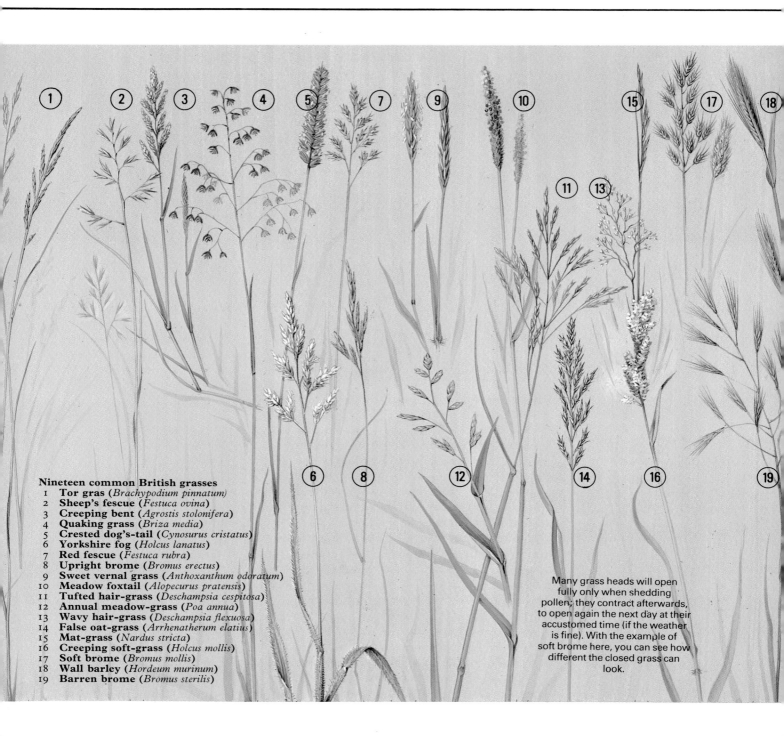

Nineteen common British grasses
1   **Tor gras** (*Brachypodium pinnatum*)
2   **Sheep's fescue** (*Festuca ovina*)
3   **Creeping bent** (*Agrostis stolonifera*)
4   **Quaking grass** (*Briza media*)
5   **Crested dog's-tail** (*Cynosurus cristatus*)
6   **Yorkshire fog** (*Holcus lanatus*)
7   **Red fescue** (*Festuca rubra*)
8   **Upright brome** (*Bromus erectus*)
9   **Sweet vernal grass** (*Anthoxanthum odoratum*)
10 **Meadow foxtail** (*Alopecurus pratensis*)
11 **Tufted hair-grass** (*Deschampsia cespitosa*)
12 **Annual meadow-grass** (*Poa annua*)
13 **Wavy hair-grass** (*Deschampsia flexuosa*)
14 **False oat-grass** (*Arrhenatherum elatius*)
15 **Mat-grass** (*Nardus stricta*)
16 **Creeping soft-grass** (*Holcus mollis*)
17 **Soft brome** (*Bromus mollis*)
18 **Wall barley** (*Hordeum murinum*)
19 **Barren brome** (*Bromus sterilis*)

Many grass heads will open fully only when shedding pollen; they contract afterwards, to open again the next day at their accustomed time (if the weather is fine). With the example of soft brome here, you can see how different the closed grass can look.

Well, here we are only a few miles inland and I am standing by a major road looking at a very different landscape from the cliffs and sand dunes we have just left behind. I can see a whole variety of man-made grasslands. This is what I like to call lowland eutrophic farmland. Eutrophic means nutrient-rich, and here there are enough potential nutrients to support lush grasses, hedgerows and even the odd bit of woodland. If I just scan the view I can see pastureland with sheep grazing. There the colour of the grass appears as a dull greeny brown. And then I can see a lot of improved pastures which are a much brighter green. In the foreground many of the fields have cereals growing in them. Remember that cereals are grasses as well. In this part of the country the farmers will be growing wheat, oats or barley. At the moment the crop is turning a rich golden

A lovely splash of yellow by the roadside provided by a thriving colony of birds-foot trefoil, *Lotus corniculatus*.

Opposite **A classic view of lowland agriculture with a rich mixture of arable and grazing land. Notice the tall hedgerows and stands of trees, all of which indicate the richness of the land.**

colour and will soon be ready for harvesting. Behind these fields the farmers have already done this and the soil has been freshly ploughed ready to be sown with winter wheat. So everywhere we look, there is a patchwork of man-made grassland held together by hedgerows. The dominant standard tree in these and the small patches of woodland is the ash, *Fraxinus excelsior*. Ash is a kind tree to grasses as it is late in coming into leaf and then it has these delicate compound leaves which allow a lot of light down to the soil.

Right now we have this marvellous view over Wierdale with Durham Cathedral in the distance. But when man first arrived here it would have looked very different. In fact, he probably would not have had a view at all as there would have been a dense canopy of forest. Today there is this marvellous diversity of habitats and, indeed, it was the prosperity that came with the clearance of the forest and the development of lowland agriculture that contributed to the wealth of the society which built the Cathedral.

We've now jumped back in the car and driven just a little further inland. I've stopped off here to take a look at a very underrated type of grassland – the roadside verge. Along this stretch it has been regularly cut up to about three metres from the tarmac. Because it has been mown we should be able to find quite a diversity of plants growing

A male chaffinch perched in a blackthorn hedge in spring. The hedges that surround the farmers' grassy fields make important nesting sites for a host of birds including the colourful finches and melodious thrushes. Without these woody corridors our countryside would be a sadder place both aesthetically and in terms of the variety of wildlife that it could support.

here. Now, I've just knelt down and immediately I can see some white clover, *Trifolium repens*, and the good old dandelion, *Taraxacum officinale*. Dandelions are one of those plants that has regenerative buds right down in the middle of the rosette of leaves. So that when the council workers come along with their mower or when you are mowing your lawn the blades go over the top of the bud and new leaves can start to grow. There are, of course, many grasses here and if we look over by the hedge, where the council mower has failed to reach, we can see if we can identify some of them.

Here we have the 'big four' grasses of our roadsides. The first one that I can pick out is the false oat-grass, *Arrhenatherum elatius*, which is big in more than one sense of the word as it is almost as tall as half a Bellamy. Now to confirm my identification I need to look somewhat closer at the grass. Here's a leaf blade and there is the sheath, so if we look at the junction we should find the ligule and, yes, there it is; a very short one, probably no more than a millimetre in length. To do the job properly you should make a careful sketch and measure it.

Now, the next grass is much, much easier to identify because its flowering panicles look

like its name – cocksfoot, *Dactylis glomerata*. The lower branches of flowers stick out at an angle that is supposed to resemble the spur on the foot of a cockerel. Again, this can be quite a tall grass; up to 140 centimetres high. If you look at the ligule you will notice that it is longer than the previous one; usually between two and ten millimetres in length with a ragged pointed tip. Cocksfoot is a good drought-resistant grass as it roots deeply and is able to tap supplies of water throughout the year.

Over here is a very important grass perennial rye-grass, *Lolium perenne*. The farmers use it a lot as it provides highly nutritious grazing for long periods of time. It has a very distinctive flowering spike with the tufts of flowers arranged alternately on either side of the stem to give it a rather nice flat appearance. The ligule on this plant is very short, like the oat-grass, but if you look closely you will see that it does have these two lobes or auricles coming off at the base of the leaf blade.

If I look around a bit I might find the fourth of our big four grasses. Now here it is. A very distinctive grass called timothy, *Phleum pratense*. This is a nice soft grass that used to grow wild in water meadows. It is named after an American agriculturalist called Timothy Hanson, who recognised its worth back in the early eighteenth century and introduced it to the United States. It doesn't do too well as a pasture grass but is very important as a fodder crop. You can spot it by its narrow, cylindrical spike of flowers, which give it its other name of cat's-tail. The ligule is blunt.

All these grasses flourish in these rich eutrophic lowlands, as do the farmers' crops. And just over the hedgerow here we can see a field of stubble; all that remains after the farmer has harvested and bailed up his cereal crop. Perhaps the farmer will burn the remains or just leave it to rot and plough it in later in the year. But the important thing to notice is that the flora of the field is completely man-managed. Except for a narrow band just by the hedge there is very, very little there that the farmer has not deliberately put in. He has used all sorts of selective herbicides, insecticides and fungicides to ensure that. So between the road and the field this little strip of verge and hedgerow represents a vital linear nature reserve that is covered with grassland. Just to make the point about how interesting these verges can

A combined harvester cutting the corn. The threshed corn is held in a large storage tank whilst the straw is thrown out at the rear. The crop here is probably a strain of barley, *Hordeum*, which, of course, is a grass.

Blue moor-grass, *Sesleria caerula*, with its blue head of flowers and boat-shaped leaves.

Right **A flowering spike of sainfoin**, *Onobrychis viciifolia*, **photographed at its most northerly outpost in Britain, a roadside verge near Durham.**

Opposite top **A very ancient form of grassland management – a deer park, which is currently playing host to a considerable number of sheep!**

Opposite bottom **A beautiful view across a patchwork of fields in the Dales. Although the grasses in the valleys are still doing very well, the presence of dry stone walls indicates that the environment is harsher.**

be, if we walk along here I will show you a plant that has an interesting story to tell.

Now, here I am standing on a fairly steep embankment alongside the road and just in front of me is an area that has only a sparse covering of vegetation. It has been kept this way probably by a combination of council mowing and accidental burning. The underlying rock is the magnesium limestone that we met down on the coast and just here I can see a rather special plant – the lovely pink and red flowering spikes of sainfoin, *Onobrychis viciifolia*. When you go on your holidays in the Mediterranean you'll find it growing in the grassland and roadsides there. It follows the limestones and chalks all the way from the sunny south through Britain to here. And that's as far as it goes. It doesn't even grow on the other side of the road. It seems as if the joint influences of soil and climate allow it to grow this far and no further. There are several other plants in this area that reach their northern limit on these magnesium limestones around Durham. But the special point of bringing you here is that if this little corner of the roadside verge became overgrown with bushes and trees, then this plant would not be able to survive and this little part of the country near Durham would not be quite as special as it is. So when you are out on your walks don't dismiss the miles of verge and look straight over the hedge. You never know what you might be missing.

Right, let's get back in the car and I'll take you to a little piece of nearby grassland and show you a species of grass that really tells you that you're 'up north'.

We've just parked the car and taken a short walk to another rather special place and all around me is a superb open grass community on magnesium limestone. Nearly every bit of this special type of grassland is under threat either from industry, who have quarried vast areas of it to make such things as fire bricks to line the great steel furnaces, or from farmers who quite logically see more profit out of ploughing it to grow crops or reseeding it. But, although there are many very rare and unusual plants here, today I want to show you a grass that before I came to the North East I'd never seen – the blue moor grass, *Sesleria caerulea*. It is one of the first grasses to come into flower in the spring and in April and May you can always tell it by its wonderful shiny blue head of flowers. During the rest of the year you can see these beautiful leaves. They have a duck-egg blue colour on the inside, rather like the lyme

grass we saw earlier on. If you look more closely they have quite distinct veins like tram-lines running along the middle. The leaf is keeled with a distinct boat-shaped tip. This grass is common up in the high arctic, and right the way across the limestones of Scandinavia. You will even find it on the tops of the limestone mountains of the Dolomites and the Alps. In fact, it might be classed as an arctic-alpine plant. So what is it doing growing down here in the middle of lowland County Durham? Well, we're not quite sure. But we do know that it grows especially well on the magnesium limestone. So this is one unique piece of semi-natural grassland – I say 'semi' because obviously without the intervention of man it wouldn't be here at all, but I am afraid the further efforts of man to manipulate his environment means that its days are numbered.

We must now move on out of these lowlands and see what grasslands we can discover further up the road.

We are now quite a bit further inland and have just pulled off to look at one of my favourite spots in the area. It is a very old form of grassland management. If we look around we will probably see some clues as to what this is. Look, there's a lovely area of grass which looks as though it is fairly regularly grazed. There are magnificent trees dotted all around and a castle in the background. But if you look at the trees you can see that they have all been browsed up to a particular height which almost certainly reflects the reach of the animals. If you start looking about you can see some rather elegant animals grazing quietly in the distance. They are fallow and red deer and, of course, this is a deer park. During the medieval times deer parks were considered important hunting and pleasure grounds for the elite of the age and many of the parks we have today are directly descended from those times. So that is another type of grassland to add to our list.

Bellamy's wild grass chase

Here I am up amongst the splendid greenery of the Dales, chewing on a stalk of the gorgeously hairy Yorkshire fog grass. The stand of rushes and the presence of creeping thistle all around me indicate that the soil has been disturbed recently and as a result the nourishing grasses are being pushed out.

Further along now and here is another good place to stop at – the village green. Today they are used as a place to walk the dog or just sit and maybe watch a game of cricket. In the past, however, they were a place of vital importance. It was to the village green that the local livestock was taken when danger loomed in the guise of predators or outside raiders. However, we'll just sit down and have our sandwiches and see how the local cricket team is faring. Not too well, I'm afraid to say. They might get a few more runs if the out-field wasn't so slow. But that is because our friends the grasses are growing so well. I can see some cocksfoot, perennial rye-grass and a new species, meadow fox-tail, *Alopecurus pratensis*.

Its now later in the day and we are further inland and I can actually see the tops of the Pennines in the distance. It is a very different landscape. Gone are the lush hedgerows with all their lovely shrubs. Their place has been taken by dry-stone walls, which make a much more effective barrier than a very, very slow-growing hedge. If you look around, many of the trees, unless they are growing in sheltered hollows, are pretty stunted. This is because we are now getting into a much harsher environment than down in the lowlands. Still, everywhere you look there are fields. In fact, I can remember seeing a wonderful British Rail poster when I was a little boy which said: 'Come to the Dales'. It was illustrated with a picture showing a patchwork quilt of different coloured greens picked out by dry-stone walls. I honestly thought such a beautiful man-made landscape as that could not exist. But there it is; a patchwork quilt.

Each one of the fields full of grass is a gigantic solar cell fixing energy from the sun's rays and doing an immense job for the farmer in feeding his livestock. Up here the climate is too harsh to grow arable crops. However, many centuries ago the climate was warmer and you can often find signs of the old lynchets formed by the ploughs of medieval farmers. Nowadays there are only cattle and sheep here.

Let's have a look and see what grasses we have growing in the area. If we start by looking again at the roadside verge I can see the same sorts of grasses that we found lower down but they are not growing quite so tall. There's a typical mixture of false oat-grass, rye-grass and cocksfoot with some Yorkshire fog, *Holcus lanatus*. No, I'm not describing the weather, that's the name of a rather

gorgeous hairy grass. I like to think that it got that name as it holds the morning mist that creeps along the hillside just above the surface. Next to it is another *Holcus* grass, creeping soft grass, *H. mollis*. They are easy to tell apart because the creeping soft grass has a little tuft of hairs on each of its nobbly nodes, rather like an ageing boy scout's knees. These two grasses become more and more important in the verges and pastures as we gain altitude. If we look over the wall we can see a very different type of grass community. The tall grasses have gone and we have a short cropped mixture of sheep's fescue grass *Festuca ovina*, and the highly adaptable red fescue. In amongst these, in full autumn fruit, are the distinctive flowering spikes of crested dog's-tail, *Cynosurus cristatus*. If you look at the spike you will immediately notice that one side is flat and the other has dense tufts of flowers. A good way of remembering the shape is to think of a dog that lives in a house and which continually bangs its tail on the floor until one side is almost perfectly flat whilst the other is bushy. I'm sure you've met one. Well, there it is: the crested dog's-tail. This grass is an indicator of acid grassland, so not the best soil but certainly good enough to keep the grass going.

If you look at the sheep droppings in the field you can see where they have been grazing. Sheep are very fastidious grazers and will keep going back to eat the sweeter tasting grasses. So after a time they can begin to change the make-up of the grass community in the field. As long as the farmer is careful and doesn't stock his fields with too many sheep no damage will be done and the grasses will continue to thrive. There are a few patches of stinging nettles, *Urtica dioica*, in the field. Now, I will tell you how they got to grow there. I can't see any cows in the field at the moment but they are certainly around as there is a whacking great cow-pat right down in front of us. If I were to lift it up I would find that the grasses beneath it had all gone yellow because all the light had been shut out. It will take quite a long time for that cow-pat to be broken down and during that time it will be releasing phosphorus and other nutrients into the soil. Now, stinging nettles are great phosphorphiles and will readily take advantage of such a situation, crowding out the grasses.

If I just cross over the road I can show you a very different type of grassy field. Here the farmer has decided to do something radically

different. He has ploughed the field and reseeded with a mixture of plants. It is a much lusher green than the more traditional pasture we have been looking at. Unfortu-nately it is not in flower but I would guess that it contains some special strains of perennial rye-grass with a little timothy grass. In amongst the grasses I can also see

some white clover which would have been planted with the grass as its roots help fix the nitrogen in the soil, providing a very cheap source of nitrogen fertiliser. It is called a short-term ley and is very green compared with the other side of the road. Mind you, to achieve this the farmer will have had to expend a lot more energy. He has had to plough it and seed it and fertilise it to get it established and will have to continue to ply it with herbicides and fertilisers to maintain its productivity. A difficult choice for the farmer.

Up here the climate is very harsh in the winter and so the sheep have to have their feed supplement during these bleak months. In order to do this the most productive areas

Above **The evening light catching the flowering head of one of our most common grasses, cocksfoot,** *Dactylis glomeratus.*

Left **Here we are right up in the Pennines. As you can see the trees have almost all gone and these summer pastures will be covered in snow for large parts of the winter.**

are often set aside not as pastures for grazing but as fields where the grasses are allowed to grow as a crop and are then cut in the summer for hay. They then become meadows and some of the meadows in this part of the world have very ancient histories.

Now we've driven a bit further along to one of these meadows and the first thing that I hope we are going to notice is the incredible diversity of the plant species growing in them. There is an interesting length of stone wall separating the roadside verge from the meadow. If we take a look, unlike our pasture and the ley, we should find that there is not too much difference between the two sides. Both do seem to have most of their plants in common. I can see quite a list: meadow foxtail, oxe-eye daisy, *Chrysanthemum leucanthemum*, tufted vetch, *Vicia cracca*, wood vetch, *V. sylvatica*, field scabious, *Knautia arvensis*, knapweed, *Centaurea nigra*. Absolutely super. And over there are some more – the melancholy thistle, *Cirsium hetrophyllum*, with its distinctive nodding head. Then there's wood crane's-bill, *Geranium sylvaticum*, lady's mantle, *Alchemilla vulgaris*, and some great burnet, *Sanguisorba officinalis* in the damper bits. The list is long which reflects partly the continuity of management over the centuries and the fact that neither the verge or the meadow are grazed but are sown at regular times of the year, which allows for a greater diversity of plants. Most of these meadow plants set their seed fairly early in the year so that the mowing doesn't cut short their life cycle. You will have probably noticed the words wood and *sylvaticum* popping up in my list. This is because some species that are considered as woodland plants in the south of England crop up here as meadow plants. All together these northern hay meadows are certainly to be treasured. It would be unforgivable if we let them completely disappear.

Still, we still have to travel a bit further if we are to reach the tops of the Pennines before the end of the day so it's back to the car.

Now we are quite high up, well over the 400 metre mark, and the landscape is starting to look decidedly different. Yes, it's moorland with patches of grassland coming right up to the edge of the road. A deep ditch beside the road to carry the water away warns us that it is a very rainy environment. The trouble with so much rain is that not only does it water the grasses but it also leaches the soils so that they will tend to be very acid and poor in nutrients. Naturally the grasses tell us that.

The sheep's fescue is still with us but here it is a rather scruffy plant. There are also some new ones. This is sweet vernal grass, *Anthoxanthum odoratum*. It is one of the easiest plants to remember. It has a fresh yellow-green colour and has a dense spike of flowers. Now, hold the spike of flowers and give it a sharp tug – usually you find that the flower-bearing culm parts company with the rest of the plant. All you do now is chew the base of your stalk and you should find that it has a lovely sweet taste. That is how it got its name and the taste is in fact coumarin, a chemical which gives hay its distinctive sweet smell. It is also said to stimulate the appetite.

The grasses up here don't grow well enough to provide hay for the sheep in winter and so when the farmer takes his sheep in during the colder months he has to bring up hay from the lower areas. In fact, many of these fells are 'stinted', which means that they can only hold a certain number of sheep each year. When most of the rules of upland grassland management are adhered to, the grasses remain as a nice tasty mixture and both the farmer and the sheep stay happy. But I'm afraid over-grazing in some areas has started to alter things quite dramatically. As we have said, sheep are fastidious eaters and will select the lusher grasses to eat and leave the tougher, harsher ones. So these unpalatable species have an enormous advantage and begin to slowly but surely take over the grassland community. Here is one of the toughest grasses of the lot – mat grass, *Nardus stricta*. Again it is an easy grass to identify with its one-sided comb of spikelets and its bristle-like tufts of leaves. I'm going to chew some of it. Ugh, horrible, stringy stuff. No wonder the sheep give it a miss. Here it is covering the ground, so the sheep are pretty hard pressed to find a tasty meal. In places you can see where they appear to have pulled it up and almost thrown it down again in disgust. A sure sign of over-grazing.

There is another type of plant up here that the sheep don't like, which takes advantage of the over-grazed land. That is heath rush, *Juncus squarrosus*. It grows in almost circular tufts with a central flowering stalk, that may be as much as twenty centimetres high, sticking out of the top. It is a tough old plant but it is ideal during the winter months for the grouse that come along and eat the seeds when all else is covered with snow.

So here we are up in the Pennines and wherever we have stopped on our journey up

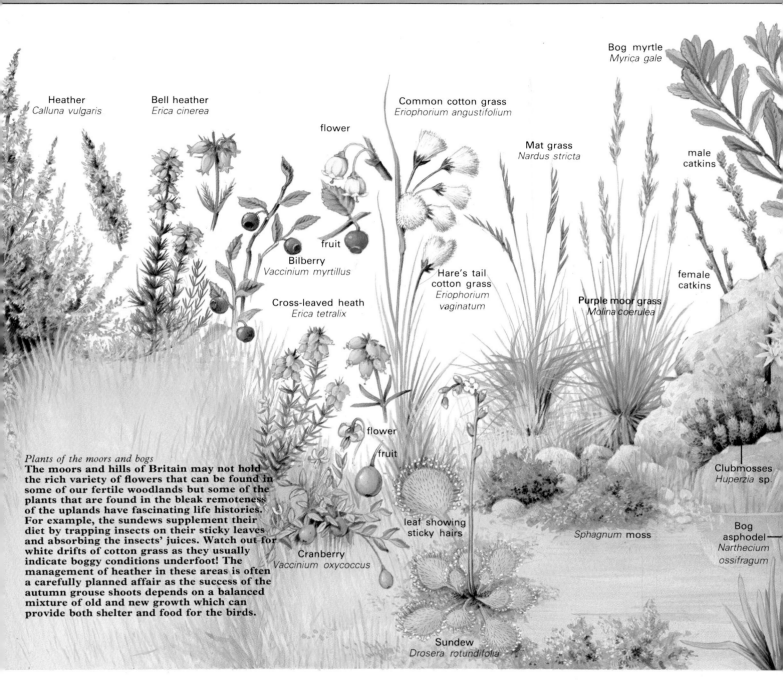

Bog myrtle
Myrica gale

Heather
Calluna vulgaris

Bell heather
Erica cinerea

flower

Common cotton grass
Eriophorium angustifolium

Mat grass
Nardus stricta

male catkins

fruit

Bilberry
Vaccinium myrtillus

Cross-leaved heath
Erica tetralix

Hare's tail cotton grass
Eriophorium vaginatum

Purple moor grass
Molina coerulea

female catkins

flower

fruit

Plants of the moors and bogs
The moors and hills of Britain may not hold the rich variety of flowers that can be found in some of our fertile woodlands but some of the plants that are found in the bleak remoteness of the uplands have fascinating life histories. For example, the sundews supplement their diet by trapping insects on their sticky leaves and absorbing the insects' juices. Watch out for white drifts of cotton grass as they usually indicate boggy conditions underfoot! The management of heather in these areas is often a carefully planned affair as the success of the autumn grouse shoots depends on a balanced mixture of old and new growth which can provide both shelter and food for the birds.

Clubmosses
Huperzia sp.

leaf showing sticky hairs

Sphagnum moss

Bog asphodel—
Narthecium ossifragum

Cranberry
Vaccinium oxycoccus

Sundew
Drosera rotundifolia

from the coast we have met members of the grasses. Right up here we also have some other members of the graminoids, the grass-like plants. We have just looked at a rush and here is a sedge. This is carnation sedge, *Carex panicea*, which has these greyish leaves that look like those of the carnations you grow in your garden. Sedges are easily told from grasses as they have a three-sided flowering stem.

Before I head back home to write up my field notes of the day, all I am going to ask you to do is to think of the importance of grasses in this world of ours. They provide an absolutely perfect cover for the soil, holding it against erosion, and protecting it from the wind and rain. They form a self-regenerating salad for the animals that come along to eat them. In many countries they provide the staple food, whether it is rice or wheat for bread. If they are allowed to grow in their own natural way they provide a special habitat for a whole variety of other plants which don't like being over-shadowed. They are tolerant of all types of uses, from having games of football played on them to providing a mini-forest for all kinds of invertebrates. All plants are important but in my opinion the grasses are the most important of them all.

scale. It is possible to resolve the different species that we can see, or many of them, to a more natural type of habitat. A fairly obvious example are chalk cliffs – both inland and sea cliffs. Other species were perhaps plants that you would find in woodland clearings and scrub. Disturbed ground, such as you might find around animal burrows, is another habitat. Plants have always exploited these disturbed or "weedy" areas. Plants have come together from all these diverse habitats to form the very rich matrix that we see here today.

'Now if we look at the species that are growing, there is another interesting point to make which concerns geographical distribution. As we are on a warm south-facing slope and in southern England, it might not be too surprising to find that many of the plants are most at home in southern Europe and here in Britain do not go much further north than the Thames. The round-headed rampion, *Phyteuma tenerum*, is a case in point. It is sometimes called the Pride of Sussex because there is more of it in Sussex than anywhere else, although I think our friends in Dorset might well dispute that. It is a beautiful plant with its head of sky-blue

campanula-like flowers. Fortunately it is quite common in this particular area.

'The flowers that are most often associated in people's minds with the chalk downs are the orchids. Somehow they possess that in-definable fascination of the exotic and are a truly remarkable group of plants. We have more than fifty different species in Britain and, of these, about thirty are found on the chalk hills of southern England. Perhaps the most characteristic is the fragrant orchid, *Gymnadenia conopsea*, with its tall spike of lovely magenta-coloured flowers. Two or three weeks ago this slope was covered with literally hundreds of them, but as you can see they have rather gone over now. Spotted orchids, *Dactylorchis fuchsii*, are also common earlier in the year but they are by no means confined to the chalk. Perhaps the most remarkable looking are those whose flowers mimic the pollinating insect like the bee orchid, *Ophrys apifera*, which can also be found on this hillside given a bit of time and patience. The sepals are a deep rose pink but the lower petal looks just like a bumble-bee, and, indeed, on the Continent, the male bee is fooled by the similarity into mistaking the flower for the female and attempts to mate

Together with the sheep, rabbits have traditionally been responsible for keeping the grassy swards of the Downs closely cropped.

Above **A male chalk-hill blue**, *Lysandra coridon*, **one of the lovely downland butterflies.**

Left **A bumble bee showing its pollen 'basket'. Some bees have been known to carry 60 per cent of their own weight in pollen.**

Opposite **Any walk across downland on a sunny summer's day will be taken against a background of singing grasshoppers. The 'pegs' on the hind legs which help produce the sound can be clearly seen.** 107

with it, transferring the sticky pollen mass onto its head in the process. When it repeats the experience with another flower cross-pollination is affected. Interestingly enough, bee orchids in Britain are always self-pollinated as the pollinating bee doesn't reach this far north. Other specialities are the tiny, little, yellow musk orchid, *Herminium monorchis*, and the pyramidal orchid, *Anacamptis pyramidalis*, both of which flower rather later in the summer.'

We were thrilled by the idea of being surrounded by such a wealth of plants and decided, for fun, to look at the species immediately around us and see how many we could locate within an area of one square foot. Faced with the challenge David got down on his knees and started counting.

'If we look at the composition of the grassland sward in detail, we can see that it consists of a matrix which is based on three different kinds of grass. Firstly, there's this very fine-leaved grass, sheep's fescue, *Festuca ovina*, which has an almost bristle-like leaf. In the old days of extensive sheep farming it was by far the most abundant of all the grasses on the chalk, which is how it got its name.

'Then, I'm afraid, mixed up with the sheep's fescue on this slope is this much more robust grass, tor grass, *Brachypodium pinnatum*, which has a flat, rather yellow-green leaf that is rough if you pull your fingers down it from the tip to base. It is very invasive and will rapidly take over the sward in the absence of grazing. So it's a thing to watch and not allow to become too abundant as it does swamp a lot of the smaller and less common species.

'The third chalk grass which can become dominant is the upright brome grass, *Zerna erecta*, which has rather long flat leaves. If it's not in flower you can always recognise it because along the margins of the leaf there is a row of hairs which are very regularly spaced. Each hair is about as long as the leaf base is broad. Mixed up with the grasses is one of the chalk sedges. Sedges are easily told from grasses by the stem which is solid and more or less triangular in cross-section as opposed to being hollow and circular. This one is the carnation sedge, *Carex flacca*, so-called because the leaves are the same colour as those of a carnation. So that makes four species. No doubt if we look more carefully we will turn up some other grasses.

'Yes, there's meadow oat-grass, *Helictotrichon pratense*, which has leaves which are more or less the same colour as the carnation. sedge. However, they are very stiff and narrow and the tip is shaped like the prow of a boat or a monk's cowl. So that's five species of grasses and sedges.

'Here is the prettiest of all the chalk grasses – quaking grass, *Briza media*, which has these very characteristic oval-shaped spikelets that quiver in the wind in a most delightful manner. The leaves of the *Briza* are quite undistinguished; they're not hairy; they're not hooded; they're not ribbed. They are, however, very obviously two-rowed with just a little twist in the leaf which is very characteristic.

'If we look at some of the other plant families, there is a whole wealth of things here. Here's a little white flower with very narrow leaves that are whorled around the stem. It is called squinancywort, *Asperula cynanchica*, and is a relative of the bedstraws. It is a typical plant of these dry chalk slopes. And here we have perhaps the most common and characteristic of all the chalk grassland herbs – salad burnet, *Poterium sanguisorba*. It is a little herbaceous member of the rose family with a compact round head of flowers. It used to be put in salads and drink and is still sometimes cultivated as a herb. And here we have the only really true chalk grassland member of the umbellifers or cow parsley family, the burnet saxifrage, *Pimpinella saxifraga*. It has a little white umbel of flowers that look very attractive. There are two or three members of the daisy or composite family here as well. This family has many species that puzzle people no end as they all look like dandelions at a first glance and are apparently impossible to differentiate. This one is a common member – the rough hawkbit, *Leontodon hispidus*. It has a very hairy leaf and if you look at the hairs under a lens you will find that they are T- or Y-shaped. There is the yellow flower-head with the very hairy involucre-bracts beneath. Amongst these is another species of yellow composite, the mouse-ear hawkweed, *Hieracium pilosella*, which has very distinctive leaves with this pure white felt underneath, no teeth around the margin and these extraordinary long hairs on the upper surface. The mouse-ear hawkweed has much paler flowers than the hawkbit. I think we have actually got a third species here which I hadn't noticed – the hairy hawkbit, *Leontodon taraxacoides*. This is much less hairy on the upper part of the stem and is smaller than the rough hawkbit.

'The little purple flowers here belong to wild thyme, *Thymus drucei*, which occurs throughout Britain on well-drained soils. Incidentally, there is another species which flowers later in the year on these southern chalklands – large thyme, *T. pulegioides*. It is bigger and has a more noticeable scent.

'Now we have to look around a little bit more. Ah, here is a member of a very important family on the chalk slopes – the legume or pea family. This is horseshoe vetch, *Hippocrepis comosa*. It has leaves composed of four or five pairs of leaflets and, unlike a true vetch, a terminal leaflet instead of a tendril. It has a yellow flower which is similar to birds-foot trefoil, *Lotus corniculatus*. But the significance of horseshoe vetch is that it is the food plant of the larvae of one of the most beautiful of all the chalk downland butterflies – the adonis blue. Other members of this plant group are important to other butterflies and we will look at that later on. The birds-foot trefoil has five leaflets and is so named because the fruits supposedly spread out like the foot of a fowl – if you have enough imagination.

'There's the round-headed rampion and here is a seedling of the small scabious, *Scabiosa columbaria*, with its toothed basal leaves. Now this is a nice plant to have in flower in our square – yellow rattle, *Rhinanthus minor*. It has this yellow flower and large calyx that becomes inflated later in the year when you can hear the seeds rattling inside it. Here is the leaf of another member of the rose family, the dropwort, *Filipendula vulgaris*, which is the chalkland equivalent of the meadowsweet, *F. ulmaria*, of damp meadows and riversides. That makes nineteen species so far.

'We are almost sitting – but I'm glad to say not quite – on two very vicious-looking rosettes of the stemless thistle, *Cirsium acualon*. It is one of those plants which is essentially southern European and its distribution in Britain is very characteristic, stopping almost dead at a line drawn from the Humber to the Severn. If you were to carry out a survey of the numbers of plants on this south-facing slope and compare that with a similar survey on the north-facing slope across the valley you would find that there are more plants on this side. So this thistle is really rather precise in its climatic preferences.

'This is the rosette of a typical chalkland member of the plantain family, hoary plantain, *Plantago media*. Unlike other plantains which are wind pollinated this plant is insect pollinated and has scented flowers with these lovely pale-pink stamens. Right next door is the rosette of the much more common narrow-leaved or ribwort plantain, *P. lanceolata*. Finally, here is the little white flower

A corn bunting perched on a field-side fence surrounded by thistles and poppies. Corn buntings are typical birds of chalk downland. These rather undistinguished-looking seed-eaters can often be seen singing from fences and posts in spring.

of the fairy or purging flax, *Linum cathar-ticum*. It is a tiny plant with glossy, hairless, egg-shaped leaves in opposite pairs up the stem and these minute white flowers. That gives us a total of twenty-two species, not bad at all.'

We agreed with David that identifying that many species of plant in one square foot of a random piece of turf was a convincing result. However, having hinted at the butterflies in the area we were eager for him to tell us more.

'The adonis blue butterfly, *Lysandra bellargus*, is still, I'm happy to say, fairly abundant in this particular locality. Sadly, however, this species, which is restricted chiefly to southern England, is rapidly disappearing from most areas as more and more of the old chalkland turf becomes "improved" or ploughed up. The adonis blue has two broods in the year. The first emerges at the end of May or the beginning of June and is in flight all through June. The second appears at the end of July or the beginning of August. So, unfortunately, we are in the gap between the two broods! The males are coloured a very intense blue, much more so than the common blue, *Polyommatus icarus*. They also have a much more distinc-tive white border to the wings which is transversed by fine black bands where the veins cross the wing. The females are very drab in comparison being predominantly brown in colour. They lay their eggs singly on the undersurface of one of the terminal leaflets of the horse-shoe vetch. They choose plants some distance apart as the caterpillars are cannibalistic. The short stubby cater-pillars which are now developing will pupate and the butterflies emerge at the end of the month in August. Another rather special blue butterfly that we find here is the

chalkhill blue, *Lysandra coridon*, which is not quite so uncommon as the adonis blue. Its range extends a little further north in Britain. The caterpillars feed on both the horse-shoe vetch and on another member of the legume family – the birds-foot trefoil. However, it does not compete with the adonis as they feed and emerge at different times, having only one brood which flies during July so if we are lucky we might see some. The males are much paler than the adonis males; they are a kind of powder blue with a distinct dark border to the wing.

'A third species of blue butterfly is the common blue, which is much more generally distributed, and, having two or three broods each year, can be seen in most months from May to September. The caterpillars of this species feed on birds-foot trefoil. Also in this general area are two other members of the "blues" – the small blue, *Cupido minimus*, and the brown argus, *Aricia agestis*. The small blue is a tiny beast, with a wingspan of only 20 millimetres as opposed to the com-mon blue which can reach over 35 milli-metres. It is darker in colour than the other three and feeds on another member of the pea family, the kidney vetch, *Anthyllis vul-neraria*. Finally we come to one more blue which is brown, the brown argus! Its cater-pillars feed on rock rose, *Helianthemum chamaecistus*, a typical chalk grassland flower, and has two broods, one in May and another in July.

Right At the bottom of the hill we found several flowering spikes of yellow-wort, *Blackstonia perfoliata*. This plant is easily recognisable with its bright yellow gentian-like flowers and fused opposite pairs of leaves. The whole plant has a distinctive greyish colour.

Below A large ant-hill garlanded with thyme, *Thymus*. The larger and more numerous the ant-hills, the older the grassland is likely to be.

A pair of six-spot
burnet moths, *Zygaena
filipendulae*, pairing
outside a cocoon high
up on a grass stem.
These brightly
coloured moths are
day-flying and can
often be seen amongst
the longer grass on
downland slopes.

111

'The more you look at these insects, the more you start to ask the obvious questions and then one begins to realise how little we know about them. For instance, why is it that in this family, the adonis blue has a blue male and a brown female; the common blue has a blue male and a bluish-brown female; the brown argus, a brown male and a brown female; while the large blue has a blue male and a blue female? No-one knows the answer.

'There is one aspect of the natural history of these insects that we do know something about and that is the relationship between the blues and ants. This is most extreme in the large blue, *Maculinea arion*, which recently became extinct in Britain. Nevertheless, the chalkhill blue also has a fascinating link with the ants, which actually search out the caterpillars and may carry them to a location close to their nest placing them on a suitable plant of birds-foot trefoil. In return for the protection the ants afford the larvae, they "milk" a gland on its back which produces a sweet juice that the ants will seem to do anything for. Indeed, in the large blue they take the caterpillar into their nest where it feeds on the ants' own larvae. It is all quite astonishing.

'A lot of people are probably most aware of the butterflies when they are out walking. But these chalk slopes have many other interesting insects. Perhaps one of the most obvious groups are the grasshoppers. The noise of their "singing" is all around us. This order of insects as a whole is tropical and even though we have a rather poor grasshopper fauna in Britain, you may be surprised to learn that we have eleven species. The ones that we can hear singing are all males as the females are silent. This "singing" should properly be called stridulating as it is not produced through the mouth like a bird's song but by rubbing a series of pegs on the inside of their hind legs against the hard outside edge of the wing cases. But then, like birds, each species has its own distinctive song, so if you know your grasshoppers' repertoire, you can impress your friends by naming them after hearing the song. If you listen carefully you can hear three different species right now. The one that sounds like a high-pitched angry bee with a continuous "zzzzzzz" noise is the stripe-winged grasshopper, *Stenobothrus lineatus*. It has a distribution which is similar to the round-headed rampion in that it is distinctly southern and does not occur much further north than the

Thames, except for a few isolated localities. Here, it is very abundant on the nice warm south-facing slope – but is generally an uncommon species. Then there are two much more widely distributed grasshoppers. First, there is the common green grasshopper, *Omacestus viridulus*, which sounds for all the world like a free-wheeling bicycle, and the meadow grasshopper, *Chorthippus parallelus*, which makes a rather feeble noise, "praah", "praah".

'Snails are another group of invertebrates that are abundant in chalk grassland. These molluscs need calcium carbonate with which to construct their shells, and what habitat has more of it than chalk? If you dig around at the base of the grasses it is quite easy to come up with a handful of snails. I have two species right here. One of them is very common and found on all types of calcium-rich habitats – chalk and limestone grassland, as well as calcium-rich sand dunes. It is called *Candidula intersecta*, and is a small, flat, banded shell. In contrast, this other one has a very different shape, like a miniature-spire and is much less common. It is called *Cochlicella acuta*, and is, like so many of the plants and animals here, more or less restricted to the southern chalkland. This one does creep up around the west coast and can be found in sand dunes. There are often similarities between sand dune habitats and chalk grassland simply because dunes collect a lot of calcium carbonate from washed up marine shells.

'A third species that we should find here is called the round-mouthed snail, *Pomatias elegans*. It looks just like a little land periwinkle and is one of the two British land snails that has an operculum – a little 'trapdoor' on the underside of the foot of the snail which seals it in when it retracts into the shell. Most of our land snails secrete a membrane across the shell if they really want to shut themselves off.'

We decided it was time to move on and have a look at the animals and plants lower down the slope. So, making sure not to put our hands on the spines of the stemless thistles, we clambered up and set off down the hill. A common blue butterfly fluttered quickly past us but there was no sign of any lingering adonis blues. However, we were to be luckier later in the year on another stretch of downland further west. The grass lower down the slope was taller but before we went any further we stopped by some odd mounds which turned out to be large anthills. Were these to be expected here? David was quite emphatic.

'Yes, anthills are very characteristic of old chalk grassland slopes and even have their own specialised plant and animal communities. The ant responsible for these is usually the yellow meadow ant, *Lasius flavus*. And although it looks fairly quiet at the moment if you disturbed it or even sat on it you would soon find out that it was very active! Interestingly, the plants growing on the top of the anthill often differ from the surrounding grassland. It has a much shorter sward than round about. This is partly because the rabbits tend to chew them down. They also use them regularly as latrines as can be seen by the large number of droppings here. There is a higher density of sheep's fescue than elsewhere and here is a common grass that we have not seen so far – crested hairgrass, *Koeleria cristata*. It is one of those grasses that extends right into eastern Europe and is an important grass of the steppes. Typical of these anthills, there is also a nice mixture of wild thyme and squinancywort.

'Anthills are one of the few examples that you can find in nature of a regular pattern of distribution. If you were, for instance, to measure the distance between these anthills, you would find that they were spread in a fairly uniform fashion about the hill. Another interesting feature of anthills is the communities of other animals that they support. If we were to be able to look inside one of them we might find a very exciting little woodlice called *Platyarthrus hoffmannseggi*, which is both blind and colourless. There is also a subterranean snail called *Ceciliodes acicula*, which is only about three millimetres long and also colourless. One of the few places that you are likely to find it is in an ant's nest. A fascinating book was written on the subject in the 1920s by H. Donisthorpe entitled *The Guests of British Ants*, and was just as large as the monograph which preceded it on the biology of the British ants themselves.'

We now moved on further down into the ranker grass. As we cut through it we noticed several new species of butterflies flying up in front of us. David took up the story.

'These are quite different from the ones that we saw further up the slope. The reason for this is primarily to do with the longer grass on which their larvae feed. The most obvious one today and to my mind perhaps the most beautiful of all our British butter-

flies, is the marbled white, *Melanargia galathea*. Although it is only black and white, the lovely marbling of the two colours, particularly when it is sitting with its wings closed and the sun is shining through it from behind, is really a most atmospheric and beautiful sight. Surprisingly the marbled white is not a member of the Pieridae or white family, which includes the cabbage white, but belongs to the Satyridae or brown family. So it is more closely related to the much more drab meadow brown and gatekeepers. A characteristic of this family is the eye-like mark towards the apex of the forewing and if you look carefully you can see that it does have such a mark. The caterpillars feed on grasses so why they should be confined to calcareous soils is a bit of a puzzle. But like some of our blues they are a southern species and are generally found south of a line drawn from the Wash to the Severn.

'The marbled white has evolved a very interesting egg-laying technique. Whilst egg-laying, female insects are particularly at risk from predators as they have to be motionless for a fair amount of time while they are laying

A mating pair of marbled white butterflies, *Melanargia galathea*, amongst the ranker grass and knapweeds at the hill bottom. These beautiful insects are confined to the downlands of southern England.

Above **A very different type of habitat with some very different flowers. This is the edge of a nearby cornfield, which has been colonised by a whole array of arable 'weed' species including poppies,** *Papaver,* **and scentless mayweed,** *Tripleurospermum inodorum.*

Opposite **If one looks closely enough there is a lot to discover in almost any stretch of countryside. This striking photograph of the flower head of a mayweed shows not only the flower's extraordinary structure but also a hover-fly and below it a diminutive thrip.**

their eggs. Most butterflies have to to search for their food plant and then carefully place the eggs on the leaf. The marbled white, however, does not have to search out a particular plant as the caterpillar feeds on most grasses and therefore the female can simply drop her eggs at random over the grassy sward without settling at all. The chances of an egg not falling on a piece of grass in a place like this are negligible. The only other British butterfly that uses this technique is the ringlet, *Aphantopus hyperanthus,* which also feeds on grasses.

'Flying around us is what must be the commonest British butterfly – the meadow brown, *Maniola jurtina.* You can find it on almost any stretch of rough grassland or hedgebank. Although they are so abundant, you will not find the caterpillars that easily. This is because the caterpillars of all the browns are fairly well camouflaged and during the day they drop to the base of the grasses, only climbing up to feed at night.

'A third species of brown butterfly is flitting about just here. This is the smallest of

the tribe – the small heath, *Coenonympha pamphilus.* This must be one of the most widely distributed of all our butterflies, being found almost the length and breadth of the British Isles on downs and heaths, wasteground and even mountain sides. It is a lovely tawny brown colour with the typical 'eyes' on the forewing. Its larvae are also grass-feeders.

'As well as the butterflies we have been turning up a few day-flying moths. Not all moths fly exclusively at night, and perhaps the most obvious of these are the burnet moths. There are two common species, the six-spot burnet, *Zygaena filipendulae,* the commonest of the two, and the five spot burnet, *Z. trifolii.* The larvae of these moths feed on members of the pea family, particularly birds-foot trefoil. The adult moths have this very distinct scarlet and dark bronze-green warning coloration. They are extremely poisonous and have a very unpleasant taste so predators soon learn to avoid them. The adults are a common sight over downland such as this in mid-summer and are especially attracted to the flower of wild marjoram, *Origanum vulgare,* and basil, *Clinopodium vulgare.*'

Further along the slope our attention was caught by a fairly tall flower with striking yellow flowers. We asked David to identify the plant.

'This is yellow-wort, *Blackstonia perfoliata*; it is actually a yellow flowered member of the gentian family. These primrose yellow flowers open during mid-day and are arranged in a loose head. The most characteristic feature of this plant, however, is the leaves. These are arranged in pairs up the stem and are joined at the base so that the stalk appears to grow up through them. Hence the Latin name, *perfoliata.* Again, it is a plant, like so many we have seen today, that is confined to calcareous soils in southern Britain.'

We started to make our way back to the cars along the valley bottom but first of all we strolled along an area of scrub. As we approached it we could hear a most peculiar song. We scanned the area with our binoculars and soon located a dumpy-looking brown bird. David pointed it out.

'Just there, sitting on one of the fence posts. It is a corn bunting with its extraordinary song, which I call "scritcheting" – and I don't mean that to sound complimentary! The corn bunting is by no means classed amongst the world's best songsters.

Nevertheless, to me, its song does sum up the feeling and the mood of the summer chalk country of the South Downs. The corn bunting is polygamous; he has quite a large territory within which several females will nest. Although he places himself rather prominently within sight of the nests it is no good watching him in order to discover the nest sites, as he never flies to the nest to feed the females while they are incubating. Corn buntings have a characteristic heavy flight and let their rather pale-coloured legs trail behind them.'

'We were now amongst the area of scrub near the top of the valley. It presented an almost impenetrable barrier of gorse, *Ulex europeaus*, hawthorn, *Crategus monogyna* and bramble, *Rubrus fruticosus*, but was obviously ideal for nesting birds so we sat down for a while to see what we could.

'We are in the middle of a hot afternoon when most bird song has ceased but we can still hear a fair amount of calling. Probably this type of scrub has one of the highest densities of breeding birds of any habitat we have. We've heard linnets, yellowhammers, dunnocks, wrens and the inevitable black-birds. The only common warbler is the whitethroat. It suffered a decline in its numbers a few years ago but this was nothing to do with the breeding success here in Britain but resulted from a severe drought in the Sahel region of the Sahara where our whitethroats spend the winter. The numbers appear to be picking up again now, which is certainly good news. We can hear its rather throaty, chuckling song just behind us.'

We walked on up to the ridge of the hill where suddenly the scene completely changed. In front of us was a vast expanse of wheat rippling in the gentle breeze; a vivid contrast to the scrub and old grassland behind us. The only noise was the gentle hiss of ripening heads of wheat brushing against each other; quite unlike the busy hum of activity we had just left behind. But every cloud has a silver lining, as they say, and this great area certainly had a very colourful one, as David explained.

'We have a great sea of wheat in front of us – one of the main reasons why so much of the old chalk downland sward has disappeared. Beside us is an even bigger sea of barley. Of course, the Downs are very productive when it comes to growing cereals and the farmers are always concerned to increase their cereal production. However, if you look around the edges of these vast fields you can still find the remnants of the old rich arable flora – in other words, the weeds. These have managed to escape the effects of the herbicides with which the crops are dressed. Some of the weeds are now becoming a little resistant to the herbicides.

'There is really a quite rich and interesting flora just here. In particular, the poppies are worth looking for. To some people they conjure up a picture of the past. There are actually five species of red poppy in Britain but the one which most of us come across is the common poppy, *Papaver rhoeas*. This eye-catching plant is the one with the big crinkly red petals with a smooth round fruit capsule. Here we have one of the four rarer species as well – the prickly poppy, *P. argemone*. The flowers, which are similar but smaller than the common poppy, are over now but we can see the main distinguishing feature – the long bristly fruit capsule. I was up here a few weeks ago and there were actually two other species of poppy here as well – so it is worth looking for them.

'There are many other weed species here. For instance, here is a large patch of the introduced pineapple or rayless mayweed, *Matricaria matricaroides*. It looks rather like a big daisy with all the white ray florets pulled off. Like so many arable weeds it is an accidental introduction and originates from South America. And here is a mix of plants which one might expect to find: knotgrass, *Polygonum aviculare*; red bartsia, *Odontites verna*; common field speedwell, *Veronica persica* (although an abundant weed it is, in fact, a native of Asia Minor that was introduced accidentally over two centuries ago) and wall speedwell, *V. arvensis*. Weeds are highly specialised plants that are well adapted to their mode of life. They have to be able to take advantage of bare, disturbed ground that appears in unpredictable places at unpredictable times. In order to do this successfully they have evolved a reproductive strategy that is different from most species. They invest in vast numbers of seeds which spread very widely so that at least some fall where there is a bare patch of fertile soil. Because of this high investment in seeds they are short-lived annuals. A short life, but a happy one! The other point about weeds is that quite often they are self-fertilising, so that if only one isolated plant becomes established it can still produce fertile seed and a new generation of plants. They also have a long flowering season with some in flower almost the whole year round.'

The rich plant communities of the downland slopes have developed in conjunction with hundreds of years of sheep grazing. The constant nibbling of the sheep has kept the tiny plants low and prevented coarser grasses and scrub from encroaching. Sadly, this type of scene is now on the decline and vast areas have been turned over to cereal production as can be seen on the hill top opposite.

We turned away from the edge of the apparently endless wheat field and took one last look over at the downland valley in which we had spent such an invigorating afternoon. But reluctantly it was time for us to depart and as we drove back alongside the cereal fields, the dramatic contrast brought home how important it is to preserve the remaining areas of old chalk downland with their very special communities of animals and plants.

A meadow walk

Francis Rose is not only one of the greatest field botanists alive today but is one of the greatest that has ever lived. He was the man who, to use the modern jargon, 'turned me on' to the world of plants. He was also my research director and, whilst I studied for my PhD, I had the privilege of walking and talking with him during the five most formative years of my career. This chapter brings you one afternoon of that magic as he takes you on a walk through one of the most magical of all types of grassland, the water meadow. In the days before the use and abuse of fertilizers, water meadows were of great importance to the local economy. The upland fields had to be manured or the crops rotated, in order to maintain fertility. Not so the water meadows, as in most winters they received a new supply of nutrient rich silts, absolutely free, from the river flood waters. They were ideal places to reap one or more good crops of herb-rich hay to dry for winter feed. It was this age-old management practice which helped to make and maintain our water meadows as sanctuaries for a great diversity of plants and birds. Perhaps, with the rising cost of chemical fertilizers, they will once again become economic entities in our river-scapes; until then, we will have to work to preserve the few that still remain.

A splendid view from the river across a large stretch of traditional wet meadowland. The apparently flat nature of the land is misleading as it is transected by numerous ditches and channels. Furthermore, the tussocky nature of the vegetation makes walking a slow but rewarding business.

A meadow walk
with
Francis Rose

When out walking by one of our many lowland rivers a nearby feature which is often overlooked is the adjoining meadows that lie in the alluvial flood plain. At first glance these marshy-looking fields, transected by numerous dykes and ditches, do not look particularly rewarding places to investigate. But until this century many of them had long histories of sympathetic management that ensured their productivity and created an environment where a great variety of plants and animals could live. Today, however, this continuity has been largely broken and many of these watermeadows have disappeared or are under threat. In lowland Britain those that remain represent some of our richest grassland habitats. So, in order to find out more we asked Dr Francis Rose, formerly Reader in Biogeography at King's College, London, now retired, and the author of many books on plants, to explore with us a typical watermeadow. On a lovely day in early July Francis took us to a quiet stretch of river in a beautiful corner of Hampshire. As we tramped down the curving path to the river he told us that the owner appreciated the need to preserve this very special habitat and that it has been designated as a Special Site of Scientific Interest. The owner consults with representatives of the Nature Conservancy Council in order to manage the meadows in the best possible way.

Dressed practically for the day and wearing our Wellingtons, we crossed the shallow, swiftly-flowing river by means of a plank bridge. From there we could see the river winding away into the distance around the area we had come to look at – a series of ancient watermeadows. Behind us, and further up the hill, fields were being worked with tractors and machines in the most modern way, a striking contrast to the tussocky land, seemingly dominated by rushes and sedges, which we now saw before us.

Francis first took us to an area that was slightly flatter than the rest and pointed out the carpet of exquisite orchids that surrounded us. Their pinks and purples stood out against a backcloth of greens. But before we looked at the plants in detail we asked him to tell us a little about the history of these places.

'Watermeadows are of special interest because of their exceptionally rich flora, a result of their very long histories and high levels of fertility due to regular flooding over many, many years.

'In previous centuries true watermeadows were carefully managed with a system of dykes, channels and ditches. In some cases a series of parallel ditches were cut across the meadow, the water levels being controlled by sluices. In the winter the water was allowed to flood onto the meadow through these ditches and to spread out on either side. When spring came the water was kept on the meadow for a time and then run off. This type of management is now very rare and can only be seen in a few places in the Avon Valley, Hampshire, and in Dorset.

'The type of meadow we are standing in today is, by comparison, much more common. There is no evidence that there were ever parallel ditches here. It is simply flooded by the river in winter, the silt enriching the soil with lime and other salts. Many of them were "laid up" for hay between March and July and after cutting were grazed by cattle and sheep. This site is too rough for hay so it is used primarily for grazing cattle.

'In the old days watermeadows were much sought after and, because of this, they were often shared. A few fascinating examples still remain. Near Cricklade, by the River Thames in Wiltshire, there is a series of old

A lovely specimen of one of our rarest meadow plants – the snake's head fritillary, *Fritillaria meleagris*. This flower used to have a much wider distribution along our lowland river valleys but it is now confined to a few sites particularly in the upper Thames Valley. Its decline parallels the change in agricultural practice as regards the use of the alluvial meadows, most of which have now been drained or reseeded. Its strange appearance is echoed in the many local names that it has acquired: 'dead men's bells' in Shropshire; 'lepers' lilies' in the west country, and 'toads' heads' in Wiltshire. It flowers early in spring before the taller plants have shaded it out.

Opposite above **A secluded patch of meadow in full flower with the purple spikes of orchids contrasting with the whites and creams of the bedstraws and meadowsweet in the background.**

watermeadows which is managed in the traditional way by lots. After the land has been cut for hay in mid-summer it becomes the common pasture of the Borough. From a natural history point of view this is of great benefit as, with several people involved, it is more difficult for anyone to decide to enclose or plough the meadows. This, however, is the exception, for in most parts of the country today watermeadows are treated as second-rate agricultural land. There is continuous pressure on these old meadows from farmers who want to "improve" them either by drainage and ploughing or conversion to ley pasture, often encouraged by government grants.

'The watermeadows we have visited today have a very rich flora and in this particular series of 200 to 300 acres well over 200 species of plants have been recorded. In the past there must have been many such sites, but now it is more common to find re-seeded pasture which often has a very low diversity of species, consisting sometimes of just rye grass and dutch clover. Apart from all of that, many of these meadows, particularly those in reach of large urban areas, have been quarried away for gravel pits.

'So it is nice to see what the old type of agricultural land was like and also to see how it created a habitat for a great diversity of plants and insects, for, if you have a great number of plants, you will also have a correspondingly large number of insects dependent on them. Here there are many butterflies and moths – the caterpillars feed on some of the plants – and dragonflies in turn feeding on other insects.

'A lot of these watermeadows probably have a pedigree going back thousands of years in one form of management or another. You never get quite the same set of species of plants and insects at any two sites. However, there is a common background of species that is found in all of them, each site having a certain individuality, which is something that one is very anxious to preserve.'

We asked Francis how we could recognise an old watermeadow. What were some of the features that marked it out from modern re-seeded pasture?

'First of all, there will be an obvious diversity of species. Even if one doesn't know what the species are, one can see that there are very many kinds of plant present. Secondly, the meadow will have a very

The green-veined white, *Pieris napi,* **is a typical butterfly of wet meadowland. The caterpillars of this species feed on various plants from the Crucifer family such as lady's smock and charlock. Unlike many butterflies it will fly on overcast days.**

colourful appearance. On ancient grassland, particularly in June and July, one will see the pink or purple spikes of orchids. The modern leys don't usually have flowers in them, except perhaps white or red clover. Also in an old watermeadow one will see the rather quaintly shaped spikes of various sorts of sedges. In the more calcareous areas totter grass or quaking grass will be there with its very characteristic panicles and there may well be marsh horsetail with its strange pointed stems with little cones on top. That plant would not be found in a modern highly organised ley pasture. It is rough and harsh, and animals do not like eating it, so farmers won't have it around.

'So old communities of this kind tend to survive where the original types of management are still, for one reason or another, maintained. The farmer may be old-fashioned or he may be conservation-minded and feel that he can afford to manage some of his land in this way. One can argue that this type of herbage is really very much better for animals to eat because of its diversity. If you watch animals grazing on recently sown ley pasture and there is some more varied traditional grassland nearby, the animals will

go and graze on that. Sometimes they'll graze along a hedge. Although it can be shown that they put on more weight if they are fed on certain types of modern ley pastures, the health of the animals, it is sometimes argued, is not necessarily better. Where there is a variety of species you tend to get more trace elements and more nutrient substances in the diet which may be important in ways which we don't yet fully understand.'

Having talked about some of the general aspects of these meadows and hinted at all their treasures, we were eager to explore them further. The most eye-catching plants around us were the tall spikes of the orchids. Francis went over to a nearby group and having inspected a few told us about them.

'We are now in an area of the watermeadow that is a bit lower than the rest. It is rather more damp and with a certain amount of grazing pressure which helps to keep out the really coarse vegetation, but not enough to suppress many of the flowering plants. Just here we can look across and see many different types of orchid in flower. Perhaps the most striking is the marsh fragrant orchid, *Gymnadenia densiflora.* There is a nice patch of them here. The common fragrant orchid, *Gymnadenia conopsea*, is present on what are probably some of the drier hummocks. One can tell the difference between these two types of orchid in several ways: the common fragrant orchid flowers in June with paler rosy pink flowers and the side sepals are pointed and bend downwards. It has a pleasant sweet scent, but with a slightly rancid overtone. The marsh fragrant orchid, on the other hand, which usually prefers damper sites such as this, flowers a little later in the year with deeply coloured pinkish-purple flowers, and the square-ended sepals are spread out at right angles. It has a rich carnation scent.

'Besides the fragrant orchids, which are so abundant here they are adding a colourful hue to the overall scene, we have the commonest of our marsh orchids – the southern marsh orchid, *Dactylorhiza praetermissa*. It is still in flower although many of the individual plants are over now. The leaves of this handsome plant are unspotted and the rich purple and pink flowering spikes can be over a foot tall. I can see some common spotted orchids, *D. fuchsii*, which has similar, but pale pink, flowers and leaves which are heavily blotched and spotted. Growing on some *Sphagnum* moss over here is a more acid-loving relative – the heath

Two hoverflies feeding on the flowers of meadowsweet, *Filipendula ulmaria*, one of the most well-known meadow plants.

Opposite **Three flowering spikes of the dense-flowered or marsh fragrant orchid** Gymnadenia densiflora. **This orchid prefers damper habitats than the common fragrant orchid** G. conopsea. **It also has a more deeply coloured flower and a rich carnation scent.**

Left **The most typical orchid of base-rich fens and wet meadows is the southern marsh orchid** Dactylorhiza praetermissa, **which has a handsome spike of rich purple flowers and unspotted leaves.**

spotted orchid, *D. maculata*. These are rather similar to *D. fuchsii* but the lower lip of the flower is less three-lobed and more triangular with a distinct loop-like pattern as opposed to spots. However, it is a potentially confusing group of orchids as not only are there often distinct colour varieties but the different species frequently hybridize. Sometimes you find a colony where it is difficult to locate a pure specimen of any species. If we had been here earlier in the year we would have found another member of the *Dactylorhiza*, the early marsh orchid, *D. incarnata*.

'Some of the more common orchids, such as the spotted orchid, produce flower spikes for several years in succession, while others, like the burnt tip orchid, *Orchis ustulata*, flower once then lie dormant for years. This can result in fluctuations in the number of flowers that appear each year. Orchids are of great interest to a large number of people, not only because of their spectacular flowers, but also because of the many interesting aspects of their biology.'

We then moved on to a more bumpy area of the watermeadow where walking was rather difficult, so prominent were the hummocks

A young frog amongst the damp meadow grasses. The unpolluted watery channels in the meadow can provide ideal sites for the frogs to lay their eggs. Ironically you are more likely to see a frog in a suburban garden pond than in today's open countryside, where many of the ponds and streams have either been drained or are badly polluted.

above the bed of the meadow. Francis went on to describe the area.

'When we look at the ground more closely, we find that it is much more interesting than it first appears. The tops of the hummocks are raised above the chalky water for most of the year, perhaps even in winter, except in times of severe flood, and are obviously somewhat leached as a result. This is reflected in the variation in the plant life found in different parts of the hummocks.

'The soil on the tops is presumably more acid than in the lower parts and in the ground in between. So on top you find a few typical heathland plants such as tormentil, *Potentilla erecta*, with its bright yellow flowers. There is even the occasional bush of heather, *Calluna vulgaris*. Also, some of the tall tufts are dominated by clumps of the tussocky purple moor-grass, *Molinia caerulea*, which flowers later in the year. This is a grass one would normally associate with damp acid heathland.

'Even the different requirements of some of the plants are accommodated, as the tormentil and purple moor-grass, which prefer acid soils, are shallow rooted, while the fragrant orchid, which is sticking out of the top here, is rooted down below in the calcareous soil beneath.

'This plant growing on the side is meadow vetchling, *Lathyrus pratensis*, one of the pea family. It is common on roadsides and here we can see it growing successfully on the well-drained hummock, rather than in the wetter spaces in between. Lower down we have some bog pimpernel, *Anagallis tenella*, which prefers damper more open conditions. Despite its name this plant is not restricted to bogs and can be found in marshes and mires ranging from very alkaline to weakly acid. It avoids the most acid bogs. For example, in the New Forest where some of the bogs are very acid you do find the bog pimpernel, but only in runnels of moving water where the pH is higher – above about 5·0. It has a charming little five-petalled flower which appears rosy pink. However, if you look closely you will find that the flowers are white with crimson veins. Another interesting point about the bog pimpernel is that, as you can see here, it is actually growing from a cushion of moss. This acts like a sponge in the wetter spells and retains its water when conditions are drier, keeping the shallow roots of the pimpernel moist.

'At the lowest level between the hummock and the floor of the meadow the soil is very chalky and we can find a number of plants typical of chalk grassland such as quaking grass, *Briza media*, and downy oat-grass, *Helictrotrichon pubescens*.

'If you look around there are a few more plants that one might expect to find on old downland turf. For instance we have some bird's-foot trefoil, *Lotus corniculatus*, and eyebright, *Euphrasia nemorosa*. In fact, this site has more in common with chalk down-land than one would think, being alkaline and also very much a product, in its present form, of human management. It is probable that there would have been swampy alder carr over much of this land at one time. This poses the interesting question: where were these plants, that we can see today, before man cut down the woods? I think the most likely view is that in earlier times the rivers were more unstable and frequently changed course, constantly producing new areas of marshland and other open habitats. Also we should not forget that in prehistoric times there were a large number of big herbivores in the countryside. These animals must have had an effect on our forests and river valleys. For example, you might have found aurochs grazing here at one time. If one thinks

further back, large numbers of bison and deer would be found and during the interglacial periods it has been discovered that hippos and rhinos were living in southern England. So in a sense when man came along with his domestic cattle and sheep he was merely replacing one form of grazing animal with another. However, one has to accept that during prehistoric times the amount of open habitat was far less than we have today. So it is regular grazing or mowing that has maintained the very diverse carpet of many small species of plant that we can see here. Without this, ranker species would soon increase, eventually pushing out the smaller plants. I think that this is an important point to remember if one wishes to conserve a site such as this. Even if you can get the co-operation of the owner or are able to purchase a site through the NCC or a local trust, just putting up a fence to keep everybody out is not good enough. This attitude is quite wrong because as we have seen the community is dependent upon sympathetic management. Nearly every habitat in Britain has been created by the presence of some form of intervention by man, such as traditional agricultural practice, and the survival

of the habitat depends on a continuity of this management. Just removing the grazing will eventually have almost as great an effect on the plant composition as actually ploughing it up. This is something which is not always sufficiently understood.'

As we walked around it was obvious that the sedges and rushes formed an important part of the rich plant community. We asked Francis to tell us some more about these superficially confusing groups.

'Sedges although apparently grass-like have solid triangular stems and have leaves in three vertical ranks. In the true sedges, *Carex*, the flowers are often grouped into a catkin-like male spikelet and several female spikelets. When there is a simple terminal spike the male flowers are found above the female. Sometimes male and female flowers are mixed in each spikelet.

'There are twenty different kinds of sedge in this area, forming quite a bulk of the herbage. Just here is an interesting one, the flea sedge, *Carex pulicaris*. This species has a single spike of flowers and the fruits that develop from the lower female flowers are about the same size and colours as fleas. Furthermore, if you gently brush them when

Two snipe feeding along a muddy water's edge. They use their long bills to probe for invertebrates in the soft ooze. In lowland Britain they will only nest in undisturbed tussocky meadows and grazed pastures where there is damp ground which will allow them to feed. The numbers of breeding pairs has declined dramatically in recent years due to the loss of this habitat.

Above **The exquisite little flower of bog pimpernel,** *Anagallis tenella*. **This plant of damp meadows and marshes appears pink from a distance but when viewed this closely can be seen to be white with pink veins.**

Right **The ragged robin,** *Lychnis flos-cuculi*, **is a widespread member of the campion family that can grow in profusion in wet meadows. Plants with robin in their name are often associated with goblins – it is considered unlucky to pick this plant.**

they are ripe, the slight pressure causes them to jump off the spike rather in the way that a flea would.

'Here is an example of a sedge that has a terminal spike of male flowers and two or three female catkins below. This is black sedge, *Carex nigra*. The little green fruits lie behind black scales, called glumes, at this time of the year. Here is another – tawny sedge, *Carex hostiana*, which has more oval spikelets and more rounded fruits with long beaks. Another very local and interesting species can be seen over here – lesser panicled sedge, *Carex diandra*, in which all

the spikelets of the dense oblong flower-head have both male and female flowers although the female ones are below the males in each little spikelet, producing little brown fruits. That's a nice sedge to find in our meadow – dioecious sedge, *Carex dioica* This type of sedge has completely separate male and female plants. The female one has small triangular pointed fruits in an oval-shaped catkin at the top of the stem, while the male plant has a small cigar-shaped catkin of male flowers. This sedge seems to depend upon fairly wet conditions and short vegetation and is a plant that is very much at risk.

'Many of the rushes are of interest as well. This group of plants are thought to be descended from the lilies which are insect-pollinated and have accordingly attractive flowers. Rushes have gone over to wind pollination and therefore, in the course of evolution, their flowers have become reduced while the stigmas have increased in size and become feathery and sticky, more readily trapping the pollen which has become more copious and dusty so it is more easily carried along by the wind. The six petals are now no more than brown scales which merely protect the bud. Sedges and

One of the first flowers to bloom in marshes and damp meadows in early spring is the kingcup or marsh marigold, *Caltha palustris*. **Its large leaves and clusters of giant buttercup-like flowers make it unmistakeable.**

A great bank of meadowsweet or 'queen of the meadows'. This sweet smelling plant grows profusely in fens and wet meadows and in less sanitary days was used as a strewing herb on the floors of cottages.

grasses have gone even further in their specialised evolution towards wind pollination and have lost their petals altogether – only scale-like glumes enclose the florets.

'In this type of habitat we have two main types of rushes: those that have a terminal, branched flower-head and leaves that are jointed inside; and those that have no leaves, a spongy pith inside the stems and a lateral flower-head. There are about three species of each type here. For instance, this is the jointed rush, *Juncus articulatus*, in which, if you carefully split the leaf open with your thumb-nail, you can see the cross-partitions inside the leaf. There is a little spray of flowers at the top of the stem where you can see six pointed, brown petals, three little pink stigmas and three stamens in each flower. Another of the jointed rushes here is the blunt-flowered rush, *Juncus subnodulosus*. The flower is a much paler buff colour with little scale-like blunt petals. The fruit is also blunt but one can always identify this rush, even if it is not in fruit or flower, by simply opening a section of leaf where one will find that not only are there cross-partitions but also vertical ones.

'Here we have two species of the other type of rush – the hard rush, *Juncus inflexus*, and the soft rush, *J. effusus*. They both have their flower-heads seemingly coming out from the side of the stem but in fact, what looks like the upper part of the stem, above the flowers, is actually a bract. The hard rush is greyish-green in colour and the stem is strongly ribbed while the soft rush has a relatively smooth stem. Both have the spongy interior pith. These rushes are very typical of these wet meadows and fens.

'If we look around now, we should find some more flowering plants. Here is a very characteristic species – ragged robin, *Lychnis flos-cuculi*. This is a relative of the familiar red campion of hedgebanks and woods but has these petals that are very deeply divided into almost strap-like forks. The delicate flowers tend to flutter in the wind like little flags. Here is the meadow buttercup, *Ranunculus acris*. It is not too common here but on some meadows can become very abundant, which causes a problem for the farmer as it is poisonous, and instinctively avoided by grazing animals. Therefore, if it forms a large part of the herbage the farmer will be tempted to plough up the meadow and reseed it. If he does that his seed will almost certainly include these flowers here – red clover, *Trifolium pratense*, and white or

dutch clover, *T. repens*. They are able to fix the nitrogen in the soil through their root nodules and therefore contribute to the overall productivity of the meadow.

'It is worth mentioning that in this diverse habitat you can find some species that are more typically found in damp woodlands. For instance, here we have the large leaves of marsh marigold or kingcup, *Caltha palustris*, whose large showy yellow flowers are long since over. Another plant that falls into this category is wild angelica, *Angelica sylvestris*.

'This little patch of fairly open meadow shows us two species that underline the nature of the pedigree of this site. First, we have an increasingly local plant, the meadow thistle, *Cirsium dissectum*. This is a plant that most people might not recognise as a thistle, because it has very feeble little prickles on the edge of an almost undivided leaf. In fact, it looks more like a knapweed. Growing next to these is a little colony of yellow rattles, *Rhinanthus minor*. This little member of the figwort family has typical yellow, two-lipped figwort flowers with a purple spotted stem and narrow pairs of leaves. It has a very inflated calyx shaped like a little pouch flattened on either side. When the seeds are ripe they rattle about inside the calyx. Like the meadow thistle, it is a plant of old meadows but unlike it, it does not seem to have a preference as to whether the soil is wet or dry, as long as it is moderately alkaline. This plant is, in fact, a semi-parasite and, although it has green leaves and can manufacture its own food, to flower successfully it needs to make a connection with one of the meadow grasses.'

As we crossed over to a wetter area of the meadow, Francis pointed out some of the commoner species of grass that were present: Yorkshire fog, *Holcus lanatus*; red fescue-grass, *Festuca rubra*, and some sweet vernal grass, *Anthoxanthum odoratum*. The vegetation gradually was becoming taller with little wet hollows that were bursting with mosses. We now started to encounter one of the most well-known of the watermeadow plants – meadowsweet, *Filipendula ulmaria*. Francis pointed out that it was also called the 'queen of the meadows'. And rightly so as the tall flower-heads were producing an almost solid mass of creamy-white. The scent that they were giving off was very sweet. This area was probably less often grazed by the cattle and that combined with the wetter regime meant that we were to find some new plants. One of the most noticeable was the

131

Above **The flowering spike of the marsh helleborine,** *Epipactis palustris.* **This charming member of the orchid family is a local plant of fens and meadows.**

Right **The tip of a marsh lousewort or red rattle,** *Pedicularis palustris,* **showing the fern-like leaves and the reddish-pink flower.**

Opposite **A yellow flag,** *Iris pseudacorus,* **with sunlit water behind. This is a plant of marshes and damper areas where the water table is permanently high.**

bogbean, *Menyanthes trifoliata,* with its large trefoil leaves. Francis told us some more about it and also pointed out some plants of interest.

'At this time of year we can see the seed capsules of the bogbean. They are quite large and each contains a number of little egg-like seeds, three or four millimetres long. If we had come earlier in the year, we would have seen its beautiful white, five-petalled flowers. They are fringed like the edge of a piece of Turkish towelling.

'Here we have the leaves of a rather nice member of the parsley or umbellifer family – pepper saxifrage, *Silaum silaus.* It is very characteristic of ancient meadows and is certainly decreasing. It has longer, more narrow and linear segments to its leaves than cow parsley. In August when it flowers you will see that it has bright sulphur yellow umbels of flowers. The name comes from the fruits that have a peppery smell, if you crush them. Another tall perennial plant of these wetter areas that we are fortunate to have here is the common meadow-rue, *Thalictrum flavum.* This is becoming quite a rarity these

A view of the dense growth of the wetter areas in the water meadow with the tall growth of marsh thistle, *Cirsium palustre*, in the centre. Habitat like this is extremely rich in plant species.

days, although according to Victorian botanists it was relatively common. Again the chief reason for its disappearance is the destruction of old meadows and the general tidying up of river banks. It has a spray of rather pretty flowers without any petals; it is the stamens that are the conspicuous part of the flower. It has compound leaves with rather narrow wedge-shaped leaflets. It used to be particularly fond of the banks of the channels which fed the water onto the meadow in the winter. To give you an idea of how scarce it is becoming, I know myself of only one other site in Hampshire where it is to be found today.

'Looking now at some of the mossy depressions in between the taller plants, we have a couple of rather nice plants. The first one is another member of the figwort family – red rattle or marsh lousewort, *Pedicularis palustris*. It has these rather attractive highly divided fern-like leaves and a reddish-purple tube-like flower with a prominent lower lip. The calyx, like its cousin the yellow rattle, is inflated. This lovely plant is now extinct in Sussex and Kent, due to drainage. Growing next to it is another plant typical of these places – the marsh helleborine, *Epipactis palustris*. This orchid is very characteristic of fenland but will also occur in old meadow systems where there are deeper hollows with more permanent high water tables. They are rather distinctive in appearance in that unlike other orchids the leaves are elliptical and pointed with strong veins and are along the stem rather than in a rosette at its base. The flower spike is rather loose with ten to fifteen flowers. Each flower has a most beautiful white lip with a yellow spot in the centre. The frilly edge to this gives it the appearance of a cravat of an eighteenth century clergyman in miniature. There are three spreading sepals which are a delicate purplish-grey on the outside and a more pinky-white on the inside. This orchid is pollinated entirely by honey bees. Unfortunately, it is far scarcer than it used to be, due to the drainage of suitable habitats.

'We are quite close to a stream and standing up conspicuously in front of us are some yellow iris, *Iris pseudocorus*, with the leaves characteristically all arranged in one plane. The familiar yellow flower is adding a splash of colour to this part of the meadows, but this plant really indicates that we are now in fen country and if we look just a little way ahead we can see the enormous tussocks of the greater panicled sedge, *Carex paniculata*,

fringing the steam. The general abundance of the bogbean just here also confirms the permanently wet conditions. So I suggest we head across to a dryer section.'

We made our way carefully through the tall ranks of flag, being careful not to trample any of the delicate plants. Soon we were walking over very different ground as a series of drier ridges across the meadows provided us with a glimpse of classic chalk grassland complete with magnificent anthills garlanded in thyme and squinancywort. The whole scene was a most unexpected and fascinating delight. As Francis picked his way between the anthills pointing out some of the typical chalk downland plants, a green woodpecker suddenly took off in front of us letting out its distinctive laughing cry. It disappeared into some nearby scrub, which was standing like Birnam Wood about to move on Dunsinane. Francis took up the story.

'If the grazing pressure was reduced or stopped the hawthorn scrub, particularly in these drier ridges, would rapidly invade the grassland which, in turn, would mean that scrub would also encroach on the wetter areas. So that willow and alder carr could take over larger areas until, theoretically, the whole series of watermeadows would disappear under a climax of oak woodland. So the balance of these places is extremely precarious. Something which must always be borne in mind when studying these sites and proposing any management plans.'

The afternoon was coming to an end, so we made our way back across the meadows trying on the one hand not to tread on any of the orchids and on the other not to fall over the hummocks. Whilst tackling this rather unusual problem we happened to flush up a snipe. As we watched it fly in a frenzied zig-zag path away from us, Francis pointed out how important these relatively undisturbed areas of roughly grazed meadow were for nesting snipe and redshank. Indeed, if the plant communities have been suffering from the loss of this habitat, the decline of the breeding populations of these birds in lowland Britain has been equally as dramatic.

As we walked back over the river and up the hill to the cars we realised that we would now look at watermeadows with their rich patchwork of flowers in a very different light. It was comforting to know that these, at least, would have a continuity of management that hopefully would ensure they were looked after for future generations to discover afresh.

Waterside walks

British rivers and lakes

MY FIRST INTIMATE CONTACT with mud and water was made in the local brickfields pond near my home in Cheam, Surrey. There many happy hours were spent learning the ways of our three species of newt and the insect fauna which inhabited their waters. My apprenticeship in the watery world was served in the ponds of Haslemere Educational Museum under the expert guidance of John Clegg and Arthur Jewell, who showed me the way around both Latin and local names. The Wandle, Mole and Thames were the first rivers in which I swam and dabbled a net. Since that time, I have come into intimate contact with rivers the world over, finding that each, though with a character of its own, can be understood by the application of the same basic rules. It was Arthur Ransome's books which lured me first to the English Lakes and then to the Norfolk Broads, to mess about in boats and look at wetland wildlife and the plants from a new angle. Since then I have never given a dry look back and waterside walks have and will always be my favourite walks.

Come splodging with me and the local experts and learn about all the things which could happen to a raindrop which has fallen onto the diversity of the British landscapes. Discover the thrills of life in a mountain stream; the process by which a river passes through youth and adolescence to maturity, as it makes its way to the sea and explore the beauty and the characteristics of the English Lakes together with the important work carried out by the various research stations of the Freshwater Biological Association.

Perhaps, most important of all, relive those days beside the local pond with new meaning and take note that the British landscapes, and that includes our rivers, streams, lakes and ponds, are changing very rapidly, and sadly, mainly for the worse. Once you have read and walked these pages, imagine what it would be like if all the ponds were filled, all our rivers and streams straightened and tamed beyond all recognition, or all our lakes given over to power-boat sports — it could happen!

WHETHER YOU ARE PLANNING to go hiking across an upland landscape or are simply intending to go out for a stroll in rural England, the focus of your walk is quite likely to be a river or lake. Waterside walks in Britain can encompass an immense variety of landscapes as a result of our diverse geology and maritime climate. This network of rivers and streams, lakes and ponds provides an important habitat for many animals and plants both in the water itself and amongst the fringing vegetation. The quality of the water varies considerably from area to area depending on the soils and management of the catchment area and this in time can have a considerable effect on the wildlife. Therefore, the richness to be expected along a southern chalk stream will contrast strongly with the few obvious animals or plants in a bubbling upland stream. Similarly lowland lakes are often much richer than upland tarns and corries.

STAGES IN THE DEVELOPMENT OF A RIVER

Classifying lakes and ponds is a relatively easy task when compared with rivers, as lakes are limited to one place and have distinct boundaries and catchment areas.

Rivers, on the other hand can run for many hundreds of miles, passing through radically different landscapes and draining different types of substrate. A simple picture of the development of a river from its source to the sea is to imagine it as containing three distinct zones: a youthful or mountain zone; a mature or foothills zone; and an old age or plain zone. These broad categories, however, fail to reflect the fact that many rivers can change from one apparent type of regime to another and then back again, depending on the immediate topography of the region they are passing through. Because of this, it is general to classify a river according to a series of recognizable zones that reflect the plant and animal life within the river. For instance, a river could be divided up by the species of fish present. This could produce four distinct zones: a headwater zone, where the stream is small and torrential and contains no fish; a trout zone, where trout is the predominant fish, here the water would usually still be torrential and subject to spates, with large boulders and rocks forming the bed of the river; a grayling or minnow zone, where these fish become dominant, here there would be deeper water

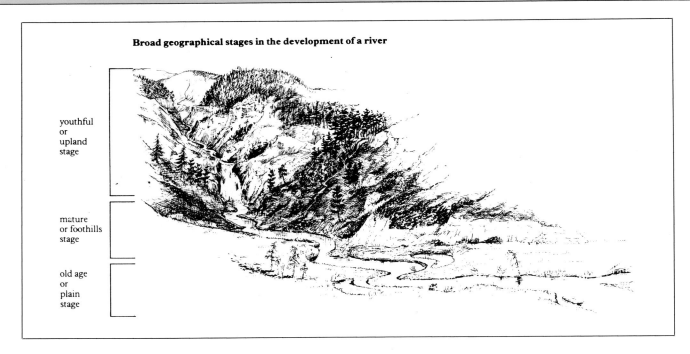

Broad geographical stages in the development of a river

youthful
or
upland
stage

mature
or foothills
stage

old age
or
plain
stage

and, although still fast flowing, silt could accumulate in patches; a coarse fish or bream zone, where the flow is slower and the river is probably meandering with large amounts of silt being deposited. A similar classification can be made using plant types with the sole presence of mosses defining the first zone, the presence of certain types of *Ranunculus*, the second, the inclusion of *Sparganium* and *Potamogeton* species, the third, and finally the last stage would be characterised by the increasing prominence of a range of flowering plants replacing *Ranunculus*.

True upland and mountain streams have very little plant growth other than mosses, as the flow is very strong and often erratic with frequent spates. In slower sections where some silt has been deposited a few flowering plants like reed canary-grass and some pondweeds can obtain a foothold. These clear tumbling waters do have large numbers of stonefly, caddis and mayfly nymphs in them and these in turn are preyed on by salmon and trout and dippers.

Lowland rivers are generally much richer in plant life but the most rewarding rivers of all these for plants and animals (and for the fisherman!) are the chalk streams of southern England. Their nutrient rich waters and stable regime means that they are an ideal habitat for a rich diversity of plants and attendant invertebrates. Because the water is mostly derived from underground springs, it has little solid material in suspension and consequently the water is usually clear. Also, the stream bed has little silt and a gravelly bottom which provides reasonable anchorage for plants. Look out for dense green carpets of water crowfoot and starwort on the river bottom and water voles busily feeding amongst the lush riverside vegetation. These are the trout streams *par excellence* so keep a watch out for trout skimming along the river bottom.

LAKESIDE BIRDWATCHING

Although the walk described in this section is through some spectacular Lakeland scenery in north west England you do not have to live near this to appreciate what marvellous places lakes are. All over Britain in recent years lake areas have sprung up creating a new dimension to the natural history of many regions. There are the gravel pits and reservoirs that supply the sand and ballast for our buildings and roads and the water supplies for our thirsty cities. Nature is always quick to respond to these new environments and given a sympathetic hand can quickly turn a bare, rather unattractive gravel pit into a delightful reed-fringed lake with plenty of wildlife to observe. A classic case is a 90 acre flooded gravel pit in a suburban area in west Kent which within fifteen years turned from a fairly unexceptional pit into one which had over 1300 pairs of fifty-five different species of birds breeding in it, all mainly as a result of a careful management policy carried out by a small but enthusiastic group of naturalists and wildfowlers.

These areas of open water are particularly important for large numbers of wintering waterfowl as compared with northern and central Europe, Britain has relatively ice-free lakes. Even reservoirs near the heart of our large cities can be teeming with exotic ducks such as goldeneyes, goosanders, pochards, wigeon and gadwalls together with black-neck grebes, red-throated divers and more. Often these birds will use these inland havens when the conditions on the coastal marshes are very severe so sometimes it is a case of the bleaker the weather, the better the birdwatching.

A tranquil scene along one of our rich southern chalk streams. Tall willows and fragrant meadow-sweet frame the picture.

Where to go

UPLAND RIVERS AND STREAMS

These types of streams are obviously very much a feature of the upland areas of north and west Britain and the rivers that flow through these regions all have their fast-flowing upland tributaries. The tributaries of the **Tay** and the **River Spey** in Scotland both have excellent stretches, although it must be remembered that public access to some of these rivers is limited as they have important salmon fisheries. It is possible to see salmon going through a fish 'pass' on their way to their spawning grounds at **Pitlochry, Tayside**. In Wales there are many beautiful

areas with upland streams, such as at **Snowdonia National Park** and the **Brecon Beacons**. **Taf Fechan** is a wooded river valley managed jointly by the Glamorgan Naturalists' Trust and Merthyr Borough Council. The **Llugwy valley** between Capel Curig and Betws-y-Coed shows many of the features of an upland river. In northern England the upper valley of **Tees** has some superb walks including the waterfalls at High and Low Force.

LOWLAND RIVERS

Britain has many superb lowland rivers, many of which have sections which are of interest to the naturalist and walker. The most famous river of them all is the great

River Thames which flows gently across southern Britain. Each area of Britain has its own major river systems – for example, the **Severn** on the west, the **Ouse** in the east and the **Tyne** and **Tees** in the north. However, some of the smaller lowland rivers which may not have has as much industrial development along their lower reaches are often well-worth exploring.

The **River Wye** which cuts a sinuous route down along the Welsh Border counties to the Severn estuary has some marvellous stretches. Particularly good areas are to be found around the **Forest of Dean** where the river has cut great gorges into the landscape. **Symonds Yat** is a popular tourist viewpoint.

Some of England's rural scene can be enjoyed at its best at such places as the **Hambledon Valley** in the Chilterns, **Windrush Valley** in Oxfordshire and **Dedham Vale** beside the **River Stour** in Suffolk, countryside immortalised by John Constable.

CHALK STREAMS

The most famous chalk streams arise in the large outcrop of chalk forming Salisbury Plain in Wiltshire and the neighbouring Hampshire Downs. They drain southwards across the coastal Tertiary deposits in the Hampshire Basin before reaching the Solent. The most well-known of these rivers are the **Avon**, **Test**, **Itchen** and **Meon**. Most of these rivers are prize fishing waters and consequently public access is generally restricted. However, if you use a good Ordnance Survey map which shows the public rights of way it is usually possible to find a stretch with a footpath.

CANALS

Most of our chalk streams have been managed over the centuries either to provide power to drive watermills or to irrigate the neighbouring water meadows. One type of lowland 'river' that has been created by man is the navigation canal. These canals formed a vast network of waterways during the first half of the nineteenth century and although, with the advent of the railways and roads, they have fallen into disuse, many have been kept-up by enthusiastic canal societies. The water in these canals is generally slow-flowing and the flora and fauna is rather similar to that which you might find in an enormous linear pond or very slow-flowing river. The great bonus with them is that the towpaths, that were used originally by horses pulling the barges, have usually been turned into public rights of way. These canals can be very rewarding places to explore for plants and animals. The **Grand Union Canal** between Kilby Bridge and Market Harborough is managed by the Leicestershire and Rutland Trust for Nature Conservation in agreement with British Waterways and has a varied aquatic and waterside flora and fauna. Some other canals that are worth visiting are the **Brecon and Abergavenny Canal**, the **Kennet and Avon Canal**, the **Basingstoke Canal** and stretches of the **Leeds-Liverpool Canal**.

LAKES

The following is a selection of lakes, lochs and loughs with public access to their margins. Many of them are artificially created areas of water either arising asa result of worked-out gravel pits or as reservoirs for the towns and cities.

These areas of water are none the less interesting for this and often contain vast numbers of wintering birds. It is suggested that you consult the local information centre or relevant body (addresses of national organisations on page 253) before intending to visit any of the sites, for further information regarding access.

1 Loch Ness, Inverness-shire. NH 50 23 This loch is known the world over as a result of its 'monster'. Frequent searches for this animal have resulted in a vast amount of information being accumulated concerning its wildlife. It is the deepest lake in Britain (130 metres).

2 Loch Garten, Inverness-shire. NH 95 18 A Speyside loch famous for its nesting Ospreys but also contains many natural history features typical of the area. RSPB reserve.

3 Loch Lomond, Strathclyde. NS 38 90 The 'Queen of Scottish Lakes'. This magnificent lake has a deep northern section and a shallow southern section, part of which is a National Nature Reserve. Whole area with the Trossachs forms one of Scotland's National Park Direction Areas.

4 Loch of Lowes, Perth. NO 05 44 A beautiful Scottish loch fringed with woodland. Ospreys breed here and there are also many species of waterfowl in winter. Good also for water plants such as water lobelia. Scottish Wildlife Trust reserve with visitor centre.

5 Loch Leven, Kinross-shire. NO 15 01 A shallow productive loch in Central Scotland. An important wintering area for a large number of waterfowl. Part National Nature Reserve, part RSPB reserve.

6 Bolam Lake, Northumberland. NZ 08 81 A country park with lake and woodland areas including nature trails and an information centre. The nearby Kielder reservoir was opened recently and has an information centre.

7 Lake District, Cumbria. The beauty and interest of the Lakes is well-known. This remarkable area has a great range of lake types with Wastwater and Ennerdale showing highly oligotrophic features and the more developed lakes such as Windermere and Esthwaite showing eutrophic features. Smaller corries and lakes, such as Angle and Stickle Tarns can be found high up in the hills.

8 Malham Tarn, Yorkshire. SD 89 66 An upland tarn with interesting geological associations. Partly owned by National Trust. This lake is the site of one of the Field Studies Centres which has an information centre and runs courses on various aspects of natural history.

9 Lake Vyrnwy, Powys. SH 98 22 A nineteenth century reservoir built high up in the Welsh mountains. Many interesting upland and water birds including dippers. Nature trails. Spectacular scenery. Part RSPB reserve.

10 Llyn Eiddwen, Dyfed. SN 60 67 An upland oligotropic lake with interesting wintering wildfowl and water plants such as quillwort and water lobelia. West Wales Naturalists' Trust Reserve. Access only along west side of the lake.

11 Llys-y-fran, Dyfed. SN 04 25 A country park in the Preseli Mountains based around a large reservoir.

12 Lough Neagh, Northern Ireland. The largest freshwater lake in the British Isles (over 400 square kilometres). There are extensive areas of reedswamp and fen along the lake margins. Nature trails can be found at Shane's Castle Reserve (RSPB) and Oxford Island. The whole area is a wildfowl refuge of international importance.

13 Rutland Water, Leicestershire. SK 93 07 A huge reservoir which is an important area for waterfowl, and waders. Part of the water has public access and part is managed as a reserve by the Leicestershire and Rutland Trust for Nature Conservation.

14 Grafham Water, Cambridgeshire. TL 15 68 A man-made reservoir which provides good opportunities to watch waterfowl with public footpaths around many stretches of the lake margin. Part of the reservoir and its margin is managed as a reserve by the Beds. and Hunts. Naturalists' Trust. Nature trails.

15 Thames Valley gravel pits. Extensive gravel pits have been excavated in the areas around London to provide building materials, etc. These pits have often been allowed to become flooded to form large areas of open water, many of which have been colonized by plants and animals, particularly water birds, which use them for roosting areas in the winter. Some have been leased or managed by local conservation groups or authorities and have nature trails. An example of this are the Broad Colney Lakes, Colney which are leased by the Herts. and Middlesex Trust for Nature Conservation.

16 Thames Valley reservoirs. The creation of large reservoirs, particularly in west and south London has provided an important new habitat for waterfowl. Special permits are required to visit most of these. However, some have limited public access and provide superb birdwatching sites. The public causeway that crosses Staines Reservoir, Middlesex, is generally good for waterfowl, especially during the winter months.

17 Wellington Country Park, Hampshire. SU 73 63 A country park centred around a series of flooded gravel pits, which have interesting wintering waterfowl. Has 'leisure' areas as well as nature trails and woodland walks.

WETLAND AREAS

The Norfolk Broads is a superb area of riverways and lakes to explore and has many reserves, many of which have limited public access. However, it is always wise to check with the local information centre or relevant body (addresses of national organisations on page 253) to confirm this before planning a visit. This list also includes some other wetland areas in Britain.

18 Norfolk Broads: Surlingham Broad – Norfolk Naturalists' Trust reserve with free access from the river. **Rockland Broad** – free access for boats. **Barton Broad** – Norfolk Naturalists' Trust reserve with access for boats. **Horsey Mere** – National trust area with access for boats. **Hickling Broad** – National Nature Reserve with access for boats.

19 Fairburn Ings, Yorkshire. SE 47 27 An RSPB reserve based around a flooded area resulting from the subsidence of old coal mines. It is well-known for its wealth of waterfowl and passage migrants. Access along public footpath with two public hides.

20 Denaby Ings, Yorkshire. SE 50 00 A marshy area created by mining subsidence. Mostly covered by flote-grass, with a superb insect fauna and large numbers of breeding birds. Owned by the Yorkshire Naturalists' Trust and has four observation hides and a field station.

21 Potteric Carr, Yorkshire. SE 59 00 An area of reed swamp, fen and open water next to the main London-Edinburgh railway. Has an impressive list of breeding and visiting birds as well as typical fen plants. The reserve was created by the Yorkshire Naturalists' Trust in collaboration

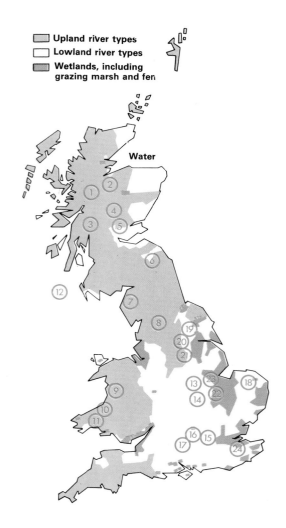

Upland river types
Lowland river types
Wetlands, including grazing marsh and fen

Water

with British Rail and is a splendid example of what can be done to an apparently unpromising area.

22 Wicken Fen, Cambridgeshire. TL 55 70 An important traditional fen reserve owned by the National Trust with a tremendous variety of marshland insects, birds and plants. There is a 2.4 kilometre nature trail.

23 Holme Fen, Cambridgeshire. TL 19 88 A drained fen reserve which is still managed in the traditional manner. Recent peat digging within the reserve and the clearing of an old decoy pond have provided habitats for plants that prefer these more open areas. National Nature Reserve.

24 Stodmarsh, Kent. TR 21 61 A rich area of open water and reed beds resulting from mining subsidence. Has large number of breeding birds and passage migrants as well as rich reedswamp and fen communities. National Nature Reserve.

A day in the Lakes

Windermere, Derwentwater, Esthwaite are names which conjure up a galaxy of holiday postcard memories from golden daffodils to bursting lungs on the final ascent to the top of Helvellyn. Eutrophic, mesotrophic, oligotrophic are not as emotive but are still words to be conjured with, for each describes a type of lake and from that description you can tell much of what you are likely to encounter on a waterside walk. Come and join me as a raindrop on its way down into Cumbria and become immersed in the subject of lakes and never again look at the contours of a map without planning a waterside walk.

A word of advice, a good map is always useful for a walk in the countryside as not only will it help you find your way there and back but it will tell you a lot about the things you will see en-route and especially about the nature of lakes. One word of caution – water is dangerous stuff and a waterside walk should be planned and undertaken with care.

A magnificent view across Loweswater in the Lake District. These beautiful lakes are the focus of many people's holiday fun and are also one of the best places to explore waterside wildlife in Britain.

A day in the Lakes

If you want to visit an area with plenty of waterside walks then one of the best places to go is the Lake District. So here I am, standing beside a beautiful lake on one of those typically rainy days in the British countryside – it is not only pouring but it also happens to be blowing so hard that the rain is hitting us horizontally. But what better time to actually explore the importance of water in the landscape? The weather doesn't really matter, as you can admire the view from the comfort of your car. But I never do that, as I like to get stuck in and have a good paddle around along the lake-side where I get wet from the top and the bottom at the same time until I almost become part of the lake itself. However, if we are going to do this we ought to understand what lakes are all about.

First of all, I can hear you say: 'What are all these lovely stretches of water doing here in the rainy old Lake District?' Well, it's partly to do with the rain, but in order to understand their origin you have to think back to 10000 years ago to the time of the Ice Ages. A great ice sheet once covered the land hereabouts, and the centre from which most of the ice radiated in this part of the world was in the high mountains of the Lake District. Gradually as the temperature rose the ice sheet became a series of massive glaciers which gouged out deep U-shaped valleys between the mountain tops. Then as the temperatures rose still further the glaciers themselves began to melt and retreat back up the valleys, depositing the material that they had picked up on the way down. Sometimes this material formed an effective barrier across the bottom of the valley. As the meltwaters from the snow and ice came tumbling down the mountains and valleys they found themselves in a cul-de-sac and slowly began to fill up the valley bottom, forming the Lakes that we can see today. Obviously there is a lot more to it than that, but all you have to do is to look at a map of the area and you can see immediately that the shapes of the lakes closely follow the great fingers of the glaciated valleys that radiate out from the centre of Cumbria. These lakes can also be very deep. For instance, Windermere is over sixteen kilometres (ten miles) long and at the deepest point is sixty-six metres (220 feet) deep, yet is only 800 metres (880 yards) wide.

Now, I reckon that if I had a chance to be something else, I'd like to be a raindrop. They travel this world for free. They don't have to buy air tickets or motor cars. They

When the rain is pouring down you can always admire the view from the car but I love nothing better than getting out there and soaking up the Lakeland scene! Here I am standing on a wave-cut platform in Crummock Water.

146

When you have a gentle slope down to the lake, where a farmer can make use of the surrounding pastures there is a good chance that the lake will be moderately eutrophic.

get evaporated up into the clouds and then off they go. It must be a blooming exciting thing to be a raindrop coming along from the west, not knowing where you are going to fall. But you can usually be safe in assuming that quite a lot of it is going to fall on the hillsides of the Lake District. Here I am imagining that I'm a raindrop and I'm about to come down on a ridge of land that separates two lakes, one called Loweswater and the other is called Crummock Water. Now, if I fall on one side of the ridge I am going to land on some nice gentle slopes amidst fairly rich pastures grazed by sheep and cattle. If I fall on the other side I'm going to land on a bleak slope with little soil cover. As I make my way down to the lake I'm going to pick up all sorts of minute particles from the rocks and the soil, and these are going to be washed along with me into the lake. So, you see, the nature of the surrounding land is going to have an important effect on the lake water itself.

If we look around Crummock Water, the amount of land that is accessible for reasonably productive farming is very low. A great deal of it looks fairly rocky and acid. This means that our vast armies of raindrops will pick up very few mineral nutrients to feed into the lake. The lake can, therefore, be classed generally as unproductive, which means that few or no plants and animals will be found in it. We can test this by looking along the shore line to see what plant and animal remains have been washed up. There is a limited strand line here with a few torn up plants and twigs. But I can't see any nice banks of waterside plants. What we have here, though, illustrates another important factor – wind action.

As I have said it is enormously windy today, in fact, it feels as if it is gusting up to a force nine gale at times. Looking out from where I'm standing (only just!) I can see waves over a foot high. I could almost be forgiven for thinking that I was standing on the beach at Brighton on a blustery day. All this wave action is going to eat away at the exposed edges of the lake, forming a series of shingly or rocky platforms that will be very inhospitable for plant growth. In sheltered bays where you don't have this wave action you have a build up of organic debris which has been slowly deposited, and this provides an ideal site for plants to colonise. However, in an unproductive lake, this process will take a very long time. These lakes are called 'oligotrophic' which is a term that is derived from the Greek: *trophe*, food and *oligos*, little

or few, as opposed to a eutrophic lake (Greek *eu*, well), which we will look at next.

Here we are only a few miles further along the road and I am currently walking across a farmer's field which looks as if it has been reseeded and fertilisers have almost certainly been put down. In front of me is a great flock of sheep and up on the hill is a small herd of cows. If I keep to the public footpath and remember to close the gates after me then I shall do no harm. Our destination is the section of path that runs along by the far side of Loweswater. Already, just from looking at this surrounding farmland, I know that we shall find a very different situation by the lake-side.

We have walked around and here is a channel that the farmer has dug to help drain his land and, who knows, it might just be carrying our raindrop. Unlike the other side of the ridge, this part of the valley has a much gentler slope and a reasonable covering of soil. So it is likely that the rainwater draining off this slope will have picked up a fair amount of mineral nutrients such as phosphates, nitrates and potassium.

This particular side of Loweswater is also

quite sheltered and if we look at the shore line we can see that it has a lot of silt deposited at the edges. However, even though the water is a good deal calmer then Crummock, the water is not that clear. This is mainly due to silt carried in suspension in the water from the stream. Earlier on in the year we would have been able to see another important factor which would affect the clarity of these eutrophic lakes – algal blooms.

Although these lakes are very deep during the summer, they tend to have two distinct temperature layers: a colder more dense layer in the deeper reaches known as the hypolimnion, and a noticeably warmer layer on top of this, the epilimnion. During the winter when the lake cools down, these layers become mixed. But in the spring the upper reaches are increasingly warmed by the sun, eventually forming a distinct layer that does not mix with the lower one. It is in this upper warm layer that most of the 'production' in the lake occurs. In particular, algae, such as *Asterionella*, a minute diatom, increase in large numbers in the spring sunshine. It is this floating mass of miniature plant life that forms the basis of the food chains in the lake,

so without them and their ability to turn the dissolved mineral nutrients into living matter the lakes would be almost dead. However, as with all things, a balance is needed. If the lake becomes too eutrophic, as a result of the farmers spraying their fields with increasingly large amounts of fertilisers or villages and towns pumping out uncontrolled amounts of effluent, the lake will soon start to suffer, as not only will the light penetration in the water be impaired but also the increasing amount of oxygen that the algae consume at night and during their decay will mean that dangerously anaerobic conditions, especially in late summer, can be produced where neither animals or large plants will be able to survive.

I like to think of the microscopic algae and the tiny animal plankton feeding on them as a very thin animal and vegetable soup. But when the soup becomes quite thick, how do the larger macrophytic plants survive as the life-giving rays of the sun will only be able to penetrate a little way beneath the surface? The answer, of course, is that they root in the rich silty bottom of the lake and stick their leaves out either on the surface of the lake or

Left **The flowering panicles of a rush. These plants have evolved flowers that are wind pollinated and the petals therefore have no need to be attractive and have as a consequence been reduced to brown scales.**

above it. If we look out across the water here, at a depth of between two and three metres, we can see the first colonisers of the lake edge doing precisely this. They are the large flat leaves of both species of water lilies that we have in Britain: the white water lily, *Nymphaea alba*, and the yellow water lily, *Nuphar lutea*. I prefer its other common name – brandy bottle – as the flowers don't last long and they then produce a wonderful fruit capsule that looks like one of the old brandy bottles. Down underneath the floating leaves are others that look partly like cooked cabbage leaves; it is quite usual for an aquatic plant to have two types of leaf.

The floating lily pads can be a problem as they can quickly cover the surface of a small pond or sheltered bay, effectively blocking out the light for everything else. However, our next zone of plants has learnt to cope with this. These larger water plants are not eaten by many of the lake animals and so they often leave a considerable amount of decaying vegetation when they die back in the winter. This all helps towards the build up of a rich organic bed of silt on the lake shelf here. As we have commented, if you live on the edge of a eutrophic lake the sensible thing to do is to grow up and out above the water so you can get to the light. This is what the next colonisers do, the perennials. These are usually large plants such as the common reed, *Phragmites*. Our chief emersive perennial here is the bulrush or common clubrush, *Scirpus lacustris*. These plants have formed a dense stand which has resulted in a further

Opposite **As soon as the Lakes were formed nature began slowly to claim them back. If one looks along the edges of many of the more sheltered Lakes one can see this process of gradual colonisation. This lovely view shows two of the initial plants that help to bind the silt and create an environment where other plants can move in. In the foreground are some rather battered lily pads of** *Nymphaea alba*, **the white water-lily and behind these is a superb stand of the bulrush or clubrush,** *Scirpus lacustris.*

Behind the stand of bulrush, the water is shallower and has been colonised by a community dominated by bottle sedge, *Carex rostrata*. The vegetation here is kept reasonably open by the grazing cattle.

accumulation of silt and organic debris, effectively pushing out the water lilies. All this is gradually raising the level of the bottom of the lake in the area. So we are looking at a process which is causing the lake to shrink. The term for this plant succession is hydroseral development. This gradual silting up and colonisation of the lake will have been continuing since the lakes were first formed over 10000 years ago. Eventually, if the process continues, the entire lake will become a swampy marsh and begin to dry until it is finally taken over by trees forming a woodland which in this part of the world is the climax vegetation.

That's the theory. Now let's get out there and have a look at the plants themselves. Ooh, it's really very cold and squelchy. I think I'll just go out as far as the start of the bulrushes. Well, here I am, the water is up to my thighs and it's blooming fantastic. It's started to rain again but I'm enjoying myself as I have found some super things to tell you about. First of all, now that I have got my head in amongst the bulrushes, I can say that they only cover about a third of the surface of the water but as they are so tall they have succeeded in shading out all the other plants. They must be over a metre high as they are above me, which means that there is more than a metre growing under the surface.

As I splodge my way back to dry land I have now come to a transitional zone between the reedswamp community with the tall bulrushes and a much more diverse community which we might call sedge fen or even sedge meadow. It is quite an abrupt change, for within a metre I have moved from a solid stand of one species to a rich mixture of bottle sedge, *Carex rostrata*, water horsetail, *Equisetum fluviatile*, and a variety of other associated plants. The few bulrushes that are growing amongst the sedges are much shorter and don't look nearly as healthy as their cousins further out. So here we can see the successional change at work. The build up of organic matter and silt which the rushes have helped to create has resulted in an area of shallower water which has favoured the sedges. Another factor is that this is probably as far out as the grazing cattle dare go. Their frequent forays out here to nibble away on the lush plant growth has also given the shorter growing sedges an advantage. The bottle sedge has this dense cylindrical mass of fruits which distribute its seeds of success. It is a perennial and uses its submerged network of rhizomes to store up food during the winter months, ready to push up masses of new shoots every spring. These weird looking plants like mini-Christmas trees are horsetails. They are the modern descendants of the giant horsetails that formed a major part of great swampy forests during the Carboniferous Period over 300 million years ago.

If I look down in between all the sedges I can see quite a few other plants. Here we have the round leaves of marsh pennywort, *Hydrocotyle vulgaris*, which, believe it or not, is a relative of the tall parsleys of the hedgerows. Its leaves look just like tiny umbrellas and if I was a gnome I would pick one up and use it to shelter from all this rain. That's lesser spearwort, *Ranunculus flammula*, a marsh-loving relative of our garden buttercup. Now, if I want to really get to grips with some of these plants I'm going to have to grovel around amongst the bases of these plants with my hands. It's very peaty and the smell that is coming off is pretty fantastic. It's like bad eggs which tells my nose that it is hydrogen sulphide, confirming that there is a lot of decaying organic matter down there. Here we have a nice little rush, *Juncus bulbosus*. This plant either forms little tufts or simply floats between the other plants. You can always tell that it is bulbous rush by feeling the base of the plant, where you will find that it has a mass of little bulbils.

Above the smell of the hydrogen sulphide I can catch something that is altogether much more pleasant – the aroma of water mint, *Mentha aquatica*. We are now in much shallower water and I can stick my hand into the ooze in the bottom and see what the floor is like. It looks just like a mass of brown decaying matter, which is what you would expect. The stringy bits are the rhizomes of the bottle sedge, but if I rub some of the deeper material between my fingers I can feel some sharp, hard bits which are particles of mineral matter that have been deposited here. So we can say that one of the reasons for the success of the hydrosere just in this bay is the mineral enrichment of the lake deposits, probably coming in from that nearby stream.

I have now moved out of the marshy fen community and I'm standing on dry ground again. We have a rather interesting situation here as the farmer has put up a barbed wire fence stretching down the hill right out into the lake and stopping in the stand of bulrushes which, as we have already guessed, is as far out as the cattle are likely to venture. This side of the fence has been regularly grazed and the sedge-rush community is still dominant in the wet meadowland. But on the protected side we have a woodland that extends almost down to the shore of the lake. It is predominantly made up of willows, *Salix*, which don't mind getting their feet wet. This type of woodland is the natural successor to the transitional sedge fen community. If we look further up the slope where the accumulation of leaf litter and fallen twigs has raised the level of the land still further, we can see birches, *Betula*, growing. These in turn can provide a 'nurse-crop' for oaks, *Quercus*, to become established. So there it is – an almost perfect example of a hydrosere, something which is going on

Above **The distinctive circular leaves of marsh pennywort,** *Hydrocotyle vulgaris*, **amongst a rich mixture of mosses, rushes, sedges and the toothed pinnate leaves of marsh cinquefoil,** *Potentilla palustris.*

Right **Where the
natural succession or
hydrosere has not
been altered by man,
woodland, which is the
climax vegetation, will
develop on the higher
land as shown here,
only metres further
along the shore from
our sedge meadow.
These are hardy
willow trees,** *Salix,*
**which, like me, don't
mind getting their feet
wet.**

wherever there is a build up of silts which can allow the plants to start colonising the fringes of these superb lakes. Now I want to show you something very different – a very oligotrophic lake, and we'll see what goes on there.

After having a gentle stroll around the farmland at Loweswater we are now looking at a complete contrast – dramatic fells rising almost sheer out of the waters at Ennerdale. The tops of the scree-covered slopes are hidden in the clouds and a strong wind is gusting across the lake surface. Any rain that is going to fall in the catchment of this lake is going to tumble and cascade down the steep slope, forming little waterfalls and swift-flowing becks. Looking at the large amount of bare rock and the thin covering of acid grassland, this rainwater is going to pick up very few mineral nutrients. This is a pretty sure sign that the lake water itself is going to be very unproductive – a highly oligotrophic lake, in other words. The result of this lack of nutrient input into the lake will be that there will be little phytoplankton. An easy way of assessing this, as we noticed in our previous lake, is the clarity of the water. So let's make our way over and see what it's like.

Here I am standing on a boulder by the lake side and sure enough the water is very clear. I can see lots of different coloured bits of fragmented rock that have probably come down from the scree slopes; they look like hard volcanic rocks. There is very little sediment and if I look behind me there is not much other than scraggy bits of acid moorland and scree, quite unlike our eutrophic farmland. Unfortunately the lake bottom shelves away quite steeply just here so we will

have to go around to another part of the lake to look at its specialised plants.

Well, we have found a section with a nice gentle shelf to it and I am actually up to my waist in this nice clear water. Looking down I can see my tatty plimsoles, which shows that it is nice and clear! Now, if I was making a proper study of the lake I would be out in a boat armed with a Secchi's disc, which is a round white board that you let down into the water to the depth where it is just visible. The depth at that point is read off and this is then used as a measurement of the light penetration in the lake. In Ennerdale it is just over eight metres (26 feet), which means that the lake is very oligotrophic. Anyway, at the depth of half a Bellamy, just here I can see a number of plants growing on the floor of the lake. They are pretty widely scattered but I can make out *Littorella uniflora*, shoreweed. That is a good name as 'littoral' means the land between the tides, and although lakes don't have tides at least it tells me that I'm dealing with a plant that grows in water. This relative of the familiar plantains is an interesting plant as it only flowers when the lake level goes down in the summer, and when it is just emergent it puts out tiny white flowers. Here is another plant with tufts of green needle-like leaves – quillwort, *Isoetes lacustris*. As I walk towards the shore the two plants are becoming more dense, almost forming a squashy green carpet. This is because there is more sunlight reaching them for photosynthesis. Over here is another underwater plant forming quite large patches all of its own. It is water lobelia, *Lobelia dortmanna*.

Opposite **Having had a
gentle stroll around
Loweswater, the
almost sheer fells
surrounding
Ennerdale make a
dramatic contrast.
Any rainwater
running off these
slopes is going to
contribute very few
nutrients to the lake
water, therefore it is
not surprising to find
that the lake is very
oligotrophic.**

Grey Heron

Coot on nest

Great Crested Grebe

Now, you needn't do a Bellamy and wade about in the water as you can often find these plants washed up on the lake shore. They all look more or less the same at first glance, but a closer look will enable you to identify them easily. The ones along the side here are already dead so it won't do any harm if I break a leaf off and look inside. A hand lens would help here, but if your eyes are reasonably all right you should be able to see enough to tell them apart. If the leaf is pointed and fairly tough and is made up inside of a solid spongy tissue, then you are dealing with *Littorella*. If it is stiff but when you break it open you can see that it is made up of four tubes which run down the whole length of the leaf, then you have *Isoetes*. This is a very interesting plant as it is a relative of the ferns. So whatever time of the year you find it there will be no flowers. But if you feel the base very gently you might find that it is all lumpy, which will be the sporangia. Don't muddle it up with bulbous rush which is a much more delicate looking plant and will almost certainly have flowers or fruit. Now,

how about water lobelia? The rosettes of leaves of this plant are quite soft and fleshy to touch and each leaf is arched back at its tip. If you are still not sure, you can break open a leaf and if you look inside you should find two whacking great tubes. If you are lucky, you might come across it whilst it is in flower and then you can see its lovely lilac-pink petals blowing in the wind above the surface of the water. It is one of my favourite plants and very, very common in certain oligotrophic lakes in Scotland.

I am now going off to look for another bay where perhaps there has been a little deposition along the shore, to see if we can find some emergent plants. A close look at a good map of the area will always help.

I have now arrived at a little sheltered bay and in amongst the stones I can see some sediment, although there is no obvious succession of plants as at the eutrophic Loweswater. Right along the edge of the lake I have found a typical plant of boggy land and more acidic waters – Bogbean, *Menyanthes trifoliata*. This is one of the easier

Moorhen

Coot

Little Grebe

Moorhen chick

waterside plants to identify as it has a three-part leaf, rather like a gigantic clover leaf. Earlier on in the year it has lovely pink and white flowers with delicate fringes to the petals. If you find one washed up along the lake side have a look at the stem. You will find that inside they are made up of a wonderful squashy tissue. This tissue is called aerenchyma. This consists of living cells with whacking great holes in between, rather like a string vest. All the water plants of the world except those that live in highly oxygenated waters have this type of tissue, which not only allows passages for oxygen to circulate from the aerial sections down to the roots but it also provides support with the minimum number of cells. I always think it interesting that if you were to look at the inner skin of a modern aeroplane you would find that its structure was remarkably similar to the spongy aerenchyma of a water plant, which, of course, the plant kingdom came up with millions of years before man.

If we look at the shore here we can see a bog moss, which is very acid and poor in nutrients. It is made up of my favourite plant – *Sphagnum*.

So we have seen two extremes in Loweswater and Ennerdale and I am sure you will find lots of variations and combinations of the two types that we have looked at today. A close look at an Ordnance Survey map can often tell you what sort of lake you are likely to find. Gentle slopes with woodland or farmland on the lake shore is usually an indication of a productive landscape and, therefore, a eutrophic lake, whereas steep, rocky slopes with short becks and little surrounding woodland could mean that you have an oligotrophic lake. Perhaps you could make a survey of the lakes of your area and put them into some type of order as they have done here in the Lake District. Another important thing to do when looking at lakes is to visit them at different times of the year, so that when you have all your notes together you can get a complete picture. Right now I don't think there is one bit of me that isn't wet through, so I'm off home to dry out and have a pot of tea before I write up my note book.

A collection of birds that can be seen on most British lakes. An important factor in encouraging these birds to breed at your local lake is the amount of vegetation cover at the water's edge. If a section of the lake has a rich band of reeds and other plants the numbers of birds breeding along the lake will increase. Disturbance is another important factor. Sometimes it is possible, if the lake is large enough, to cordon-off part of the lake from water sports thus leaving a 'quiet' area where the birds can feed and nest in peace.

An upland river walk

In the grounds of Kindrogen Field Centre there is a seat with a plaque which records the fact that Queen Victoria took tea at that place overlooking one of the headwaters of the River Tay. There could be no better place to do just that or to take a waterside walk, and there could be no better guide than Brian Brookes, warden of the centre. As he bounds along the bank, his immense enthusiasm and knowledge bubbles over almost as fast as the clear water, which flows over the waterfalls. Think of the problem the aquatic animals have of living in such a place, battered by the rushing waters and in danger of being swept away by spates or even crushed by moving boulders. Yet life in such tumbled waters has its compensations. There is plenty of oxygen, dare I say, always on tap and a good supply of food washed in from the banks or from upstream. You couldn't want a better start than a mountain stream walk to your adventure through waterside Britain.

A classic view of an upland stream cutting its way through the Scottish mountains in a characteristic V-shaped valley.

An upland river walk
with
Brian Brookes

When you take a walk along the banks of one of Britain's lowland rivers and savour the apparently tranquil scene, it is worth remembering that most of our major rivers have a very different beginning. Probably they start their long journey to the sea from springs or snow meltwaters high in mountains and, for a while, will be characterised as a cascading brook cutting a path down through rocky uplands. These early stages of development have their own distinct associations of plants and animals and have the added bonus of sometimes being found in magnificent scenery. In order to find out more about these upland streams we travelled to the mountains of Scotland to visit Brian Brookes, warden of the Kindrogen Field Centre in Perthshire. In the glorious July sunshine, Brian led us out to the headwaters of one of the tributaries of the River Tay, right up in the heart of the Scottish Grampians. As it turned out, a good road followed the river valley and so, after only a short walk, we found ourselves standing amidst towering mountains scanning miles of heather-covered moors and listening to the distant calling of grouse echoing across the glens. A few yards down a slope from us was a sparkling stream but the real beginnings of the river were right at our feet. We sat down on a great granite boulder whilst Brian began to unfold the story of the headwaters of this particular stream.

'At the moment we are about 2000 feet (625 metres) above sea level and here we have found one of the many places where there is water coming down the hill and out of the ground in the form of springs. Now, one of the first things to look for, when you find a spring like this, is the type of rock that is predominant in the area as this will affect the richness of the water. Interestingly, this area has a very mixed collection of rocks. Some of them are very acidic, like this schist; there is a lot of granite but there are also bands of limestone. This is very important as where the water has been in contact with this limestone it will have dissolved some of the minerals and will consequently be relatively rich, whereas in other places the chemicals in the rock are largely insoluble and the waters at the spring head will lack any mineral nutrients for plant and animal growth. It just so happens that the spring we have before us now is very rich in lime and other chemicals and this shows immediately in the vegetation that is growing around the spring. There are great cushions of mosses actually at the very

A spring at the headwaters of our river. This one has had a rather colourful start! The bright red colouring is a deposit associated with the oxidization of ferrous compounds brought to the surface in the spring water. A very ancient form of bacteria is involved in this process and derives its energy from the conversion. The great clumps of mosses around the spring indicate the mineral richness of the water.

160

point where the water is seeping out of the ground. There is also a great diversity of higher plants such as sedges, rushes and grasses. Particularly eye-catching is the yellow mountain saxifrage, *Saxifraga aizoides*, which is forming a ribbon down each side of the stream. At this time of year it has these beautiful yellow flowers with orange spots near the base of the petals. It is a very good indicator of calcareous influences. If there is lime in the water we are assuming that we probably have quantities of other important elements for plant life such as magnesium and iron. Indeed, as far as iron is concerned we can actually see places where there are considerable rusty brown deposits associated with the oxidization of ferrous compounds. Bacteria will be involved in this process and will themselves be deriving energy from the conversion of ferrous to ferric iron.

Further into the valley we can see the stream itself which is bubbling and crashing over boulders and pebbles. The bright yellow flowers are yellow mountain saxifrage, *Saxifraga aizoides*, **which gives an indication of the lime-rich nature of this particular catchment area.**

This young ram is taking an intense interest in our survey of his salad lunch!

'Looking around we can see some other plants which indicate the very rich nature of this spring. There is a lot of totty or quaking grass, *Briza media*, and a common plant of our lawns which you might not expect to see up here – *Bellis perennis*, the daisy. In a place like this, however, they are an indication of limey conditions. There are also some sedges such as this tawny sedge, *Carex hostiana*, and right at our feet are the tiny white flowers of fairy flax, *Linum catharticum*.'

To one side of the spring the ground was more open and muddy which on closer inspection showed the tracks of many animals. We asked Brian what could have caused such a trampling of the spring.

'Well, it's an absolute quagmire, isn't it? It is in fact another spring area and again the water must be rich in nutrients as the surrounding vegetation is quite luxurient. Considering we are surrounded by extensive areas of pretty tough old heather, this little oasis of lush grasses and other plants is going to attract grazing animals. In this part of the world the biggest and most important animals, apart from the sheep, are the herds of red deer. So what we can see here is ground that deer have churned up while they have been grazing on the succulent vegeta-tion. In the summer the hinds and the stags form separate herds. The hinds, which will have with them the calves that were born in June, form large herds of maybe one or two hundred animals. They tend to keep a little further away from these main roads. If we went over to the other side of the hill we would probably see a herd down in the glen. The stags, on the other hand, keep in smaller groups and wander a little more. So probably it is a small group of stags that has made all this mess.

'Later in the year the stags begin to fight each other and go off on their own to collect as many hinds as they can. Each stag then defends his harem against all comers which, as you can imagine, leads to a certain amount of fighting and noise. Also at this time of year muddy areas such as this are used by the stags as wallows. They deliberately roll over and over on their backs in the wet mud and coat themselves in a dripping layer of ooze. I'm not sure whether this simply cools them off or makes them appear more frightening to aggressors during the fighting.'

We made our way carefully around the spring and headed a short distance down the slope to the main stream. However, before we looked at this in any detail Brian pointed

out that the other side of the valley was worth looking at first. It certainly looked damp and we clambered over to take a closer look. Brian explained why he had brought us across.

'This area of the hillside is a most exciting place for a naturalist. It is what is known as a calcareous flush, which means that it is an area with water rich in minerals seeping out of the ground, like the spring that we have just looked at but much more expansive. An appreciation of the importance of these areas really takes you on to the whole question of the origin of a stream or river. In the first instance, precipitation in the form of rain or snow is obviously the start of the whole process. The water in the stream is derived either directly from this rainwater falling into it or from water that has drained laterally from the surrounding catchment area. The bulk of the water arrives via this second route and therefore the type of soil around the stream is very important. In this area the soil is rich and limey, but just a little further down the soil is sandy and covered with heather and therefore the input into the stream at that point in terms of nutrients is going to be far less. There are many plants that tell you immediately whether you are on acid or limey soil. Further down on the acid side is hard fern, *Blechnum spicant*, bilberry, *Vaccinium myrtillus* and heather, *Calluna vulgaris*, whereas here we have more of the yellow mountain saxifrage, eye-bright, *Euphrasia*, and alpine lady's mantle, *Alchemilla alpina*. Also here is a species of cotton grass with a wide pale green leaf called *Eriophorum latifolium*. This type of cotton grass only grows in calcareous damp areas, whilst further along in the acid area you can see another type of cotton grass, *Eriophorum angustifolium*, which is common in acid and boggy areas and has long narrow and much darker green leaves. So if you can differentiate between these two types of cotton grass you can immediately say whether you are by a base-rich or an acid site.

'If we just look at a couple of the plants here I will be able to show you an interesting reproductive mechanism that a lot of these upland plants use. Here we have some viviparous fescue grass, *Festuca vivipara*, and instead of producing flowers at the top as one might expect, it has these little plantlets, each of which can just break off and get blown or washed away and immediately start to grow into an identical plant. The alpine bistort, *Polygonum viviparum*, has it both ways as it produces conventional flowers at

Sheep can be found grazing right to the tops of many of our mountains therefore many of the more interesting 'alpine' plants are found on inaccessible gullies and crags. In the Scottish Highlands also look out for soaring golden eagles and distant herds of red deer browsing on remote slopes.

A close-up view of the moss, *Campyllium stellatum*, showing the golden-yellow star-like tips to the fronds.

The alpine bistort, *Polygonum viviparum*, clearly showing the conventional flowers at the top of the flowering stalk and the little bulbils in the lower part. This mixed approach to reproduction gives the plant a better chance of producing offspring in the short unpredictable summer season.

the top of the inflorescence and little bulbils lower down. Again, if these were broken off they would form new plants. The higher up you go into the hills the more bulbils and the less flowers you find so there is a direct relationship with the altitude. This is quite significant as at this height there are practically no annual plants because the risk of the seed not surviving the winter or failing to produce seed in the short summer is so high.

'Typical plants of these wet areas are the butterworts. They occur on both basic and acid sites and are able to add to their nutrient intake by trapping insects. They have a rosette of yellow leaves with sticky upper surfaces which work on the fly-paper principle. When the insect is well and truly stuck, the leaf secretes an enzyme which gradually digests it. They have these beautiful purple flowers. However, the predominant vegetation here are the sedges and rushes. In between them are these lovely mosses and liverworts. Here again, if you are up to identifying them, they will also confirm the wet and limey nature of the area. For example, here is a moss, *Campyllium stellatum*, whose leaves are quite narrow and

spreading, making these bronze or golden-yellow stars at the tips. And there is a lovely little flat thalloid liverwort with a purple frill around the edge; it is called *Preissia*.

'This is an interesting plant if you are interested in the evolution of plants – the club moss, *Selaginella selaginoides*. It is actually more closely related to the ferns than the mosses. If you move up the evolutionary scale this plant is the first one you come to that produces spores of two kinds – big ones that form the female part of the life-cycle and little ones that are the male part. In lower plants the spores are only of one kind.

'Whilst we are here right at the headwaters it would be a good point to discuss an important physical feature of the stream itself. If you consider that the water has just emerged from these springs, once it is in the stream and out in the open it is going to be subject to rapid changes in temperature. On a hot summer's day like this the rocks will become quite warm and the water tumbling over them will become warm as well. At night the opposite will happen. Further to this, the temperature changes with the seasons can also be very extreme. But the

nearer to the source of the stream you go the less variation you have as the water coming out from the rocks is of a fairly constant temperature. So although the water feels cold today, in winter it may still be flowing when the rest of the landscape is frozen solid. Some of the animals that are found in these headwaters rely on this constancy of temperature. In particular there is a little flatworm which we might be lucky enough to find here. What we need to do is search among the stones on the stream bed, especially the flat ones sitting on sand and gravel which have a current of water underneath them. What we are looking for is a little flat worm-like animal which will be on the rock surface. Ah, there we have a very, very small one. It is a dirty creamy-ochre colour with sharp ear-like points at the front. It is gliding very slowly across the surface. It is a very primitive little animal and belongs to one of the flatworm families which includes the tape-worms and liverflukes. This is a free-swimming animal called *Crenobia alpina*, and it is very fussy about the temperature of the water in which it lives. It is essentially an animal associated with very cold arctic-type tundra conditions which would have been prevalent here in the immediate post-glacial period about 10000 years ago. In places the

The common butterwort, *Pinguicula vulgaris,* **is a typical plant of the wet areas of north and west Britain. They are able to add to their nutrient intake by trapping insects on the sticky upper surfaces of the leaves. The leaf secretes an enzyme which gradually digests the insect.**

conditions are still similar – obviously there is more vegetation now but the water temperature is probably comparable and so this relic of the glacial fauna has managed to survive in the headwaters of these streams.'

We placed the rock carefully back in the stream and moved on down the valley to a nearby bluff. Having looked in detail at the micro-habitats afforded by the headwaters of the stream we now altered our gaze to the overall landscape. To say that it was impressive was certainly an understatement but what were the forces that had formed it and in particular what part did our stream play in the overall pattern?

'First of all it must be remembered that the underlying rocks are extremely ancient – over 350 million years old – and that the mountains have been formed by a series of tremendous upheavals, producing durable metamorphic rocks. But these rocks only form the skeleton of the landscape. In order to understand the scene we see today we have to look at a much more recent time, geologically speaking, when the land was under ice.

When you look at the view up here you will notice that there is very little solid rock visible and that most of the landscape is actually covered with a deposit that is hiding this rock. We are looking in fact at a landscape which has been produced by glaciation. If we go back to the depths of the ice-age this area would have been covered by a thickness of ice between a quarter and half a mile in depth. Certainly far higher than the tops of these mountains. So we have to think in terms of a great ice sheet rather than individual glaciers. This sheet slowly radiated outwards from the main area of precipitation in Scotland which was then, as now, the western side of the Highlands. So material from this western region would gradually have been pushed outwards to be eventually deposited all over these hills. As the climate improved the ice sheet began to thin and at one stage the tops of the hills would have begun to poke out through the ice-sheet and the ice movements be guided by the shapes of the intervening valleys. Gradually the sheet would have broken up

A splendid view of an upland glaciated valley showing the broad flat bottom and the truncated spurs. Notice how the river, despite its size, is meandering across the level valley floor.

into a series of glaciers and it is these glaciers, still propelled by the weight of ice behind them, which went down glens like this and gouged out the wide U-shaped flat-bottomed valleys, cutting of any spurs.

'Eventually the climate improved to the point where the movement of the glaciers itself began to slow down until it became stagnant and began melting away. At this stage, there was a lot of water running from the glacier and from ice further up the valley which would have brought more material down and deposited it in between the chunks of ice and along the sides of the valley, particularly as a gap opened between the glacier side and the valley. The stones in these deposits are very smooth and rounded, confirming that they were transported by water. If we were to look at material higher up on the hill slopes which was deposited straight out of the ice we would find that it was much more angular and sharp.

'So looking south we can see the wide flat-bottomed valley we have today with the river running in the centre. However, off to our

left is a very different shaped valley. This one is much narrower with a V-shaped cross-section. The gradient is quite steep and the stream is flowing quite rapidly down the valley centre, tumbling over little waterfalls and around large boulders. As it goes it will be washing away some of the rocks and gradually deepening the valley. So this valley is the result of erosion by the stream and not by glaciers. Another pointer to this is that the stream is running in a series of zig-zags resulting from deflections from its course produced by obstructions such as hard rocks. We can only see a short distance up the valley as there is an interlocking series of spurs. A glacier would have produced a much straighter valley and removed the spurs.

'Further along where the stream has entered the main glaciated valley it is flowing much more slowly, the gradient is less but is still moving from side to side. The curves are much bigger, however, producing a more sinuous wave-like pattern in contrast to the zig-zag that we had earlier. The bottom of the valley is filled, as these hillsides are, with glacial material and the river is continuing to erode it away. Just below us it has cut into some of the glacial mounds to produce a steep, flat slope which is far more typical of a water-worn slope than one produced by glacial action. However, obviously the overall shape and size of the valley has nothing to do with the present river.'

Before we moved on, we took one last look at the river meandering down the centre of the glen, the water catching the mid-day sun. What animal life lived amongst the rocks and boulders? Were there likely to be any fish lurking in the deeper pools? These were questions which we were to look at next. Brian took us to a stretch of a nearby river which he has studied in detail over the years and where we could look closely at the river and its life.

'We've now come to a more mature phase of a river although it is still one that is dominated by fairly fast flow and has many boulders of all sizes in its bed. Before we look at the animal life, it would be an idea just to appreciate the range of environments that make up even a short stretch of river such as this. We are standing next to a fairly deep pool with a relatively calm surface whereas just upstream there is quite a rough area with a low waterfall. Also notice how the water flow is much faster in the middle of the river. This has an important effect on the distribution of the boulders and pebbles on the

river bed. For example, you can see that nearly all the large boulders are in the centre and as you move out to the sides they are progressively smaller. This is because in the slower flowing sections some deposition is occurring. However, the flow is still too fast generally for the finer silts to be deposited. Also, remember that a river like this will change substantially from season to season. At the moment it is quite shallow and a great deal of the river bed is exposed but during the winter the water level will be considerably higher, as can be seen from the debris lodged in the bankside tree two metres above the current water level.

'All in all, then, as a habitat for animals this is not a particularly hospitable site when compared with most other freshwater sites. Looking at the water cascading along between the rocks it is obviously going to be difficult to find any animals living on the water surface. Whereas on a pond you might find pond-skaters running around, the river, even now, is running at more than a metre a second, so a pond-skater would have to be moving incredibly fast just to stay where it is. Similarly in the main body of the water only the larger vertebrates such as salmon and trout are going to be able to swim fast enough to take advantage of the environment. So where are the majority of river animals going to be found? The animals will obviously need to anchor themselves to something and therefore, not surprisingly, we have to search the river bed for the small invertebrates. So let's have a search around under these stones.

'Immediately you will notice that there are a lot of algae on the surface of the stones and trapped in between the rocks and pebbles are all sorts of plant debris – pieces of grass, leaves, twigs etc. This tells us that a lot of potential food in fact comes from other systems outside the river. Things fall in all the time; besides the plants, insects drown in the river in quite large numbers. So we can assume that quite a lot of the river animals will be scavengers. However, there are quite complex relationships within the river. For example, we can see a lot of zig-zagging chironomid midges flying above the water. The larvae will be important scavengers on the river bed and in turn will be a major supply of food for the fish population. Perhaps, the best way of beginning to unravel the web of relationships in a river like this would be to look at the life histories of some specific animals.

'Remember when you disturb the river

Above **In contrast to the wide U-shaped profile of the glaciated valley this side stream has worn down its own V-shaped valley.**

bed be sure that the boulders are carefully replaced as you are undoubtedly endangering the lives of many small animals if you just haphazardly throw them back.'

Brian had brought along some plastic dishes and a sturdy looking net and soon the water in the dish was writhing with dozens of invertebrates that he had collected. Brian gently picked out a few and told us about them.

'We have two or three dozen insect larvae here, most of which are mayfly nymphs. We can identify them as such because they have these three very long tails. These are sensory organs and in some species like this one they are almost as long as the rest of the insect. The nymph is obviously adapted to living in a fast flowing river as it has a wide flat body and limbs so that it can fit underneath stones and lie close to the rock surface. Its behaviour is also adapted and if you watch them in the

Opposite **The river at a more mature stage. Although the volume of water has increased the bed of the river is still dominated by large boulders and stones which offer a variety of habitats for river animals.**

169

Mayfly nymphs of these fast flowing mountain rivers are adapted to cling tightly to the rock surfaces and have developed streamlined profiles in order to lessen friction with the water. Notice the rows of flap-like gills along the abdomen and the characteristic three 'tails'.

river you will notice that they do not swim but will run across the stones, always hanging on tightly. In these fast flowing rivers which are constantly tumbling and crashing over the rocks, the water contains a lot of oxygen and the animals that live here tend to be dependent on these high oxygen levels. That is one of the reasons why they don't look too happy in the dish. One of the things they are doing, if you look very closely, is beating their gills, which are in pairs along the side of the abdomen. These 'gills' are ventilating organs and create a current of water over the body so that the insect can absorb as much oxygen as possible. If we were to watch them in the river we would notice that they hardly move their gills as there is sufficient oxygen. This species of mayfly, which is typical of stony rivers, is called *Ecdyonurus venosus*. Together with it we have another closely related mayfly called *Rhithrogena* whose gills have become enlarged and are no longer mobile. They

overlap and form a sucker with which it attaches itself to the rock surface. So if you were to keep a mixture of *Ecdyonurus* and *Rhithrogena* nymphs in a dish of still water you would find that the latter would soon die as they would be unable to ventilate. There is also some suggestion that the gills might be used in helping the animals to swim and stabilise themselves.

'So if we are to find these kinds of insects in the river we should look in places where the water is moving moderately fast, where there is a good supply of oxygen and also where there is a food supply. This leads us to some of these medium-sized flat stones which have a good current of water underneath. With luck, we will find an insect hanging on upside-down facing the current. Here's a good example, it is a stonefly larvae. It looks at first glance not too dissimilar to the mayfly larvae but does, in fact, belong to a separate order of insects – the Plecoptera. They have two, instead of three, long sensory tails and some of them are quite big. Certain species, such as *Perla bipunctata*, can be as long as three or four centimetres including their tail, and take as long as three years to mature. What we have here is one called *Dinocras cephalotes*. Interestingly, the gills of stoneflies are not on their abdomen, as in mayflies, but are on the thorax at the top of their legs, looking like little pieces of cotton wool. If we put one into still water it can't beat its little fluffy gills so it will start to do 'press-ups'. The shorter the supply of oxygen, the more furiously it will do its 'press-ups' in the same way that a mayfly will beat its gills faster.

'Like the mayflies, the stonefly adults emerge in early summer. The adults are rather drab-coloured but are big and spectacular looking and still retain the two tails. They lay their black eggs in frothy bubbling masses in between stones up above the water level – hence the name, stonefly.

'Our dish also contains some freshwater shrimps, *Gammarus*, which can be found in practically any river or stream in Britain providing the water has a fairly high calcium content. They are mostly scavenging animals although they do eat algae. Their behaviour is interesting in that they respond very quickly to light, for example, in a dish like this they will always swim to the part that is in shadow. This indicates that they are essentially nocturnal, and spend the day hidden under stones. They have a daily dilemma in that they are under the stone during the day but the algae on which they

marus swimming upstream as, given a current, this shrimp will swim into it. This enables them, when the river is not in spate, to make up for the effects of drift.

'We can also see some representatives of another important group of freshwater insects – the caddis flies. The larvae of these flies use material from the river to construct cases within which they live. The case is attached to a silk envelope which they spin around themselves before starting to build. This one has a beautifully constructed case made up of small grains of sand, little pieces of quartz and flakes of mica. Each species has a different type of case and this one is round in section with a slight curve along its length. We can tell which is the oldest end because the diameter of the case increases as the developing insect adds material at the front end. The larva crawls around with its abdomen inside the case and is able to stick its head, thorax and legs out in the front. In these fast flowing waters perhaps a better strategy might be to fix your case to a large rock and wait for the food to come to you. Indeed, in the river here are a lot of *Agapetus* species which do just that. There is another caddis fly, called *Hydropsyche*, which simply spins itself a case of silk. This becomes elaborated into a funnel-like web which catches food carried along in the current, just like an underwater spiders' web. If you have a clear stream you can sometimes look down into the water and see what are apparently crescent shapes on the bed of the river – these are the entrances to their silk nets. But for filter-feeding *par excellence* you want to look into the waterfall areas where the water is flowing fastest. This is where we find the larvae of the black flies, *Simulium*. Quite contrary to many of the other animals they seek out the lightest places rather than the darkest ones and this concentrates them on the outer surfaces of the rock where the water is fastest. They also respond to the current itself, moving towards the fastest flowing water. Here, from glands on the head, they spin themselves a little pad of silk which is attached to the rock. They hook their posterior end, which has great cones with curved teeth, on to the pad and then go limp in the water, extending their mouth parts which are like sieves. There they lie in the current catching food by filtering the water. When they move from one place to another they simply spin another pad and loop themselves onto it and by using the silk pads as a series of stepping stones they slowly get around.

The stonefly nymphs only have two 'tails' and if you look carefully you can see the feathery gills on the thorax at the top of the legs. This is a *Dinocras* nymph, which is typically found in clean mountain streams.

feed at night grows on the top surface. They therefore have to make this rather tricky manoeuvre from the bottom to the top and back again. If you fixed a net in a stream facing upstream and regularly monitored it every hour you would find that very few *Gammarus* were caught for most of the time, but there would be spectacular numbers being swept along by the river at sunset and sunrise when they were making this transition.

'This brings up the subject of drift. No matter how careful you are, at some stage, if you are a small invertebrate, you are going to be swept downstream. For the insects, this is not a very great problem as the adult insect, be it a mayfly or a mosquito, will always fly upstream to mate and lay its eggs, thus compensating for any downstream drift of its larvae. But what do the shrimps do? If you could fix your nets facing downstream you would find that you would still catch *Gam-*

The salmon has an extraordinary life cycle that begins as a fry high up in the headwaters of upland rivers. The young salmon or parr then remains in the river for a year or two before moving to the lower reaches as a smolt prior to going to sea. It will then stay at sea feeding in the rich waters off Greenland for some years attaining its full adult status, before eventually returning to its natal-headwaters to breed.

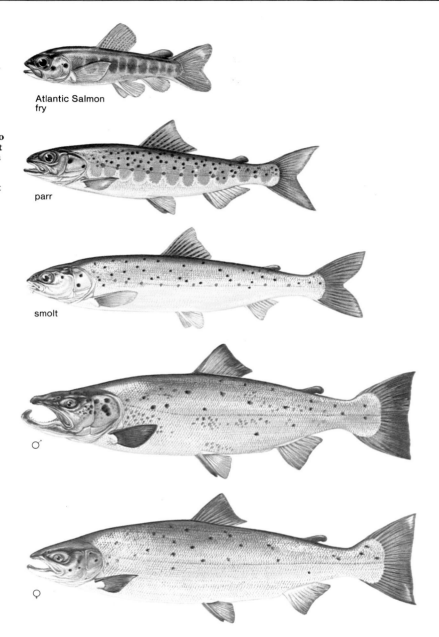

Atlantic Salmon
fry

parr

smolt

♂

♀

'These are just some of the many invertebrates that are to be found on the river bed. As we have seen, some, like the *Simulium,* are filter feeders, others, like the big stonefly nymphs are carnivorous and will eat the herbivores and scavengers. But they all in turn will be prey to the larger vertebrates such as the fish, which are near the head of the food chain. A river like this will have large numbers of brown trout, and at certain times of year salmon. The trout, which are entirely freshwater fish, will be feeding and growing in this part of the river but will move up to the headwaters to breed and spawn. These trout will be feeding mostly on the stonefly and mayfly larvae and the *Gammarus.*

'The salmon, of course, are a very different story. However, there will be, even with the river as low as this, a large number of salmon here. But if you were to catch any you would find they were only four to six inches long (15 centimetres). This would be because they would be the very young stages of the salmon, hatched from eggs laid up in the very headwaters of the stream in the middle of winter. They will have moved down to this part of the river as very small salmon called parr and will spend a year or two in the river, feeding and growing very slowly. At this stage they look very much like trout and can be difficult to distinguish from them. They do have, however, very pronounced dark marks all the way down the side which the trout usually do not, but this is not infallible. Eventually they become much less colourful and rather more silvery, with few strong patterns. They are turning from parr into smolt and this is when they move further down the river before finally going to sea. They stay at sea for some years, apparently the time varies from salmon to salmon, feeding mostly around the waters of west Greenland. But in the end they always return to breed. Amazingly they are able to retrace their way right back to the headwaters where they were spawned. The adult salmon will have grown phenomenally in the period at sea – these are the fish we generally think of as the salmon. The cock and hen fish, as they are called, will move up the river always swimming against the strongest currents. When the rivers are low, such as now, they will hang back until there has been some heavy rainfall and then when there is a surge of water down the river, the salmon will begin to move up. At this stage in their life cycle they don't feed as they undergo some very fundamental changes on their return to freshwater. One of these is that the whole of the gut tends to atrophy. This presents a problem for the angler, who has to catch the salmon by annoying it rather more than by tempting it to eat. Sometimes this long journey up the river means that the fish arrive in the spawning grounds in pretty poor condition and afterwards they normally die. These spent fish are called kelts, and in the early part of the spring you can find four or five of these emaciated dark red kelts washed up along a hundred yard stretch along here. Some of them manage to get back to the sea where they regenerate their digestive system and will return to breed again.

'Another group of vertebrates at the top of the food chain are the birds. If you are visiting a stretch of upland river it is always worth looking out for the delightful dipper. They like these rivers, with plenty of boulders to perch on and fast clear water with plenty of invertebrates to feed on. You will often see this dumpy dark brown and white bird flying low and straight over the water and landing on a protruding rock in the centre of the river. There it will stand dipping and bobbing up and down, doing "knee-bends". If you get a good view another point to look out for is its eyes. For the dipper, like most birds, has a third eyelid, a nictating membrane. This shows up white in the dipper contrasting with its dark head. Suddenly it will just pop off the boulder to feed in the

river. However, unlike a wader, which would paddle around poking into the shallower areas, the dipper will actually go under the water and walk on the bed, held down by the force of the water pressing down on its back. Here it moves along upstream turning over stones with its beak and fishing out the crustaceans and insect larvae which are hidden underneath. Dippers often nest in bridges and stonework or occasionally in overhanging trees. They will then construct a very big nest out of twigs. Each pair has a definite stretch of river which is their territory and they patrol this regularly. The number of territories on a river will directly reflect the amount of food available and therefore the productivity of the river.

'Another bird that is typical of these stony rivers is the grey wagtail. If you just get a quick glimpse of one travelling upstream with its typical bounding flight the most noticeable feature, despite its name, is the bright sulphur yellow belly and perhaps the black bib of the male. They hawk over the surface of the river, picking off the adult mosquitoes, midges and mayflies. Like the dipper they breed along the banks of this river, perhaps in a clump of grass hanging down over a boulder or beside a waterfall in a rock crevice.

'Whereas these birds, to some extent, feed, like the fish, on the profuse invertebrate life in the river, they are predators that, in a sense, come further up the food chain and can feed on the fish themselves. It could also be said that they are from partly outside the river ecosystem. If we look along the bank of the river in sandy places or where there's a little muddy backwater we might be lucky enough to see the webbed tracks of an otter. If you are very lucky you might see a stream of bubbles in mid-river followed by sight of a flat wedge-shaped head and long whiskers.

The dipper is a familiar bird of rocky upland rivers and streams. It has developed the ability to actually walk under the water, where it catches insect larvae and crustaceans on the river bed.

173

But unfortunately there are very few otters and more often than not when you see a large carnivore along a river it turns out to be something rather smaller and darker, much more weasel-like – a mink. These are usually escapees from fur farms and can be a fairly serious threat to river fisheries because they seem to kill a lot of fish and eat very few of them. In contrast the number of otters is so small in this part of the world that the amount of fish they kill is relatively insignificant.'

While Brian was telling us about the otter we scanned the river with the vague hope that we might actually see one. But, of course, we had no such luck. We returned our stonefly nymphs carefully to the river. Brian had certainly shown us some of the rich natural life that can be found in these upland streams and rivers. But an important part of the overall equation was still to be brought in – the effect of that arch transformer of all things – man. We drove downstream to Blairgowrie to discuss some of his uses and abuses of our rivers. Brian took up the story.

'We have now come much father down the river system where the river is much bigger. The volume of water being discharged at this point is something like four or five times the volume that we were seeing further up. The increased volume means that the potential of the river in terms of energy and therefore as a source of power has increased tremendously. Whereas in the glens man used the river to drive small mills for grinding flour, we are now in a situation where a considerable source of energy could be trapped for industrial and semi-industrial purposes. This source of power is the key to the growth of Blairgowrie in that the prosperity of the town was built on the success of the mills along the riverside here. Although they are sadly no longer in use they started originally as flax mills for linen and soon after that were associated with the growth of the jute industry in Dundee. The mill we can see upstream has still got its great water wheel which right until the present day contributed to the power requirements of that mill. For most of the mills, the water power over the years was initially supplemented and eventually largely replaced by coal. However, it is interesting that one mill actually went back in its last days to the river again, using it as a source of power supply to drive its own small hydro-electric turbine plant. So this is a very significant relationship between the river and man.

'Not all of man's relationships are quite so happy, I'm afraid. We do get examples all along the river of its being used for the disposal of waste, rubbish and effluent both domestic and from farms and industry. This has a considerable effect on the river and its life. You can actually gauge to what degree a river is polluted by the types of plant and animals that are living in it. For example, we were only able to find the stonefly and mayfly larvae earlier on because there was practically no pollution at that point. If the pollution was uncontrolled the river could easily be reduced to a lifeless habitat. There are, of course, many types of pollution. Moderate organic pollution from sewage can be regarded in a river like this as a slight enrichment of the river system and many of the animals in the river may well depend upon such organic input for food. We often see a lot of fungi in river water showing as a grey felty growth on the surface of the rocks. This will spread dramatically if you increase the degree of organic matter in the system and it can begin to cover the algal growth in the river itself. Other forms of pollution can

be much more insidious. One can think of instances of toxic effluent going into a river and having a dramatic effect on the river life. Other forms of pollution can be important in some areas. Even a power station may be using water from a river as a coolant and then discharging warm water into the river. This thermal pollution may have its good and bad points. Mining and quarrying may appear to be innocuous yet the very fine suspended material discharged into a river can, for example, clog up the gills of the fish. A well-aerated river such as this with its rapids and tumbling waterfalls can take a degree of organic pollution because of the high levels of oxygen for biological activity, but slower flowing reaches can become stagnant and the river life severely affected.

'One final point that we should remember is that just as at the headwaters, the chemistry of the water here is dependent on the surrounding land use. The chemicals will depend partly on the geology over which the river has come and partly the soils through which the rainwater has percolated and in turn the use to which man has put the landscape. If it is an arable landscape the farmers will probably have used a great deal of artificial fertilizers and many of these, especially the nitrogenous ones, are likely to be washed away from the fields and will eventually end up in the main river. Application of fertilizer to forestry land will also result in chemicals, such as calcium phosphate, being washed into the river system. All this will immediately affect the nature of the plant and animal systems in the river. So it is important to be aware of all these diverse influences when looking at a river system.'

Brian certainly was not exaggerating about the tumbling waterfalls along the river as we were standing beside a spectacular series of gullies and rapids carved out of sedimentary conglomerate rock. It had been a superb day and despite the fact that we had seen so much, from the mountain-side springs to this magnificent stretch of river lined with mills, we had only really scratched the surface. And I for one am looking forward to visiting these upland rivers again for another look, and who knows, I might even catch a glimpse of the elusive otter.

A lowland river walk

All rivers pass through a process of maturation as they make their own individualistic way down from source to sink in the sea. In their youth, they rush headlong down tearing away at any rocks which dare to impede their progress. In maturity, they meander through flatter country, the combined might of the waters, derived from their tributaries, creating almost as much as they destroy. The pulse of a river reflects that of the landscape while the vegetation along its margins and the wildlife and fish which visit and live within its waters, reflects the health of that same landscape both in natural and man-made terms. Thanks to the growing body of knowledge concerning the life of our rivers, at last many are being made cleaner and gross uncontrolled pollution is a thing of the past – although eutrophication is still an increasing problem. Nigel Holmes is one of our greatest river walkers, recording the facts of change in terms of plant and animal communities. He usually records his data on floppy discs for computer retrival, here he records it all so everyone can understand!

An idyllic lowland river scene with alders shading the far bank and a carpet of water lilies and fringing bur-reeds in the foreground – all classic signs of a river flowing over clay.

A lowland river walk
with
Nigel Holmes

The majority of rivers in lowland Britain have been substantially affected by the activities of man who uses them as a source of both water and power supply; as a means of disposing of large amounts of waste products and, not least of all, for navigation from one region to another. Nature, in its way, has adjusted to these many demands and it could be said that man may have created as many new habitats for river plants and animals as he has destroyed. In some areas, where there has been uncontrolled releasing of industrial and sewage effluents into the river systems, this balance has been dramatically upset and the river life has largely disappeared. However, we were fortunate to discover a stretch of river, near to the great industrial conurbation of Birmingham, that has largely escaped these more excessive problems and displays a marvellous diversity of lowland river plants and animals.

It was a thundery day in early August when we travelled up to meet our expert for the day, Dr Nigel Holmes, a member of the Nature Conservancy Council's scientific team, and whose job it is to ensure that the precious heritage of wildlife in Britain's rivers is adequately considered from a nature conservation point of view. Luckily, the storms had largely passed over and we were able to kit up in our wellington boots and macs hopeful of a fascinating afternoon's stroll.

We started our walk from a bridge where the river was no more than five metres (15 feet) wide. On one side of us were marshy pastures where a small herd of cattle were quietly grazing. The river was flowing quite swiftly but, unlike the Scottish mountain stream we had seen earlier in the year, it was fringed not with boulders but with luxuriant stands of reeds. While we surveyed the tranquil scene, we asked Nigel to tell us about the background to this little river.

'This is the River Blythe which rises on the mudstones south of Solihull and comes down east of the Birmingham Exhibition Centre to flow into a larger river, some seven kilometres (four miles) from here. It is a gem of a lowland river that has a reasonable quality of water and which, ironically, flows into what is reputed to be one of the worst polluted streams in the country – the River Tame – which runs right through Birmingham then into the Trent. On a clear day you can look from this gentle rural scene downstream to the power stations and factory chimneys along the Tame.

'You are probably asking yourselves why this stretch has remained unpolluted? This river has perhaps escaped some of the fate of the Tame and the Trent simply because it is too shallow to be navigable by large boats for most of its course and this has probably contributed to the lack of any large industrial sites along its length. There is some treated sewage input from nearby Solihull, but not enough to radically alter its chemistry.

'The type of rock that a river flows over is critical in determining its regime and the Blythe has an interesting mix of mudstone and sandstone overlain in areas with boulder clay. If you are in an area dominated by clay, which is a very impervious substrate, the rain runs straight off the land and into the river

system. Therefore, the level of the river rises and falls exceedingly fast. Some on the clay areas of the Weald, for example, will rise and fall as much as five metres (15 feet). This feature is very noticeable as the bridges are generally very high above the river. Rivers which flow over a porous substrate, such as chalk, are very different as rainwater collects in underground "reservoirs" to be gradually released into the system. If you look at a bridge over a pure chalk stream you will probably find that it is no more than 30 centimetres (one foot) above the surface of the water, reflecting the very small amount of rise and fall. This river has an intermediate flow regime, as the mudstones and sandstones have a certain porosity. However, the

areas overlain with clay are much more susceptible to sudden changes, so the banks are not as shallow as on a chalk stream.'

The plant life was obviously an important component of the natural community and we asked Nigel to tell us what were the most typical plants of our lowland rivers.

'It is very difficult to say what is typical, as, depending on exactly where you are within a river, you will find different assemblages of species. Every section of river provides its own habitat. For instance, as we walk downstream from here we will go from gravel stretches into silted clay areas, where we will find very different groups of plants. However, generally the plants that are typical of lowland rivers are the ones that will grow in

The River Blythe near Birmingham showing that you don't have to go to the Constable country to find some beautiful stretches of lowland river. The dark green stripes in the water are beds of *Ranunculus.*

179

The familiar leaves and fruits of branched bur-reed, *Sparganium erectum*, one of the most typical fringing plants of our lowland rivers.

tight-knit rigid rosettes of leaves. So we can see that not only flow but also the nutrient status of the water is important in determining which plants you can find.

'In very slow-flowing rivers and backwaters, you can find plants that are not rooted at all, such as the duckweeds, *Lemna*, which simply float on the surface and are able to reproduce fast enough to replace numbers lost downstream. These may also be found in faster flowing lowland rivers at the edges where a marginal fringe of vegetation protects them from being washed away. In southern England, a floating fern, *Azolla filiculoides*, may often be seen. This has fine hairs covering its surface which hold raindrops that glisten in the sun.

'An important type of plant that one finds in lowland rivers are those which, although rooted underwater, have a substantial part of their growth above the water surface. Of the smaller emergent plants, which will have some leaves underwater and some above, an interesting example is the river water-dropwort, *Oenanthe fluviatilis*. I mention this plant as it is an important species in the British Isles, which requires conservation consideration. It is a common plant in southern lowland rivers only, especially in those which have a base-rich element, yet it is probably the only aquatic plant in Great Britain which is more common here than anywhere else in the world. This dropwort is confined to Europe and contrasts with many of our other plants deemed to be "rare" or "endangered". They are often other plants which may be just hanging on here, yet may be common or even pest species elsewhere in Europe, or in other continents.

'The fringing reeds are another example of the emergent river plants. If the river flows through what used to be a wetland area its banks may now constitute the only remaining wetland environment. We often find on these banks what might be called relic species of the former general wetland plant community. Plants like the common reed, *Phragmites communis* and reedmace or bulrush, *Typha*, are examples of this. There are many more species that we could discuss and we shall be looking at some as we make our way downstream.

'Looking down the bank of the river, an obvious feature are the willow trees, *Salix*, that are present all along the edge. The two most common willows on the edges are the white willow, *Salix alba*, and the crack willow, *Salix fragilis*. Both are frequently

deep water – some of which never reach the surface. The pondweeds, *Potamogeton*, are an example of a family that are rooted in the river bottom and can either remain totally underwater or have leaves that reach the surface. The broad-leaved pondweed, *Potamogeton natans*, has both floating and submerged leaves. Another group of plants that grow under the water are the starworts, *Callitriche*. This group has different species growing according to the nature of the water. If you have a very acid lowland stream, such as you might find in the New Forest of Hampshire, you will find *C. hamulata*, which has long linear leaves with spanner-like tips. In the more sluggish sections of a river you might find *C. stagnalis*, which has more oval-shaped leaves. Where the water is more basic or calcareous and still reasonably sluggish, you find *C. obtusangula*, which has very

planted. These are very much part of the lowland river scene and the ones here have been traditionally cut, as they are mostly pollarded. This means that the branches have been cut back regularly at about two to three metres (six to nine feet) above the ground. This provided a supply of poles for rural industries and kept the shoots out of reach of the browsing cattle. In recent years, with the decline in these industries and the shift in farming emphasis, the cutting has usually been carried out by the water authority as the overhanging branches might create a hazard to obstruct the flow of the river. Also, this remedial cutting might prevent the whole tree from falling in. The other main riverside tree is the alder, *Alnus glutinosa*. This apparently sombre tree has distinctive pendulous male and round female catkins which appear before the leaves. The seeds in the woody cone-like fruits are sought out by flocks of siskins and redpolls during the winter months.

'Different trees have different values for wildlife. For instance, the otter is much more likely to have a holt in an overhanging ash or sycamore, because they tend to form large boles which bow out so that the otter can

Where there are bays and obstructions along the river course some of the plants of slower flowing waters are able to colonise the water surface, such as the minute duckweeds, *Lemna*. Further along the river are some pollarded willows which are another common feature of these rivers.

Seen in close-up the metallic greens of this female banded agrion, *Agrion splendens*, are quite breath-taking. This lovely insect can be seen fluttering along riverside vegetation for most of the summer.

excavate a small cavern underneath in which to hide. Insects and fish, on the other hand, can use the shelter of the more matted root systems of the willow and alder.

'Trees also often provide the only permanent, solid objects at the water level in lowland, slow flowing rivers. They therefore provide the base on which aquatic mosses attach themselves. The two most common ones are *Fontinalis antipyretica* and *Rhynchostegium viparioides*. These plants will be typical on man-made structures such as weirs and bridges.'

Whilst Nigel had been describing some of the plant life, a brightly coloured damselfly

had been flying in and out of the fringing reeds, its bright metallic colours catching the afternoon sun. We asked Nigel to tell us some more about the insects of the rivers.

'The most obvious insects and probably the most interesting to the walker and amateur naturalist are the dragonflies and damselflies, Odonata. Some of the larger dragonflies have territories which they patrol regularly, fighting off any intruders. As they feed in flight during daylight, they provide spectacular displays. As they are so noticeable they are very good indicators as to the health of the overall habitat. In recent years we have lost four of the forty or so species in

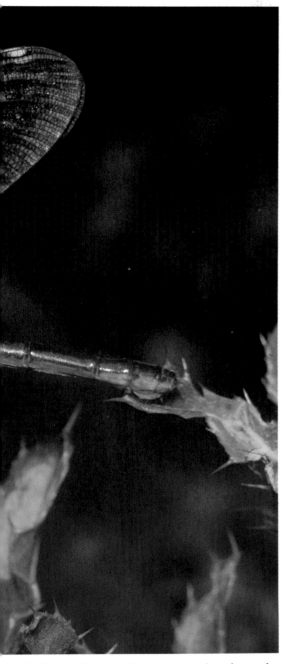

A fine stand of the common fringing grass, reed sweet-grass, *Glyceria maxima*.

Britain, which makes one wonder about the numbers of species we have lost from other not-so-well known insect groups. Many of our dragonflies prefer unpolluted still or very slowly moving waters, but there are a few that like rivers.

'In a weedy section like this, with its mixture of slow and fast flows, you might find the scarce libellula, *Libellula fulva*, although due to the pollution of many of its former sites, it is now very local and only found in southern England. The damselfly that we can see here is one of our commonest species, the splendid agrion, *Agrion splendens*. The ones with the metallic blue colora-tion are the males and the green ones are the females. Both *Agrion virgo* and *A. splendens* prefer fast flowing streams in lowlands which have gravel bottoms. Although many damselflies and dragonflies preferentially frequent still waters, others have an obligate requirement for moving waters. The White-legged Damselfly, *Platycnemis pennipes*, is one such example, being immediately identi-fied by its white tibiae on the middle and back legs. It occurs only in the southern half of England and lays its eggs on floating vegeta-tion. There are also twelve small red or blue damselflies, the common blue damselfly, *Enallagma cyathigerum*, being typical of sluggish lowland rivers with plenty of mar-ginal vegetation. The majority of British large dragonflies prefer to breed in still waters yet the green *Gomphus vulgatissimus*, which is confined to South England and

Wales, breeds in running water, as does the more widely distributed large yellow *Cordulegaster boltonii*.

'Other insects that you might find in well-oxygenated rivers with some gravel on the bottom are the mayflies, Ephemeroptera, and stoneflies, Plecoptera. The former small insects, with their two or three long tails, are probably better known by fishermen than entomologists. The latter, the stoneflies, usually bigger and drab, have two characteristic tails in the nymph stage. The caddisflies, Trichoptera, can be abundant in the lowland rivers. In one such as this, you will find three types of nymphs or larvae: those that live in the gravelly sections and make cases of small pebbles; those that are associated with particular plants, for example, some will use fragments of the watercrowfeet *Ranunculus*; finally, those that are free-swimming and attach themselves to the various surfaces by spinning spider-like nets.

'Feeding on the large numbers of insect larvae and crustaceans that are found in these rivers as well as the plants, are the fish. In a river like this we have all three of the main fish zones. The section we are in at the moment called the trout zone, as it has a fast flow which makes it well-oxygenated and has a shallow, gravelly bottom where the insects, which the trout will feed on, live. Further downstream where the flow is not quite as fast and the river is deeper, is the grayling zone – but because of the influence of the clay I would not consider it to be very good for that species of fish – it is also sometimes called the minnow zone. Then we have the slower weedy stretches, which comprise the coarse fish zone. I would think that you would have dace, roach, gudgeon and chubb along there. There is a fisherman just downstream and if he's had any luck we should find out if I am right.'

We started off down the river and stopped to ask our angler how he was doing. The recent storms had made the water rather turbid but he was in good spirits. He had caught a few dace and knew there were plenty of roach, gudgeon and minnow along that stretch of river. Even a few trout wandered that far down, he confided in us. This nicely confirmed what Nigel had been saying, but Nigel went on to point out that the zone categories are very broad and that in some areas, such as rivers in East Anglia or those flowing through the Fens, the slow coarse section may last for many, many kilometres and there may be no real grayling or trout zone worth considering. It all depends on the geography of the area.

The bank along this stretch was thick with stinging nettles, *Urtica dioica*, which made walking rather painful but we felt we should not simply ignore them, as every plant has its own story to tell. So we asked Nigel if there was any reason for them to be growing in such profusion.

'It is said that stinging nettles are an indication of rich soils, which is partly true but in many river systems they are usually an indication of disturbance. If you have a bank that is dominated by them it probably means that you are looking at a part of the river that has been dredged and the rich spoil that has been left on the sides has been colonised by the nettles. Once they are established they are very difficult to replace. Here we can see that we are on what I suspect is a recently cut channel which has been created to by-pass the natural meander which you can make out as the depression running across the corner of the field behind us.'

Further along the bank we came to an area that looked far more interesting – a rich variety of plants were fringing the river. We asked Nigel to identify them.

'Here are some nice colourful plants that are highly typical of a lowland river – the great willowherb, *Epilobium hirsutum*; over there is some purple loosestrife, *Lythrum salicaria*, with its spines of purple flowers. Alongside it is a very common plant of these river banks, *Glyceria maxima*, reed sweetgrass, which looks like a smaller version of the common reed. If we look right down at the water's edge, we can see drifting in the current the submerged leaves of bur-reed, *Sparganium*, and next to that are these darker fine-leaved patches. This is a member of the pondweeds, that I mentioned earlier. This particular one is *Potamogeton pectinatus*, fennel pondweed. It is a very common plant in lowland rivers which are nutrient-rich as it can tolerate a high degree of pollution. Where you have clear unpolluted water you have the water buttercups but as soon as the water becomes cloudy then it is nearly always replaced by *P. pectinatus*. It is a very adaptable water plant. Further out in the centre of the river here you can see the bent leaves of the bulrush or clubrush, *Scirpus lacustris*. This species, like the yellow waterlily, *Nuphar lutea*, is very characteristic of rivers on a clay substrate. Most people would think of the waterlily as occurring only in very slow or ponded conditions but, in fact, it will tolerate a fairly fast flow providing it has the right depth and a clayey bottom in which to root. The yellow water-lily has two types of leaves – the floating leathery leaves and thinner cabbage-like leaves which remain under the surface. Therefore, if a boat were to come along and chop off the top leaves, it has always got these crinkly lower ones which can carry on the task of photosynthesising. In this respect it is unlike the white water-lily, *Nymphaea alba*, which has only the large surface leaves. This may well account for the decline of the white water-lily and it is found now only in clean, relatively undisturbed water. This combination of yellow water-lily, bulrush and fennel pondweed with reed sweet-grass and bur-reed on the muddy banks should always tell you that you are in a slow-flowing river with a clay substrate.

'There is a stretch of the River Windrush in Oxfordshire where the river splits into two channels, one goes over a fairly gravelly substrate while the other is clay and although there is no difference in the water between the two channels, their floras are totally different. In the one with the gravel it is almost totally dominated by the brook crowfoot, *Ranunculus calcareus*, and the river crowfoot, *R. fluitans*. In the other stream, where you have the clay, it is all bur-reeds, yellow water-lily and bulrush, simply because the habitat is different.

'Where the substrate of the river is very loose and silty you will only find those plants, such as the starworts, Canadian pondweeds, *Elodea*, and hornwort, *Ceratophyllum*, which are shallowly rooted and able to cope with the unstable floor of the river. Plants, such as the water-lilies, need to root into a more solid substrate and if there is a layer of silt they either have to be able to grow up through

Two parent mute swans keep watch over their eight cygnets which are feeding on the rich harvest of river vegetation. Although the young can fly after about four months, the family party may well remain together during the winter months.

Above **A large hoverfly feeding on the terminal flower-head of water-mint,** *Mentha aquatica.*

Centre top **A yellow waterside carpet of great yellow-cress,** *Rorippa amphibia,* **typically growing half-in and half-out of the water.**

this, which presents problems for new shoots as this layer is often very anaerobic in rich systems, or they are unable to put down roots. It might appear to be alright for one season but when the plant dies back for the winter then tries to put out its tender new shoots in the spring, they are just smothered. This problem is not always appreciated by river engineers who widen a river course to cope with periods of flood and find that during the summer season the low flow in the river is so dissipated that silt, which would otherwise be moved on, is deposited across the river bed. A further problem is that any plants that root in this silt are washed away if the river flow suddenly increases.'

We now made our way further along the riverside. Ahead of us was a herd of cattle which were drinking from the river. This part was obviously a regular drinking spot as

the bank had been broken down and the edge was well trampled. This provided an interesting series of habitats for waterside plants, as Nigel explained.

'Cattle trampling can actually increase the diversity of the plant community, as it keeps the surface disturbed and open, allowing annual species to get a hold, whereas normally they would have to compete for space with the tall growing perennials that crowd the bank. Here we have a rich mixture of both low-growing perennials and some annuals that are straggling from the muddy flat bottom of the bank into the river. First, there is water mint, *Mentha aquatica*, which is on the landward side where it doesn't become too wet. Then we have another member of the labiates – gypsywort, *Lycopus europaeus*, which has deeply toothed leaves and tiny white flowers borne in whorls around the stem. Right on the water margin we have two plants – water forget-me-not, *Myosotis scorpioides* and great yellow-cress *Rorippa amphibia*. This last plant is appropriately named as it is truly amphibious and will grow both on land and in water. At certain times of the year it will produce a fantastic yellow carpet of flowers along the bank. There are actually four types of watercress, two others of which have yellow flowers: *Rorippa sylvestris*, which is rarely found in lowland rivers because it prefers to grow amongst loose

pebbles in unstable situations; *R. palustris*, which is more frequent, growing in marshy and muddy cattle-trampled areas such as this. In chalky and base-rich rivers is the well-known white-flowered watercress, *Rorippa nasturtium-aquaticum*, which grows best in base-rich mud.

'You will have noticed that a lot of these plants have the word *aquaticum*, *palustris* or *fluviatilis* in them which simply denotes that they are found in either aquatic, marshy or river habitats. For example, here we have *Alisma plantago-aquatica*, which is the common water-plantain. It has these leaves that look like those of a plantain but it belongs, in fact, to its own separate family.

'Just here is an interesting plant. This is trifid bur-marigold, *Bidens tripartita*, which is a fairly uncommon annual of these trampled sites. The term "trifid" implies nothing sinister but refers to the trifoliate leaves. When the fruits ripen they have little barbed spines on top which presumably fasten on to animals that brush past to drink at the river, so dispersing the seeds. The more common, nodding bur-marigold, *Bidens cernua*, occurs in similar situations but has long undivided leaves and a drooping flower-head. We also have here two other annual plants that grow well in these more open situations. First, here is toadrush, *Juncus bufonius*, which has small pale green flowers and narrow grooved

leaves. Then, next to it, we have a very small specimen of celery-leaved buttercup, *Ranunculus sceleratus*. It has these little yellow flowers and a good specimen can grow to over ninety centimetres (three feet) with a thick stalk and large lobed leaves.'

The opposite side of the river had a low vertical clay bank with many holes arranged along it above the water level. We asked Nigel what might have made these.

'Vertical banks are often important for nesting birds. If they are high enough you might find sand martins nesting in them. Where the nesting holes have been unavoidably destroyed it has been found that the martins will use sections of pipe pushed into the bank. But these holes are too low. I would guess that they were made by water voles when the bank was slightly lower and it has since been eroded away to expose them to

Above **A small fly resting on the flowering spike of water forget-me-not,** *Myosotis scorpioides*, **a common plant of river-sides throughout Britain.**

Above **One of the more local riverside annuals is this member of the composites – trifid bur-marigold,** *Bidens tripartita.*

view. Water voles like well vegetated banks to hide amongst. This enchanting rodent is often unkindly called the water rat but it doesn't look like a rat at all, having a much more rounded head with small ears and a shorter tail. They are almost exclusively vegetarians, unlike the other common water-side mammal – the water shrew. This is a voracious carnivore, like all the shrews, and will eat anything from worms and small insects to tadples and small fish. It is a good swimmer, like the water vole, and can be easily recognised by its small size and contrasting black upperparts and lighter underside.

'A much rarer animal of our lowland rivers is the otter. We do not know why so many otters have disappeared from lowland England. There are various theories which include factors such as the extra disturbance of very rapid and intense land drainage work; the effect of pesticide run-off from neigh-

bouring farmland and generally increasing disturbance along our rivers. It is almost certainly due to a combination of factors. There is so much sympathy for the otter that certain areas, which have a suitable range of habitats, have been designated as otter "havens". In some places in East Anglia they are transplanting otters back into the wild but this has to be carried out very carefully as the otter has a mammoth range, for instance, a dog otter will travel anything from ten to twenty kilometres (six to twelve miles) in a couple of days.

'Looking again at the range of plants that we have along the bank here, we have a curiously named plant – the skullcap, *Scutellaria galericulata*. The name refers to the shape of the calyx which is supposed to resemble a leather helmet worn by roman soldiers, called a *galerum*. This is a fairly common plant of banksides, though its numbers have suffered from the drainage of many of its former marshy haunts. It has small blue tube-like flowers. Here is another plant with blue flowers, though admittedly of a very different shape – *Veronica beccabunga*, brooklime. This member of the figwort family is very common along our lowland rivers. It has blunt fleshy leaves and a tall spike of deep blue flowers. There are two other speedwells that are found along rivers – blue water-speedwell *Veronica anagallis-aquatica*, and pink water-speedwell *V. catenata*. The former is found typically in chalkstreams, and is fairly widely distributed, even being found in the oolite streams of Derbyshire. *Veronica catenata* has pink flowers and, although it is more catholic in its requirements, it is less common, probably because it is not as robust as *V. anagallis-aquatica*.

'Growing in the water's edge we have a rather striking plant – arrowhead, *Sagittaria sagittifolia*, with these white three-petalled flowers and very imposing aerial leaves shaped appropriately like large arrowheads. Interestingly, the arrowhead has three different types of leaves: these arrow-shaped ones, then floating on the surface we can see some, which more closely resemble the leaf of a broad-leaved pondweed and finally, submerged in the river, are more strap-shaped leaves, which are very undulant. This one is in a bay where the water is rather sluggish so the aerial leaves are dominant but where there is more flow the linear, submerged leaves become dominant and you could mistake it for a different plant – in fact, they look rather like the leaves of the bur-reed, *Sparganium emersum*. A similar pheno-menon occurs with bulrush, *Scirpus lacustris*. Most people know this plant as a tall emergent plant, forming dense bankside stands, but it can grow in a good current and it will then have long submerged leaves and no flowers.

'Around the base of the burreeds in this bay are some duckweeds which, if you remember, are free-floating plants. This is the common duckweed, *Lemna minor*, which consists of a simple flat frond or thallus, only two to four millimetres across, and a single long root hanging down below. In very sluggish rivers you might find fat duckweed, *Lemna gibba*, which has an air sac underneath the thallus. In dykes you will find a larger duckweed with a tuft of roots, *Lemna poly-rhiza*. It is not really a river species but you might discover it where a slow-flowing river is fed by a dyke filled with this plant. Both *Lemna gibba* and *L. polyrhiza* produce special winter forms which sink to the bottom of the river or pond to lie dormant until the spring when they bud-off new free-floating forms. There is a fourth species that

you might find – this is the ivy-leaved duckweed, *Lemna trisula*. This species tends to remain predominantly submerged some-times carpeting the bottoms of rivers which have clear water. It has strange translucent fronds that usually form branched colonies that look like groups of tiny ivy leaves.'

As we were peering down at these unusual little plants, a mute swan glided serenely past looking at us. This was the first swan we had seen that day and we asked Nigel if they were a common sight along the river.

'They seem to be alright along this stretch but unfortunately our population of swans is generally suffering rather badly from lead poisoning. Although, in many things, the fishermen are our allies it does seem that one of the main causes of this is discarded lead shot left by anglers. Like many birds, swans habitually swallow pellets to aid their diges-tion and, in doing so, take in lead shot from the banks and river bottoms. This then builds up, eventually affecting their nervous system. Sometimes it affects their gut muscles so that they starve to death even though their crops may be full. Disturbance and even vandalism has not helped matters

Lowland rivers and canals are the haunt of this small member of the grebe family – the dabchick. Here the parent bird has just brought a small fish to the surface to feed its chick.

Along deeper, slow-flowing sections of the river the bizarrely shaped leaves of the arrowhead, *Sagittaria sagittifolia* **can be seen. This plant has, in fact, three distinct types of leaves – submerged strap-like leaves, floating pondweed-like leaves and the arrow-shaped aerial-leaves.**

and I'm afraid in some areas already the population of mute swans has decreased dramatically. A simple thing to help prevent this that any angler can do, is to make sure that the lead weights and split shot they use are not discarded or left on the banks where the swans can reach them. It is important that people realise that lead shot on the bed of the river or discarded in the thick vegetation on the bank are both as potentially lethal to the swan.

'Other birds that you might hope to see along here are moorhens and coots, the latter preferring slower flowing rivers. I know that there are kingfishers along here but that is a bird you have to have a great deal of patience to see.'

A little further down the river was a classic meander in the river which clearly showed that the river was still making its own course along this part of its length. Nigel took up the story.

'Here we can see a meander with its typical eroding and depositing sections. What is happening is that on the opposite bank the flow is cutting deeply into the edge and making a vertical bank, and on this side you have the deposition of any gravels that have come downstream. If this was a more silty river, this bank would have a deposit of silt,

probably colonised by reed sweet-grass. So here we can say that the river is being allowed to do its own thing. Often when river engineers "improve" a stretch of river they will try and cut out the meanders, as we saw further up the river. Even if they leave them in, they will frequently dredge so that the typical shelving profile is taken out. If we look just down stream of the meander we can see that after the deep pool section there is an area where the river is much shallower causing the surface to look fairly turbulent – this is called the gravelly riffle section which will be well oxygenated and will be colonised by *Ranunculus*, in this case, the river crow-foot, *R. fluitans*. If the meander continues to develop naturally the curve will become more and more pronounced until the river will break through the thin strip of land between the two ends of the curve, cutting off the original bend to form a new channel and leaving an ox-bow lake. The pond-like habitat that you get in these cut-off ox-bows can be very rich and, if it is still periodically replenished from the river during flood times, the water will remain relatively fresh which is better for the aquatic life.

'We are now walking beside a more gravelly section which in early summer is white with the crowfoot flowers. Having just seen a natural meandering section we now have a very straight stretch which has been made by man, almost certainly to divert the river away from the railway, which runs alongside just here. It still has a gravelly bottom but soon we will be coming to a section where the river water has been ponded back because of a mill. One further point we should mention here is the algal growths that occur in these rivers. When the water becomes nutrient rich, possibly as a result of sewage input or the drainage of heavily fertilized farmland, the algae tend to do better competitively than the higher plants and can become a dominant feature of the river vegetation at certain times of the year. In this stony section with its reasonable flow you will find a species called cotweed or blanketweed, *Cladophora glomerata*. It can become so prevalent that it smothers the other plants. Another filamentous alga that you find in lowland rivers is *Enteromorpha*, which is related to the blanketweed you find on the coasts. It is a very characteristic algae, forming long green tubes, often more than a metre long. In East Anglia a bright green carpeting alga, which has an almost pelt-like look about it, is *Vaucheria*. Large "blooms" of these species are looked upon as a sign of secondary pollution and on decompsition can severely deplete the oxygen content of the river water. In undisturbed rivers subjected to an increase in nutrients, it is usual that the larger plants will rebutt the damaging growth of the algae due to two main factors: firstly, they already occupy some of the prime sites in the river; secondly, they often produce substances, which they release into the water, that subdue algae growth. In a recently dredged river such a balance is lacking and these are the areas where algae problems are greatest.

'Here we are just a little further along and the river has changed character yet again. There are bur-reeds growing out into the water and patches of water-lilies that tell us we are back on a clay substrate. Growing here are the two species of *Elodea* water-weeds. The Canadian waterweed, *Elodea canadensis*, was introduced in British rivers over 100 years ago (1847) and rapidly spread throughout Britain's waterways to such an extent that it became a threat to navigation, clogging up canals and rivers. In fact, a Minister was appointed to control the problem in the 1860s. Interestingly, this plant was spreading vegetatively as there was only the female plant present. The vigour that this

coloniser had in the nineteenth century appears to have gone and it seems to have reached a steady state. However, another member of the same genus, *Elodea nuttallii*, was first noticed in East Anglia in 1975 and has since spread to many parts of England and may well be replacing *E. canadensis*. It is particularly prevalent in deep, nutrient rich waters with sluggish flows.

'Further along here the river banks appear very different to the fairly open sections that we have just seen. This is because as we approach the mill the water has been held back and consequently there has been a lot of deposition along the banks which are now much more silty and muddy. Colonising these sections are large stands of reedmace,

The linear nature of our riverside habitats mean that introduced plants can sometimes spread rapidly. The case of the aquatic Canadian waterweed has been well documented. The Himalayan balsam, *Impatiens glandulifera,* **is another case. This plant is another introduction, this time from North America, orange balsam,** *Impatiens capensis.*

The dense bank side vegetation provides a superb habitat for water birds such as this moorhen.

Typha latifolia, and encroaching out into the open water are amphibious bistort, *Polygonum amphibium*, and great yellow-cress *Rorippa amphibia*. An interesting plant to look out for is the orange balsam, *Impatiens capensis,* which is an introduction from North America and can be found by many lowland rivers in southern England. The larger Himalayan balsam, *Impatiens glandulifera*, although only introduced in the last century, has spread throughout the river systems of Britain. This plant has a number of interesting local names such as policeman's helmet, after the colour and shape of the flowers, and jumping jack, which refers to the fact that when the fruits ripen they burst spectacularly and scatter their seeds along the bank and into the water.'

We then made our way up onto a road bridge that crossed the river. Here we had a

view of the mill laid or leet, which formerly would have taken the water from the river to power the mill wheel. It was obvious from the almost pond-like nature of the water that it had long been in disuse. The 'pond' was fringed with a band of reeds, laced with flowering plants and the surface of the water was broken by patches of yellow water-lilies. A perfect habitat for dragonflies and other water insects. Running off from this still area of water was a narrower channel which eventually joined the main course of the river on the other side of the mill. Here we were confronted with a very different spectacle to the quiet scene we had just been surveying.

'Here we can see some river dredging work in progress. The idea is to attempt to recreate a natural channel at about three-quarters of a metre (two feet) below the present river bottom. The usual management practice is to

As the river approached the mill the water became increasingly ponded-back resulting in a thick band of reedmace and bur-reed fringing the river and large amounts of water-lily growing over the open surface.

Dredging in progress. The crane with its giant bucket has been taking material from the bed of the river and dumping it on the adjacent field. This highly expensive operation is essentially to help the farmer grow more cereal crops by stopping the river from flooding in winter.

scrape off the top soil adjacent to the river and put it to one side, then scrape out the river bed and use that to raise the level of the bank, covering this with the original top soil. This means that the land can still be utilised by the farmer. It has a dual purpose as it stops the floodwater spilling into the fields and provides an accessible area for them to dump the spoil. You can see that they have found a mix of clays and gravel in the river bed. It is a very expensive operation and one often questions the overall cost benefits of such schemes. The purpose of this is to allow the farmer to change from using this adjoining land as pasture to arable. As pasture the land can often be helped by periodic flooding from the river as the deposited silts will enrich the land. The fishing fraternity obviously are anxious to maintain the quality and type of river as it is above the mill and, in that sense, are important allies of the conservationists when it comes to objecting to the proposal of such schemes'.

We had certainly appreciated our walk along this stretch of river. The feature which had been most surprising was the variety of habitats that these more natural lowland rivers could provide – the open fast flowing sections with their plants twisting and turning in the current; the more tranquil slow sections with the insects darting from flower to flower along the bank; the shade of the

riverside trees and the unexpected view around the meander. It would be a sorry day if this was all reduced to the bland uniformity of a simple 'drainage channel'. Happily, there are still many hundreds of miles of walks by our lowland rivers that provide a refreshing glimpse of our natural heritage in all its forms and fortunately, there are people like Nigel keeping a careful watch on them.

Coastal walks

British coasts

'OH, I DO LIKE TO BE BESIDE THE SEASIDE!' I have said it, shouted and even sung it, and what is more I really do mean it. There is no better place for a budding naturalist to get his or her feet wet than the seashores of Britain. Just look at a map of the British Isles – there's lots of coastline in relation to land area. That is one of the advantages of living on an island, but even better, just look at all the indentations; there are miles and miles of excitement and always something more to look at just around the corner. Add to this the varied geology of Britain ranging from the hard, acidic granites to the soft, erodable limestones and all the rock types in-between, all exposed to the force of the waves; the large rivers depositing their products of erosion; onshore currents washing material from one area to another; the fact that the west coast is bathed by the warm balmy waters of the North Atlantic Drift and the east faces the chilling winds coming down clear across from the Arctic and the Urals; and what have you got: diversity and that is the spice of life.

If any of you are now saying, 'Oh dear, diversity – that means there is going to be lots of different things to sort out, lots of names to learn.' Please hold on, for despite this diversity all our coasts have one thing in common: tides; and it is the tidal cycle that adds order to what would otherwise be a very confusing world. Every day, twice a day, the tide comes in and goes back out again and as it does this it exposes and resubmerges an area which is called the littoral zone. Any plant or animal living between the tides has got to put up with these drastic changes in its home environment. Add to this constant cycle the effect of crashing waves, torrential rain, biting winds, hot summer sun and cold winter frosts and you have a very harsh habitat. The end result is that very few plants and animals, albeit from a wide range of groups, have evolved to be successful denizens of the littoral zone.

I reckon if you learn to identify forty or so different plants and animals that wherever you might be on the British coast you should be able to feel at home. You then will not only be meeting with 'old friends' but will immediately notice what is new and exciting. In other words, a little knowledge of the most common and abundant members of our seashore life will open the doors to the diversity of life hiding in the rock pools and along the beach. But don't forget to look out for all the marvellous birds that take advantage of all these sources of food, especially along our lovely muddy estuaries. Many of them have travelled thousands of miles to enjoy the wealth of plant and animal life around our shores.

The coastline also has a tremendously interesting group of land plants growing along its higher reaches and one of the most exciting things a natural historian can do, after he has had a good splash around down in the littoral zone, is to discover how these plants have colonised the shore.

Good beachcombing!

The seashore can be a dangerous place so if you are planning to make a trip, remember:
- Always check the tide tables and the weather reports
- Always tell other people where you are going, and don't go on your own unless it is unavoidable
- Dress properly; it can get mighty cold and the rocks are very slippery. I find a pair of training shoes with good soles ideal for scrambling about
- A trip to the local museum is a good idea when planning your trip and can save holiday time
- Never, repeat never, collect a live animal or plant. When it comes to shells and other flotsam, only collect what you need. There are others following in your footsteps

---

BRITAIN HAS SOME OF THE most varied and beautiful coastal scenery in the world and this is matched by the tremendous diversity of plants and animals that live on our shores. Probably only a coral reef contains as wide a range of animal types as can be found on a stretch of our rocky shoreline. Before we look any further at this diversity we must understand the prime governing factor controlling life on the shore: the tides.

THE TIDES

Probably the most conspicuous feature of any seashore around our coasts is the daily rise and fall of the tides. These are caused by the gravitational pull of the moon and the sun. A high or low tide occurs approximately every twelve hours and at least one period in every month the tide reaches its maximum flow and ebb. This happens about two days after a full moon and a new moon and is called a *spring tide*, although it bears no relationship to that particular season of the year. Between the periods of the spring tides there is a time

31 Sands of Forvie, Grampian. NK 02 27 National Nature Reserve. Extensive sand dune system with good plant succession leading to dune heath.

32 Tentsmuir Point, Fife. NO 50 27 National Nature Reserve. Well-developed system of sand dunes with good plant succession leading to afforested dune heath.

33 Lindisfarne, Northumberland. NU 15 44 National Nature Reserve. Large dune system on Holy Island and on the mainland at Ross Links. Superb area with a wide range of coastal habitats.

34 Gibraltar Point, Lincolnshire. TF 55 58 Nature reserve managed by the Lincolnshire and South Humberside Naturalists' Trust. Area of dunes and saltmarsh with sand and shingle beaches. Bird observatory, see page 122.

35 North Norfolk Coast. Good areas of sand dunes all along the coast notably at Hunstanton, Holme, Scolt Head and areas of Blakeney Point.

36 Sandwich Bay, Kent. TR 36 60 Area of sand dunes which is good for both flowers and bird life. RSPB, National Trust and Kent Trust for Nature Conservation joint reserve.

37 Studland Bay, Dorset. SZ 04 84 National Nature Reserve. Extensive area of dunes which have become stabilised to form dune heath. Good range of plants but noteworthy also for its fauna which include some of our rarer birds and reptiles.

38 Dawlish Warren, Devon. SX 98 79 Local Nature Reserve. Area of sand dunes showing dune succession. Also good for bird watching across the estuary in winter.

39 Braunton Burrows, Devon. SS 46 32 National Nature Reserve. Most extensive sand dune system in the South West, with dunes reaching 30 metres in height. Occasionally used by the Ministry of Defence. Excellent dune flora and fauna.

40 Whiteford Burrows, Glamorgan. SS 44 95 National Nature Reserve. Area of sand dunes and saltings. Good for both botanising and birdwatching. Worth visiting Oxwich Burrows on the south side of the Gower Peninsula, also a National Nature Reserve.

41 Cors Fochno, Dyfed. SN 65 95 Nature Reserve. Coastal stretch has a good series of sand dunes with a duneland nature trail.

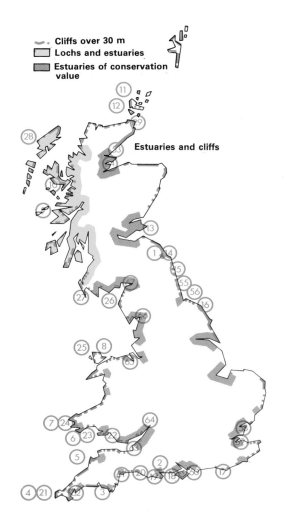

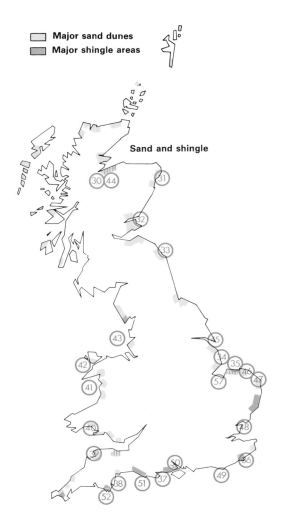

A mixed flock of Dunlins and Knots taking flight at the edge of the Solway Firth. The larger wading birds on the are Grey Plovers. The large numbers of waders and wildfowl that winter along Britain's estuaries and coasts make them internationally important.

42 Newborough Warren, Gwynedd. SH 40 68 National Nature Reserve. Extensive area of excellent dunes showing plant succession.

43 Ainsdale, Merseyside. SD 28 10 National Nature Reserve. Large area of dunes showing succession through to pine plantation. Interesting fauna including rarer reptiles and amphibians.

SHINGLE

The following is a selection of shingle bars and spits from around our coasts. The beaches of South and East England are frequently fringed with shingle on the upper shore. Because of the unstable nature of shingle, some of these sites are particularly prone to erosion from trampling. Also certain more isolated stretches may have nesting birds, so make sure that it is all right to walk over them first, particularly in spring.

44 Culbin Sands, Grampian. NH 95 63 An area of shingle and sand bars, including some lagoons. The mainland is heavily forested.

45 Spurn Point, Humberside. TA 40 11 A three-mile spit which has developed on the north side of the Humber estuary. Local Nature Reserve with a bird observatory at the point.

46 Scolt Head, Norfolk. TF 81 46 National Nature reserve. A fascinating area of saltmarsh and shingle with good botanic and birdwatching interest. It is important to avoid the terneries in spring.

47 Blakeney Point, Norfolk. TG 00 47 National Trust. Extensive area of shingle with interesting plants. Mostly maintained as a bird sanctuary as there are large colonies of nesting birds.

48 Orfordness, Suffolk. TM 40 46 Vast area of shingle – one of the largest spits in the country – diverting the Alde eleven miles southward. Interesting shingle plants to be seen.

49 Dungeness, Kent. TR 07 18 Prominent coastal headland developed by successive beaches. Good birdwatching as well as interesting flora.

50 Hurst Point, Hampshire. SU 32 90 A four-mile shingle spit stretching out towards the Isle of Wight, with Hurst Castle at its tip.

51 Chesil Beach, Dorset. SY 67 75 Famous shingle beach forming an eighteen-mile bar from Portland in the east to Bridport and also enclosing the extensive Fleet lagoon. The beach is unusually high in places, reaching up to 10 metres, with extensive areas of Shrubby Seablite on the landward side.

52 Slapton Sands, Devon. SX 83 44 Shingle beach enclosing Slapton Ley. Field Studies Centre at Slapton village.

ESTUARIES

The British Isles is fortunate in having some superb estuaries. The following is a selection from around our coasts. If you are intending to visit any of these it is suggested that you check at the local information centre where they will tell you the best areas to go to and the places with public access. Always seek local information and permission.

53 Dornoch Firth, Scottish Highlands. NH 81 88 Estuary with extensive saltmarsh. Good birdwatching in autumn and winter.

54 Cromarty Firth, Scottish Highlands. NH 75 72 Large area of sand and mud flats as well as saltmarsh.

55 Lindisfarne, Northumberland. NU 15 44 National Nature Reserve. Interesting area of sand and mud flats. Good birdwatching.

56 Teeside, Cleveland. NZ 55 28 Large estuary near industrial conurbation but with some extensive mudflats and saltmarsh. Good birdwatching in winter.

57 Wash, Lincolnshire/Norfolk. Vast area of estuarine mudflats and saltmarsh of international importance. Good places to visit are Gibraltar Point, Boston Point, Holbeach, Ouse Mouth, Snettisham and Hunstanton.

58 Walton-on-the-Naze, Essex. TM 27 25 Large area of tidal marshes and mudflats. Good winter birdwatching.

59 North Kent Marshes, Kent. TQ 85 75 Large area of tidal marshes and mudflats around the Medway and Swale Estuaries, showing all stages of development. Good birdwatching area.

60 Portsmouth, Langstone, Chichester Harbours, Hampshire/Sussex. SU 75 05 Series of inter-tidal inlets with large areas of mudflats, saltmarshes and rough grazing. Good vantage points at Farlington Marshes and Thorney Island. Worth visiting Pagham Harbour along the Sussex coast.

61 Exe Estuary, Devon. SX 99 85 Large areas of mudflats exposed at low tide which provide good birdwatching during the autumn and winter.

62 Fal Estuary, Cornwall. SX 85 42 Series of sheltered inlets with mudflats which provide some interesting birdwatching.

63 Bridgwater Bay, Somerset. ST 29 47 National Nature Reserve. Interesting area with full range of estuary habitats, including sand and mud flats as well as saltmarsh.

64 Slimbridge, Gloucester. SO 72 05 Wildfowl Trust. Good views of high saltmarsh and rough grazing. Excellent for wildfowl in winter. Well worth visiting the Trust's collection.

65 Dee Estuary, Clwyd/Merseyside. SJ 25 27 Vast expanses of mudflats and saltmarsh. Large area is a National Wildfowl Refuge. Good birdwatching.

66 Morecambe Bay, Lancashire/Cumbria. SD 38 75 Huge area of inter-tidal sand and mud flats of international importance. Holds probably the largest over-wintering population of waders in Britain.

67 Caerlaverock, Dumfries. NY 04 67 National Nature Reserve. Extensive sand flats and saltmarsh. Visited in winter by large numbers of geese.

Bellamy's Seaside

On a day trip to the sea? Fed up with building sand castles? Well, take a look along the beach and you will be surprised what you will find in the way of marine life. I can hear you saying, 'What, any old beach?'. To answer that question I went to one of the nearest stretches of shoreline from my home in County Durham. It is nothing at all special – I would even say that it is rather ugly and yet I spent a whole day happily dabbling around and I will go back again and again.

Here I am just about to get my feet wet beside a rock pool at the seaside.

Bellamy's Seaside

I have often said that given any piece of our seashore, a naturalist should be able to find enough to keep him or herself busy for hours without moving more than one hundred metres. So, today, I have come to prove it, and the area I have chosen is one of the less salubrious stretches of the coastline of the North East of England. If the Industrial Revolution didn't actually start here, most of its developments happened hereabouts. Ever since industrial pollution was invented this stretch of beach has had more than its fair share and today it lies close to the mouth of one of the world's busiest industrial rivers.

The shoreline is not a pretty site. The beach, which was originally formed of magnesium limestone, is now covered with debris of varying sorts: concrete, house bricks, pieces of glass, wood and the inevitable plastic, you name it and it's here. All this is backed by a gaunt Victorian seawall. Yet in amongst all the human bric-a-brac, I guarantee that there will be many living things of great interest.

I always start at the strand line, for there, in amongst all the jetsam that has been washed up, I can usually find specimens of everything I will see lower down the beach. What is more, this is the one place in which collecting the odd specimen to take home will do no harm because all the things here have come to the end of their natural life span. They have all died and have been dumped high and dry by the tide. So you can have enormous fun here, searching for the best piece of seaweed or the best shell for your collection. But please, only take what you want because you must remember that you are not the only pebble on the beach, there will be plenty of other beach-combers coming along and they do not want to be disappointed.

Here is a great mass of seaweed all tangled up together. There are nine different sorts in all, the most abundant being a dull brown colour. Seaweeds are the common term for the marine algae, and the 'browns' are by far the largest and most common on our cool temperate shores.

These must be the commonest of them all: the wracks; everyone knows these. They are the seaweeds that aunty always brings back from her day at the sea to act as a barometer: wet and slippery when wet; dry and brittle to the touch when dry.

Whether or not you believe in their weather forecasting properties, a close look at a brown seaweed will reveal that it is quite unlike your average garden plant in that it is not divided into root, stem and leaf. Each consists of a single plant body – a thallus. They are fixed to rocks or, in some cases, pebbles, by a holdfast which may be disc shaped, like a sucker, or branch-like, as in the root of a land plant. One major difference is that true roots penetrate down into the substrata whereas the branches of the hold-

Not everybody's idea of the perfect holiday beach but nevertheless there is much for a seaside naturalist to explore, from the seaweeds at the base of the seawall to the dried-out flotsam amongst the pebbles.

fast can only stick on to the surface. Another difference is that the holdfast branches dichotomously, which means that at each branch point it divides into two equal halves. Compare the branching of a holdfast with that of the root or come to that, the shoots of a garden plant and you will find that the branching in the latter is much more complex and, in biological terms, much more advanced. The seaweeds were doing their thing in the seas of the world millions of years before there were any land plants. I defy you to find a dichotomously branched plant growing in your garden. I also defy you to find seaweeds uninteresting once you have taken a close look and learnt about their weird ways of life.

Here is a piece of Spiral Wrack, *Fucus spiralis*, and, yes, it is in fruit, there on the end of each branch is a swollen portion. If I hold it up to the light each swelling looks as if it has got a bad dose of measles. Each of these is a fertile conceptacle and the spots are the reproductive organs which either contain sperm or eggs. In this case they have already been released into the sea and some of the eggs will have been fertilised and some of them will have been carried out to sea. If they are lucky, they will end up on a bare piece of rock where they can develop into a new wrack plant. If you want to find out all about their reproduction you will need a microscope and a lot of patience. However, even with them high and dry on the strand line it is easy to see the differences between the three main species: Spiral Wrack is a small brown seaweed with a spiral twist to it. Bladder Wrack is the one with double 'poppers', one on each side of the thick mid rib. But don't muddle the 'popper floats' up with the fertile conceptacles. Serrated Wrack is the largest of the three which, as its name suggests, has a serrated edge to the blade, rather like a saw. Now we have got these basic differences plugged into our minds, a trip down the beach should let us into the secrets of their ecology, the way they live.

However, here there is no need to move all that far because flanking the beach at this point is a magnificent seawall, as Victorian as its makers, a masterpiece of the mason's art, fashioned from beautifully shaped blocks of stone. This wall will weather anything that the North Sea can throw at it for many centuries to come and the local marine life has cashed in on this fact and made it their home. From a distance it looks as if someone has been along with a gigantic brush painting broad horizontal stripes, with lurid green at the very top then four shades of brown and finally at the bottom a lovely mixture of deep reds and purples. This is the classic zonation of the normally gently sloping seashore truncated into some 2·6 metres of vertical seawall. Why, I could give a whole term's degree course in marine biology without moving away from this wall. Even though it is entirely man made, highly polluted and on the east coast of England which is not famed for its marine biological interest. A closer look at the wall shows that the zonation is much more complex than it appears at first. At the top there is a mixture of green seaweeds, which includes one which can only be described as 'dirty green'. Close up it looks like a series of little bladders which may have a silvery appearance due to trapped air. This is *Prasiola stipitata* (sorry about the name it doesn't have an English one!). It is a plant which appears to thrive on organic pollution for its natural habitat is the splash zone of rocks in seabird colonies. Apparently human sewage is as rich in phosphates and nitrates as are seabird droppings, for the *Prasiola* is certainly doing well here.

Mixed in with this are masses of a red seaweed called *Porphyra umbilicalis*. This is the famous Laver Bread which makes the traditional Welsh breakfast so tasty; not that I would collect it for eating along this shoreline.

In amongst this upper zone is the first of the wracks, the small but very tough Channelled Wrack. This is easily identified by the fact that the blades are channelled rather like a rolled human tongue. If you are unable to roll your tongue, then find someone who can and check out the features of *Pelvetia canaliculata*.

Below this rather mixed zone the three larger wracks have established themselves into clear bands. Firstly, there is Spiral Wrack, *Fucus spiralis*, then below that is the Bladder Wrack, *Fucus vesiculosus* and then at the bottom is the Serrated Wrack, *Fucus serratus*. A close look will show you that in the centre of each zone, each species of seaweed forms a monoculture in which no other seaweed can grow. In such a crowded place the competition is going to be very fierce and only the fittest will survive. It would appear that evolution has fitted each sort of wrack to thrive best in one particular tidal range. Within that range, however broad or narrow, that particular species will

A whole degree course in marine biology on one exposed, rather polluted section of seawall. The broad brush strokes of algae clearly show the shore zonation: green seaweeds at the top followed by *Pelvetia canaliculata*, *Fucus spiralis*, *Fucus vesiculosus*, **and** *Fucus serratus*, with the red seaweeds becoming increasingly prominent towards the base. See the opposite page for a closer look at some better specimens of the important brown seaweeds.

Channelled Wrack, *Pelvetia canaliculata.* **The tips of the frond in the centre are swollen to form reproductive bodies. This seaweed is found on the upper shore.**

Spiral Wrack, *Fucus spiralis.* **The tips are swollen conceptacles and the bad dose of 'measles' are the reproductive organs, which either contain sperm or eggs.**

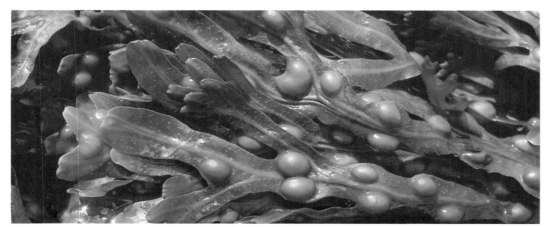

Bladder Wrack, *Fucus vesiculosus.* **The 'poppers' on either side of the mid-rib are air-bladders which add buoyancy to the seaweed. This is a typical plant of the middle shore.**

Serrated Wrack, *Fucus serratus.* **The toothed edge of this seaweed of the lower middle shore makes it easy to identify.**

be able to reign supreme, filling all the available habitat space. Only at the margins of each zone is there enough room for other species to find space for their holdfasts.

When you are next down at the seaside take a close look at these seaweeds, poke about in amongst the wracks and try to prove me right or wrong. As you do this you will learn a lot about the plants themselves. For a start, they will all feel very slippery and are certainly not very nice to walk about on, but without that slippum the plants would be scraped to bits by the waves which wash them back and forth over the rocks. This slippum is produced by the plant and that takes energy and no plant is going to waste energy just to make the occasional budding algologist fall flat on his face. One second fact that becomes very obvious is that in the crowded world of the seaweed zones there is little or no room for a new plant, even of the same species, to get a foothold. One important thing for all organisms that live fixed to one spot in a crowded world is the need for an efficient method of dispersal of their young. Each year countless billions of fertilised seaweed eggs go to waste carried to the wrong place by the vagaries of wind and tide. They are either eaten or fall onto stony ground in the sense of the biblical parable. However, the few that survive are sufficient to fill the spaces on the shore vacated by the death of other plants.

The last zone at the foot of the seawall is a livid red-purple colour, covered with a mixture of several different types of red seaweed. Of all the types of seaweed, the 'reds' are amongst the most difficult to identify so at this juncture I think we will just say that they are a lovely colour and pass on down the shore.

The seaweed zonation we have seen on the wall is also present on the shore itself but in a much more extended form as the width of each zone is dependent on the angle of the slope. So in order to see the 'red' zone I will have to do a lot of walking . . . oops! I have slipped into a rock pool. The zonation on the beach is also a much less regular business! The seawall had a relatively even surface whereas here, the slope is very uneven with deep pools and rocks sticking up in-between. The main factor determining the zonation is the fluctuation of the tide in relation to the point on which seaweed is trying to grow. . . . there I go slipping into another pool. Despite these irregularities the zonation is there and each of the main types of wrack faithfully adheres to its own special environment.

The seashore is a very special place and should be treated with the utmost respect: slippery rocks and a turning tide can land the unwary in all sorts of trouble. You should always check the state of the tide before you venture on to the beach and, however interesting you find the terrain and its inhabitants, always remember that tides have no respect for scholarship. I always like to follow the tide down and finish my study just after low water. It is all too easy on a rising tide to linger at a particular spot for just too long and find yourself cut off with, at the very least, a wet route to safety above the high tide mark.

Today, I have not followed my golden rule and the tide is already on the turn and I am going to have to be careful. Here I am close to the low tide mark and it must be a neap tide because the water is still lapping around the lower zones of the Serrated Wrack and the large plants of the next zone are only just protruding above the water. However, here in a large rock pool, which is in places almost a metre deep, all is revealed. The pool is almost filled with a tangle of kelp and I can see three different species from the edge here. A tangle of kelp! Please excuse a rather in-joke, you see the other common name for the kelps is 'tangles'. If you have never smelt the tangle of the isles then take it from me that it is the aroma of seaweed. The kelps boast among their numbers not only the largest seaweed around the coast of Britain but also the largest seaweed in the world.

The two which are most abundant in my pool are the Smooth-stalked Kelp, *Laminaria digitata*, and the Rough-stalked Kelp, *Laminaria hyperborea*. Both consist of a large well-branched (always dichotomously) holdfast, a long flexible stalk or stipe and a rather hand-like blade. There is one with last year's blade, all tattered and torn, still attached to the new one that has developed this season. The kelps are perennial plants and the holdfast and stipe increase in size throughout their life while a brand new blade is produced each year. Around our coasts, the Rough-stalked Kelp lives the longest and can become a very large plant. What is more, it is possible to tell how old they are. Take a holdfast, remembering that there are plenty washed up on the strand line so there is no need to damage a living plant, and cut it in half length ways. You will probably need a strong penknife to do this. It will now be easy to see that the branches of the hold-fast come off from the stipe in a series of levels or whorls. Very roughly the number of branch levels gives you the age of the plant in years. If you inspect the cut surface you have made you should find that each branch level is marked out within the stipe tissue by a dark line. These are like annual rings in a tree trunk and counting them will give you a more accurate measure of the age of the plant. But please be careful because false lines not connected with a branch level can lead you astray. It is the number of branch levels that counts and not the number of branches, so be careful and if you find one which is more than 15 years of age, then you have probably made a mistake.

The Rough-stalked Kelp always stands out from the others by the fact that its stipe is covered with a sock of red seaweeds. The knobbly surface of the stalk of this kelp provides a safe anchorage for epiphytes and the fascinating thing is that these grow in distinct zones along the stipe.

The commonest epiphyte hereabouts on the kelp's stipe is *Rhodymenia palmata*, the Edible Dulse, a lovely chewy seaweed (but please do not try and eat it along these polluted waters). Although it comes in a variety of shapes and sizes it can often be picked out by its dark red colour, producing deep purple reflections. Another epiphyte is *Ptilota plumosa*, this seaweed has repeatedly branched

A trip to the seaside would not be the same without the mewing cries of gulls providing a backdrop to the ice-creams and holiday buckets and spades. This is a selection of some of the more common species that can be seen around our beaches and harbours.

fronds which give it the appearance of a bird's feather. Then there is *Membranoptera alata*, a very descriptive name for a beautiful plant, each one of which consists of a dark red midrib fringed with a transparent membrane-like blade. Often growing close to the holdfast are the exquisite fronds of *Phycodrys rubens*, this plant looks like almost transparent oak leaves, or in some forms they are lobed so as to resemble the leaves of holly. Please don't get this one muddled up with *Delesseria sanguinea*, which produces much larger transparent leaf-like fronds, which resemble neither the leaves of oak or holly.

But now I have got my feet wet I am going to explore the pool in a bit more depth. . . . Ooh, it's cold, but that's what the large seaweeds really like. The warm balmy waters of the tropics may be okay for coral reefs but they are death to the large seaweeds, which only thrive in the cool temperate waters. So much so that many of our seaweeds put on much of their growth and complete their reproduction in the cooler waters of spring. One reason why a seaweed hunt is always best at Easter.

It is lovely and slippery, sloshing about in amongst all the kelps and yes, I have found

A living-graph. This collection of Rough-Stalked Kelps (*Laminaria hyperborea*) shows the typical growth pattern of the kelps. The older ones on the right-hand side of the 'graph' have still got their collection of epiphytic red seaweeds attached to the stalk. The holdfasts also will have an exciting array of plants and animals living in them. This collection of kelps for our growth curve were all washed up, so don't go out and pull up any of these super sea-weeds.

The red seaweeds are certainly not the easiest of plants when it comes to correct identification. You will need a good guide, a lens or microscope and a lot of patience, but believe you me it is well worth while. I got hooked on the seaweed bug whilst on a course at the Dale Fort Field Centre in Pembrokeshire run by John Barrett, who will be looking at some of our more common marine animals on another walk.

Even without names, the red seaweeds that you can collect from the strand line provide hours of interest and before we leave the beach I will show you what to do with them.

the third of the common kelps: *Laminaria saccharina*. This one, like the others, has a branched holdfast and then a thin short stipe leading to a great flamboyant undivided blade which is crinkled down the middle, rather like a modern with-it dress shirt. These can grow up to 2·4 metres in length but, of course, here in a rock pool, growth will be more difficult due to all the bashing about by the waves.

You know we humans are very lucky. We visit the seashore when we want to and when the weather cuts up rough or it gets too cold we can nip off home. Not so for the creatures of the sea, they have to stay put and the ones that live on the shore have to put up with the roughest, toughest environment on earth. Think about it. When the tide is out in the summer up goes the temperature, the water evaporates and you are covered in a crust of salt. There is some around the edge of our rock pool. No wonder the green seaweed looks so anaemic. Next moment it is pouring with rain and you are washed clean with almost pure distilled water. In winter exactly the opposite happens: down comes the rain and a quick snap of frost freezes you solid, then back comes the tide and you are thawed out in salty water. What a way of life, no wonder the greatest diversity of the shore-line is found in the deeper rock pools, where at least some of these fluctuations are smoothed out.

What else can I find. Well, at the moment all the fronds of these common kelps are lying as it were, flat on their faces, all mixed up. When the tide comes in the buoyant salt water will bring them all to attention and they will float upright in the swell. The best way to see this is to join the British or Scottish Sub Aqua Club and learn to dive and look to the waters. I well remember my amazement at swimming through the kelp 'forest' with all the stipes erect and the fronds displayed to advantage intercepting the dappled rays of the sun. I also remember how amazed I was when one of the kelps, which I had grabbed to steady myself in the swell, came off in my hand. Well, it didn't come off, it came up, holdfast, substrate and all. It was attached, not to solid rock, but to a group of pebbles. The Crinkled Kelp appears to enjoy this method of attachment and each year as the new blade grows it begins to act as a buoyant sail and it will lift the pebbles clear of the sea bed and float them along in the currents. This is an extraordinary thing to see underwater especially if a whole forest of Crinkled Kelps are on the move. Research by a group of amateur divers has shown that pebble transport by kelp plants can be very important in the build up of shingle banks, which are one of nature's own forms of sea defence. If you find a deep enough rock pool you can try out the kelp sails for yourself; see how well they carry their load of pebbles.

My feet are beginning to get cold and the tide is certainly well on the turn so it's time for me to make my way up the beach and as I do, I am going to collect seaweeds (but only those that have already been broken loose by wave action and cast up on the beach). The small ones go into a polythene bag which has got sea water in the bottom so that they can freshen up. The large kelps, and today I am concentrating on the Rough-stalked one, I will just carry along. There must have been a bad storm recently because there are lots and lots washed up. What I am looking for is one of each size from the smallest to the biggest and I am doing this for a very special reason. . . . Yes, I reckon that I now have enough and all I need is a sandy beach and before your very eyes I will give you a lesson in seaweedology.

There we are, absolutely perfect. You can

do this for yourself: draw a straight line in the sand and starting with the smallest kelp lay your collection on the beach with their holdfasts touching the line. Then lay the next biggest and the next, until you have put them all down with the longest ones finally at the right. Now join the tips of each frond up with another line in the sand and what you have got is a perfect growth curve.

What is more, using the technique described earlier you can age each one of the plants and this will mean that you have plotted a 'living graph'. The curve produced by joining the tips of the fronds has a very special name, it is called a sigmoid

Searching for the best pieces of seaweed along the strand line can be great fun. What is more, this is the one place in which collecting the odd specimen to take home will do no harm because all the plants here have come to the end of their natural life span.

A Rough-stalked Kelp with a forest of epiphytic red seaweeds growing along its stipe. Red seaweeds are very difficult to identify but these are mostly *Rhodymenia palmata*.

curve. When young, the plant grows very slowly but after the first couple of years it speeds up into what is called its 'exponential' phase. If you are good at maths you will understand when I say that over that part of the curve the growth of the plant it is undergoing compound interest. If mathematics isn't your strong point then just stand back and admire the kelps' growth curve. Eventually the growth of the older plants slows down as the plant reaches its 'senescent' phase of growth. Eventually it will die, perhaps its buoyant size is just too much for its ageing holdfast, so that it is ripped up by the next storm and we can pick it up on the beach. Remember in nature nothing goes to waste and these rotting seaweeds that make such a nasty smell, provide food for a whole cross-section of creepy crawlies, fungi and bacteria all of which help to break them down eventually leaving the beach clean and healthy.

Before you discard your all-action growth curve take a close look at the holdfasts. As the plant grows, so too does the holdfast and as the latter is made up of all these whorls of branched branches each provides a complex inner space which creates an ideal habitat, a protective home, for a whole range of animals. What is more, as the kelp plant grows so does the volume of the homes in the holdfast. Unfortunately by the time the holdfast has been washed up on the beach all the sensible mobile animals have moved house. However, some will not have been lucky and their remains will be there, still well and truly entangled with the branches.

I went round the world three times to make a series of television programmes about the various major steps in evolution – *Botanic Man*. During that time I met David Attenborough's team doing much the same thing to make his own series, *Life on Earth*. Yet I can guarantee that with a little patience you can see a cross-section of the diversity of the life that we saw on our travels here on the coast, and much of it inside kelp holdfasts. Each of the holdfasts is covered with a felt of mini-plants, single-celled and colonial diatoms, and, in amongst them, are colonies of bacteria. It is this living mini-carpet which helps make the rocks so slippery. There in the largest holdfast, is what looks like a piece of orange rubber, that is a Breadcrumb Sponge, *Halichondria panicea*. It is an aggregate of many millions of cells all working together to produce a very special way of life and certainly it is a lot more complex than the single-celled plants and animals.

Sea anemones are almost everywhere hereabouts. They belong to a group of animals called the Cnidaria which capture their prey by the stinging cells on their tentacles. Here on the kelp is a close relative – a hydroid, a little branched colony looking much more like a plant than an animal. The Cnidaria are simple animals with a sack-like gut; food caught by the tentacles are pushed into the mouth and once digestion is completed inside the body, waste is voided back out through the mouth.

There, poking out of one of the holdfasts, is a lovely green paddle worm. I will lift him, sorry it, they're hermaphrodite, out and put it back in the water where it belongs. This is a much more advanced sort of creature. It is made up of a series of segments and has a one way gut: food goes in at the front and waste goes out at the back – a much more advanced form of creature than the Cnidaria. Another worm, *Spirorbis spirillum*, has built its home on the Crinkled Kelp, this is a little coiled tube shining white and almost translucent against the surface of the kelp. That has probably been washed up from quite deep water and is showing its most characteristic feature: its tube is coiled in an anticlockwise direction. Compare it to the much more abundant homes of *Spirorbis borealis*, whose tube coils in the opposite direction. This is by far the commonest one on the shore and likes to grow on the wracks.

The next group, the molluscs, are virtually everywhere. They are very complex animals and come in a number of basic shapes and forms. There are those with one shell valve, like the winkle over there. Others have two shell valves and by that pool I can see a great knot of mussels which have this feature. The local people used to collect luscious oysters from here before pollution got in the way and those were also bivalve molluscs. The most advanced form of molluscs are the squids and octopuses, but I'm afraid we are unlikely to see one today, although I have seen enormous squid washed up on the shore only a few miles from here. Cuttlefish bones (the white things budgerigars sharpen their beaks on) are not uncommonly washed up on the beach. These are the internal shells of squids and I think that is the nicest thing about the molluscs – when they die of natural causes they leave behind an eminently collectable souvenir, the shell. Well, at least most of them do. So

Above **Beadlet Anemone** (*Actinia equina*) with its tentacles retracted – a member of the Cnidaria, the animals with stinging cells. It is lying next to a saw-toothed blade of Serrated Wrack.

Left **A Green Paddle Worm**, *Eulalia viridis*, sliding across a rock encrusted with barnacles. This member of the Annelida, segmented worms, is a predator on the barnacles, one of the most numerous animals of our rocky shores.

215

Where there is a suitable anchorage on a rock, competition for space is extremely fierce. Therefore you often have several living organisms living on top of each other, all feeding on the feast of plankton brought in at each new tide. Here we have mussels and limpets, members of the Mollusca, encrusted with barnacles, members of the Crustacea, waiting for the sea to cover them.

you never need collect a living mollusc.

Next in the evolutionary ladder comes the animals with jointed legs, the members of the Arthropoda. Lift up a nearby stone and they will come at you from all directions, but remember to put the stone back with care or you might well squash them. Their armour-plated exoskeleton may protect them from their enemies but not from a carelessly placed rock. If I look around in this gully I should be able to find some of their discarded external skeletons. . . . What have I got here? A Shore Crab's nipper and the carapace (upper shell) of a tiny Porcelain Crab. Both of these are just right to put in the marine section of my home museum. What is more, they have been dead and dry for a long time and so won't smell the house out. Now that's not a piece of crab but the arm of an ophiuroid, a brittle-star. This animal belongs to the great group of Spiny-skinned Animals, the Echinodermata. These include the sea urchins, sea cucumbers and sea stars. I will not use the terms starfish, because they are not fish at all.

While on the subject of fish, you have to be quick to see them in the rock pools let alone catch one. Whilst walking across this stretch of beach I have seen several darting for cover under the weeds in the rock pools. They are too quick for me but then, of course, I am a botanist. However, that rapid movement introduces us to the advantage of having a backbone against which muscles can work very efficiently. Next time you eat fish for dinner remember you are eating those power packed muscles which drive the fish through the water with such speed and grace. While thinking about the vertebrates, the animals

with backbones, take a look up and there are several gulls flying over head – a backbone plus warm blood and anything is possible!

Then, of course, there are the mammals. There are plenty further along the beach playing sand castles. This one is half in and half out of a rock pool, but it wouldn't be a rare sight to sit here where I am and see a seal's head bobbing out there in amongst the kelp fronds which are almost submerged. What a morning, I've now got lovely wet feet. We've seen some super plants and seen the whole panoply of evolutionary effort and I didn't have to move much more than a hundred metres. That's why I do like to be beside the seaside.

But now to work. I will now have to write up my notes in my all-important field note-book but unfortunately as usual like most of my things it is now soaking wet. However, I will have to remember to copy it out into my big notebook as soon as I get home. And then also I must deal with all those seaweeds in my plastic bag. When I'm home, I take each specimen out one by one and float them in the sink or a bowl filled with ordinary tap water where they spread themselves out beautifully. I then put a piece of paper under the seaweed (the bond typing paper is best) and lift the paper up very carefully, and with a bit of teasing I find that it has arranged itself on the paper. Next, after I've let it settle down, I lift it out of the water and allow the seaweed to stick itself down on the paper with its own mucilage. Then what I have to do, is to make sure before I press it, that it doesn't stick to the paper I'm going to put on top. Therefore I cover the specimen with a piece of muslin, and then make a newspaper sandwich, remembering to change the newspaper regularly for the first day or so. Meanwhile, I have put my heaviest books on top to press everything down nice and flat and there you are – a perfect specimen. You should then put your piece of paper with its seaweed in your pressed seaweed book. The red seaweeds collected from the strand line can be super to have, and every year I use some of them to make my Christmas cards. In future, if you do get really interested in the seaweeds and learn to identify them, then you should label them and say where, when, and how they were found – and then the seaweeds become a record for the future. Who knows, we could then use your collection in many years to come as valuable evidence for the changes in the sea life around the coast.

HOW TO PRESS YOUR OWN SEAWEED

1 First float your specimen in a bowl so that the fronds spread out flat; 2 slide a piece of paper carefully under your seaweed and 3 gently place it on some sheets of newspaper, 4 making sure that it is lying flat. 5 You should then lay a sheet of muslin cloth over the seaweed. 6 This protects it from the sheets of newspaper which you place over the top. 7 It is important to replace the newspaper at regular intervals whilst the seaweed is still wet. 8 You should hold the seaweed sandwich down with some of your heaviest books and when it has dried you have a perfect pressed specimen for your seaweed collection.

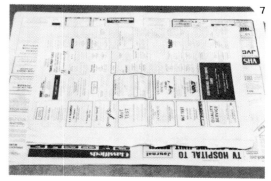

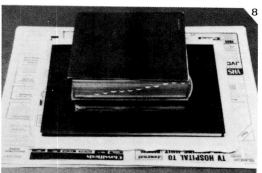

Rocky Shorelines

To me and many thousands of marine biologists John Barrett is a very special person. He and his team at Dale Fort in Pembrokeshire have introduced many of us to the wonders of marine life. Here he is in splendid form walking with care and immense knowledge across his home patch, the wonderfully rich rocky shore at Dale. The only thing that is missing from the real experience is the cry of the gulls and the taste of good Welsh tea at the end of a satisfying day in the field.

The rocky shoreline at Dale, covered in seaweeds and providing a home for a vast array of animals.

Rocky Shorelines
with John Barrett

One of the most exciting places for a naturalist to explore is a stretch of rocky coastline at low tide. Britain has some superb lengths, particularly along our northern and western coasts. We went down to one of the many lovely bays on the Pembrokeshire coast to see what we could find. Our guide for the day was John Barrett, who has written and lectured on the life of our shores for many years and who was co-author of the first field guide to the animals and plants living there.

We started our walk as the tide was going out across a slippery belt of seaweeds. Before we went too far, we asked John to describe some of the problems of living in this habitat and something of the principles that controlled the distribution of plants and animals in it.

'Probably only the coral reefs of the world contain as great a variety of types of plants and animals as live on a rocky shore. This variety includes representatives of all the major groups in the animal kingdom (the Phyla). Since all are animals of the sea and not of the land, they all breathe oxygen which is dissolved in seawater. Also many feed directly on that primary source of food in the sea – the plankton.

'Drifting in the surface layers of the sea are living organisms in numbers beyond computation. At least 800 animals, each larger than a bacterium, will be in the next mouthful of seawater the reader swallows when swimming. These are the 'flesh' – the meat – of the plankton.

'When the prophet cried that all flesh was grass he was searching for consolation and not asserting a biological truth. Nonetheless all flesh in the sea depends for food on microscopically small single-celled plants called diatoms – 20000 of the largest and several millions of the smaller in a bucketful. Diatoms aggregate a greater weight per acre of sea than do fully grown potatoes in an acre of field. They far outnumber the animals in that mouthful of seawater. Diatoms are the first link of every food chain in the sea and on the shore.

'The dangers of living on a rocky shore are considerable. First of all, being marine, the animals must never dry out. So all are adapted in one way or another to resist desiccation by wind and/or sun when the ebb tide has left them in the open air. They also have to avoid being washed away during a gale. The gale may rage for two days, with twenty tons of water in each cubic yard of each wave crashing onto the shore. Then, next day, when all is quiet again, the little animals are exactly where they were before the gale blew up.

'The ebb and flow of the tide is a dominant control in the distribution of life along a rocky shore. Tidal characteristics confine many common plants and animals within horizontal layers – the technical word is 'zonation'. Nothing shows zonation on a shore better than the big brown seaweeds called the wracks.

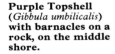

Purple Topshell (*Gibbula umbilicalis*) **with barnacles on a rock, on the middle shore.**

'At the top, around mean high water of spring tides, is a zone dominated by the Channelled Wrack, *Pelvetia canaliculata*; just below, at mean high water neaps, is the Flat Wrack, *Fucus spiralis*. In the middle of the shore is a layer of Egg Wrack, *Ascophyllum nodosum*, which, where it is sheltered from waves, lies over the rocks as a dense mattress, almost excluding all other plants and animals. Below the Egg Wrack comes the Bladder Wrack, *Fucus vesiculosus*, with its paired bladders which pop so readily when dry. Then lower down again, at about low water of neaps, is the Saw Wrack, *Fucus serratus*, which is easily identified by the edge of the frond having teeth along it rather like those of a saw.

'This outline pattern of zonation is complicated by wave action. For instance, Egg Wrack is mechanically feeble. A mass of it may dominate the middle of a sheltered shore, but, as soon as the angle changes to admit a greater pressure of wave action, the Egg Wrack is increasingly torn away by those waves. Even small waves shorten it to the point that it cannot brush off the barnacle larvae from the rocks at that delicate moment when they settle as adults from the plankton. As the exposure increases the length of the wracks decreases, so the area of open rock surface increases, allowing the number of barnacles to increase until they dominate the exposed shore from about the middle downwards. A square yard of surface may accommodate up to 60000 barnacles. The number along a mile of coast is, indeed, large.

'The zonation of winkles is easy to see. In the splash zone, above high water mark, is the tiny Small Winkle, *Littorina neritoides*. Lower down, at much the same level as the Flat Wrack, comes the Rough Winkle, *Littorina saxatilis*. (Some specialists argue nowadays that this one name may cover four separate species.) At midtide level on less exposed shores is the Edible Winkle, *Littorina littorea*; slightly lower, with the Bladder Wrack, comes the Flat Winkle, *Littorina littoralis*, which is coloured either dark black-green or bright yellow.

'These Flat Winkles are much the same size and shape as the bladders in Bladder Wrack. Until quite recently it was thought that, at low tide, the 'yellow' winkles hid from hungry waders underneath the seaweeds while the 'green' ones stayed on top, made safe from detection by their shape and colour. By the simple test of counting the

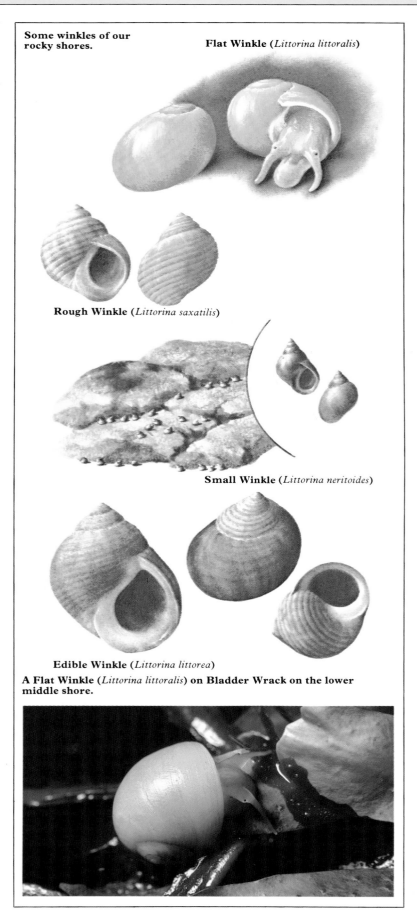

Some winkles of our rocky shores.

Flat Winkle (*Littorina littoralis*)

Rough Winkle (*Littorina saxatilis*)

Small Winkle (*Littorina neritoides*)

Edible Winkle (*Littorina littorea*)

A Flat Winkle (*Littorina littoralis*) on Bladder Wrack on the lower middle shore.

numbers of the two colours on and under a sample patch of wracks anybody can confirm that this hard worn notion is not true!

'Like all the other winkles, the Small are male or female. They copulate and then release fertilized eggs. Living so high up the shore, there is a biological advantage if all the Small Winkles in one area synchronize this release to coincide with the time of high-water spring-tides in winter, just at the time when there is the greatest chance that splash from a gale will wash down those eggs into the sea. There they hatch, and then pass through their various larval stages in the plankton which precede settlement as adults on the shore. At the time of settlement they have a magic capability (instinct) within them. When covered by water they crawl upwards; when becoming uncovered by the ebb tide they move into dark cracks in the rocks. This gives protection from passing predators. Then, when the new flood covers them again, the urge to climb reasserts dominance over the urge to hide in the dark; so up they go again. In the end they find their way right up to the top of the shore. A remarkable journey for a snail which may be less than a fifth of an inch long (5 millimetres).

'The Rough Winkle avoids these hazards by giving birth to fully developed young. Although living at a slightly lower level on the shore than the Small, the Rough has a second advantage in the evolutionary race out of the sea onto the land. Its gills show the first signs of modification towards being lungs. It can 'breathe' very damp air. So, in, say, a million more years, we may find Rough Winkles amongst our lettuces!

'The Rough is well adapted to resist all degrees of wave action. A snail's shell is made up of a series of whorls. Given a snail's shape and asked how it could be strengthened to resist the hammer blows from stones crashed onto it during a gale, a mechanical engineer would say that the incision between successive whorls must be deepened. This is just how evolution (survival of the fittest) has worked in the Rough Winkle. Compare one from a very exposed shore with one from shelter and it is hard to believe that the two specimens belong to the same species. However, a series of shells collected in a sequence from exposure to shelter will show a gradation of modification (adaptation) linking the two ends of the series (a biological cline).

'The topshells, common on all but very exposed rocky shores, are different from the winkles in that they do not copulate, but release their sperm and ova into the sea. Fertilization then depends upon the chance meeting in the sea of the ovum with a sperm, which are meanwhile at risk in the food chains.

'Another difference between winkles and topshells is that topshells have a little hole in the centre of the mouth of the shell which indicates the hollowness of the column round which the shell is built. Since winkles have a column which is solid, they have no hole in the middle of their mouths.

'The topshells do not come as high up the beach as the winkles. On many, the Purple, *Gibbula umbilicalis*, flourishes at about mean sea level and the Grey, *G. cineraria*, downwards from low water of neaps. The

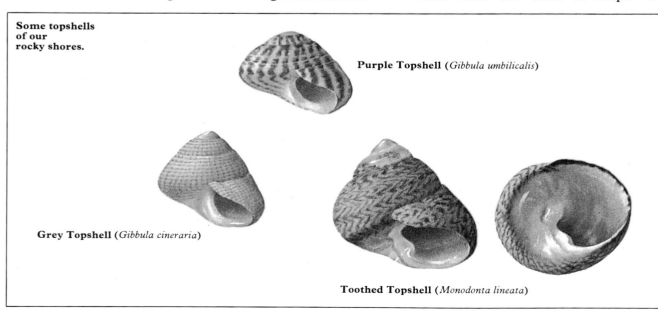

Some topshells of our rocky shores.

Purple Topshell (*Gibbula umbilicalis*)

Grey Topshell (*Gibbula cineraria*)

Toothed Topshell (*Monodonta lineata*)

Toothed Topshell, *Monodonta lineata*, has a shining mother-of-pearl mouth and zig-zag markings on its shell. It is otherwise much the same size and colour as the Edible Winkle, which is found in the same places.

'A feature common to both winkles and topshells (and many other snails and worms) is the operculum. When the animal pulls itself into its shell, the entrance is stoppered by a round leathery disc. This operculum holds in moisture, so saving the owner from being dried out. It is also an effective barrier against entry by a hungry predator.

'The limpet is an animal characteristic of all rocky shores. The conical shell can be as much as 2 inches (6 centimetres) across but it is usually somewhat smaller than that. The limpet clings to the rock by a sucker foot with proverbial tightness. Each lives in its own 'home' which is ground out by circular muscular pressure to fit the shell precisely to the rock. Soft rock is ground to fit the shell; but the shell is ground to fit hard rock. So, no matter what the nature of the rock, there is always a watertight fit between it and the limpet shell. Just before the ebb tide exposes the animal to the danger of desiccation the shell is pulled down tight onto its home, so retaining water in the tissues of the limpet and in the empty spaces in the shell round the body. Even so, all the oxygen in the trapped water would be used up before the returning tide could replace it, if it were not for the limpet's ability to lift its shell that fractional distance from the rock that allows oxygen from the air to percolate in but does not allow the water inside to leak out.

'When the tide covers them, limpets move about feeding. They have, like the winkles and topshells, a long tongue on which are hard chitinous teeth. It is a nice coincidence of organic chemistry that these teeth are of the same material as the hard wing-cases of beetles. The limpet tongue is rolled out and then withdrawn so that the hooked teeth on the underside scrape off diatoms lodged on the rock or slivers from the surface of larger seaweeds which are then ingested by the limpets.

'When on these feeding sorties they travel several feet from their "home", but they

These are four species of limpets that can be found along the British coast. *Patella aspersa* and *P. intermedia* are generally found lower down the shore line than the Common Limpet, *P. vulgata*. The Blue-rayed Limpet, *P. pelucida*, is often found attached to the fronds and holdfasts of *Laminaria* on the lower shore.

Patella vulgata

Patella aspera

Patina pellucida

Patella intermedia

Limpets (*Patella*). The one on its back shows its sucker-foot, ringed by its gills, with its head and tentacles protruding to the left. Dogwhelks have eaten some of the barnacles. The grey patch is the calcium carbonate base from which all the plant cells of the seaweed, *Lithophyllum* sp., have died off, perhaps eaten by limpets.

Rocky shore dominated by Acorn Barnacles (*Balanus balanoides*) and so exposed that only residual tufts of wracks just survive.

always return to it before the ebb tide exposes them again. It is easy to test the ability of limpets to return to their homes from various distances and angles. Gently knock off two or three and mark them with spots of nail varnish. Dab the same code of spots beside their "home", from which you tapped them. Now put the limpets a measured distance away in some damp place – sideways, upwards or downwards. When the tide comes in they will be off feeding; before it goes out again they will have secured themselves on their "homes" – up to a distance limit which your experiment will determine.

'We have already noted the wide zone of barnacles in the lower half of exposed shores. The barnacles' relationship to crabs and woodlice was not discovered until 1833 when their larval forms were first recognised. Up to then they were counted as molluscs. Most barnacle species have six external plates which are often fused together. An Australian invader with only four plates was first noticed in 1945. All species have two more plates within the protection of the outer ring which, when covered by the tide, slide open to allow "legs" to emerge which kick rhythmically to establish an in-flow of seawater laden with oxygen and food.

expose the surface of the rock to which it was attached. This exposure gives barnacle larvae the chance they need to attach themselves.

'Next Dogwhelks move in, which eat the barnacles. The mussel clumps developing round what was temporarily an area of living barnacles are now free to spread across the dead barnacles' shells, until, once more, the new mussel clump is washed off and the barnacles can again use the rock surface newly cleared of mussels. So the cycle turns.

'The attachment of mussels is by sticky threads which are extruded through the narrow end of the shell. The threads are something like the guy ropes of a tent but, unlike a tent's, they attach only the front end of the mussel. This leaves the shell free to flex to changing angles of the press of the waves. Had the shell been fixed firmly throughout its length, it would quickly have been smashed off by water pressure.

'Mussels feed by drawing in a flow of water through an inhalant tube ("siphon") extension of its body. Just as for so many

'On an exposed shore largely dominated by barnacles you often find a mass of mussels amongst them. The relationship between the density of mussels and the density of barnacles is intricate. The larval mussels, which are in the plankton, at the time of changing to adults are chemically attracted by the already existing attached adults and they fix themselves onto these adults. More and more come in, drawn to the same site by the 'scent', so that large lumps of mussels are built up, attached to the rock only by those at the bottom of the pile. Eventually the clump gets so big that a wave coming in at the critical angle can smash it off and so

other animals, barnacles, for instance, this water contains oxygen for breathing and plankton for food. Fine hair sieves attached to the mussel's gills separate the food from the fine silt and sand suspended in the water which falls down into the bottom of the shell until released into the sea by opening the shell.

'Meanwhile the food is carried from the filters into the digestive tract by the water flow. In its passage through the tissues of the mussel the water has had added to it eggs or sperm which are then squirted out through the exhalant siphon with the waste water. Each mussel passes a pint of seawater

Barnacles feeding. In effect, these crustaceans are attached to the rocks by their head ends and their thoracic appendages have become filter-feeding organs.

225

through itself every 12–15 minutes. The danger of sucking in water that was waste from a neighbour is avoided by all squirting out the waste with something like eight times the force available for sucking in. So waste is jetted too far out into the body of sea water to be recirculated until it has been recharged with food and oxygen.

'To ensure the stability of the adult population the chances that a mussel egg will be fertilized are increased by the release from the males of many times more sperms than the 25 million eggs emitted by each female. The chance is still further improved

when all the adults synchronize this release with the time of the same summer spring tide.

'Despite the astronomical initial numbers twenty four hours later only 170,000 swimming larvae survive beneath each square yard of water over a mussel bed. Of these less than fifty survive to be adults. The rest have been eaten. For instance, each of those hundreds of thousands of acorn barnacles living hard by, constantly kick in a flow of water from which they extract as food, mussel eggs, sperm and larvae amongst all the other planktonic titbits. Those who

Mussels, barnacles, limpets and two much abraded Purple Top-shells, compete for space at about mean sea level on a rocky shore.

think that these reproductive processes are wasteful are thinking too narrowly of the species and not of the total community which are dependent on each other for food and thus for survival.

'The Dogwhelk, *Nucella lapillus*, is a common mollusc where barnacles flourish. It eats them. The Dogwhelk's thick, elongated and rough shell has a hollowed extension of the mouth through which a tube-tongue can be extruded, the end of which is rimmed with a circlet of hard points. The whelk forces its tongue against the thinner internal plates of the barnacle and screws an entrance by twisting its tongue. Then it can suck out the barnacle meat. Any population of barnacles contains many empty cases – all of them cleaned out by whelks.

'After copulation the female whelks deposit capsules of eggs in deep cracks at low tide level. They are massed together like stalked grains of wheat. Only five per cent of the 300–1 000 eggs in each are fertile. After some four months the remaining ninety-five per cent will have been eaten by the few that hatch and now emerge about 1/16th inch (1·5 millimetres) long. They do

not attack barnacles until they have grown to about a quarter of an inch (6 millimetres).

'Three or four little lumps are often to be seen in the mouth of a Dogwhelk shell. They indicate a period when the food supply was too scarce to allow steady growth. When food is plentiful the shell begins to expand again and those little lumps disappear up into the increasing size of the shell.'

Having looked at the commonest molluscs we moved down the shore to see what else was about. We quickly lit on some sea-anemones.

'The commonest anemone on rocky shores, and particularly in pools, is the dark crimson Beadlet, *Actinia equina*. The name comes from the circlet of cornflower-blue spots which you will see if you gently fold

Dogwhelk (*Nucella lapillus*) feeding on Acorn Barnacles.

Beadlet Anemone
(*Actinia equina*); **the protruding mouth can be seen at the centre of the tentacles.**

brush against them. They then fold down upon the luckless meal and slowly force it towards and, then, into the mouth which is located within the circle of tentacles. Some anemones have spring-loaded narcotic darts attached within their body with which they can tranquillise a struggling captive and so prevent it damaging their mouth. The meal is then digested quietly and the waste material ejected.

'Some of the larger sea-slugs, including the Common Grey, *Aeolidia papillosa*, having eaten a sea-anemone, are able to separate out from the body of the anemone the stinging threads complete with the mechanism for their release and then to pass the whole apparatus up into their own back; what was the poisonous armament of the anemone now defends the slug that ate it.

'The Snakelocks, *Anemonia sulcata*, is common around mean sea level in rock pools. It is usually a rather dull khaki colour but some are magic apple green, with the tentacles shading through to an exquisite watery blue-purple tip. The Snakelocks cannot close up its tentacles; they constantly writhe in memory of Medusa.

'Although rock pools are such a feature of rocky shores it is misguided to expect that they always hold a lovely selection of plants and animals within them. The dangers of living in a pool are not at once obvious. For instance, summer sunshine may heat up the water far above the temperature of the sea; winter's cold may cool it equally far below

back the top of the column of the anemone. Out of water they are but blobs of dark red jelly, quite different from the flower-heads of tentacles that open when the tide returns.

'Anemones are simple animals, related to jellyfish. They have only one entrance to the body. This is the mouth at the time of feeding, but, when the meal has been digested, the inedible bits and the body waste are excreted through what was the mouth and is now the anus.

'Under water the sticky tentacles wave gently, waiting for some tiny animal to

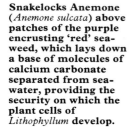

Snakelocks Anemone
(*Anemone sulcata*) **above patches of the purple encrusting 'red' seaweed, which lays down a base of molecules of calcium carbonate separated from seawater, providing the security on which the plant cells of** *Lithophyllum* **develop.**

sea temperature; a pool may even freeze. Heavy rain may wash out all the salt water and leave the pool almost fresh; hot sunshine may evaporate the water to the point that it becomes supersaturated with salt, with salt crystals shining round the edge. Only a very few animals are adapted to survive such heavy physiological strains. Big, deep pools are the real treasure houses.

'However, on the surface of even quite small pools you may well find tiny blue creatures, either singly or, more often, aggregated in lumps supported by the surface tension of the water. These are wingless insects called *Lipura maritima*.

'All insects breathe atmospheric oxygen through little tubes in the side of their bodies. In *Lipura*, the cross-section of these tubes is so small that the surface tension prevents water from penetrating into them and so drowning the insect. To guard against being drowned, if it is washed back into the sea by waves and then held below the surface in a cold water layer, the insect's body is covered with downy hairs within which it traps bubbles of air that provide enough oxygen to last five days. So it has only to get its breath, so to speak, once in five days during which the chances are that it will have been washed back onto the shore again.'

We turned again to hunting among the rocks and seaweeds. John soon pulled out a fine Shore Crab, *Carcinus maenas*, its rich green shell glistening in the sunshine.

'You can readily recognise him because he is the only crab which has three blunt teeth between the eyes and five sharp ones on either side of the shell. The last joint of the back legs is flattened for swimming but is still sharply pointed enough for walking. In the true swimming crabs this last joint is as rounded as a paddle blade. The tail is tucked under the shell; the male's is narrow, pointed and 5-jointed; the female's roundly broad and 7-jointed. Under the female's tail you may find a sandy coloured, granular bunch of 150000 fertile eggs which she carries for several months before they hatch into planktonic larvae. After undergoing six changes of form in the sea they eventually settle as adult crabs about an eighth of an inch (3 millimetres) across.

'Carrying their "skeleton" outside their body they would be unable to grow larger were they not adapted to rid themselves periodically of its constriction. When the time comes to grow, the crab creeps for

Below **Springtails** (*Lipura maritima*) **are wingless insects, here supported by surface tension on the water of a pool; they are the only common intertidal insect.**

Bottom **Shore-crab** (*Carcinus maenas*) **amongst Sea-lettuce; the light is reflected off the three blunt teeth between the eyes and some of the sharp points on either side.**

Broad-clawed Porcelain Crab (*Porcellana platycheles*); **because it is out of water all the body hairs are lying flat.**

shelter under a rock or deep amongst seaweeds and then the line of weakness, which runs along the back of the shell, is split open and the body forces out backwards. All is removed including the gills from the gill-covers, the eyes from their stalks and the legs are extricated right from the tip end. After three to four days the new shell will have hardened out, one third larger than the old one. Starting with a shell 3 millimetres across and increasing in size by a third at each change, how many changes does a crab undergo before it has reached its full size of 150 millimetres across?

'While most of the cast shells are quickly smashed to pieces by the waves, some, caught by currents, accumulate along the high tide line of saltmarshes and in very sheltered nooks along a rocky shore. If you find such an accumulation you will know that no catastrophe has smitten the local crabs, when you note that all the shells are split along the line at the back.

'Sometimes you will find under the tail of a crab, not a granular lump of eggs, but a smooth, grey mass which is the reproductive parts of a parasitic barnacle, *Sacculina carcini*. This parasite has larval stages exactly like the acorn barnacles', but, at the change to the adult state, instead of settling on rocks it settles on a crab's jaws from where it grows threads throughout the host's tissues through which the parasite absorbs food. Eventually a sac of reproductive parts of the parasite appears under the tail of the female crab. If it is dangerous for the host to have a soft shell, it is equally dangerous for the parasite. So the growth of the parasitic barnacle inhibits any change of shell by the host. After the parasite has released sperm or ova into the sea it dies and the crab at once reverts to its normal rhythm of life.

'Here we have a much smaller, rounder crab, one with long antennae and with its flat nippers and body covered with fine hairs. This is the Broad-clawed Porcelain, *Porcellana platycheles*. They are about half an inch (12 millimetres) across and common under stones, where the hairs help to secure them into the muddy sand. They do not catch food with their nippers but, instead, they fish for it by casting out a sticky, web-fine net from their mouth to which the planktonic food adheres as they suck the net in again.

'Whereas crabs have ten legs, including the nippers, the porcelains appear to have only eight. The last pair are there, but are folded under the tail and have become part of the crab's reproductive apparatus. This position of the back legs indicates the relationship of these porcelains with the hermits and lobsters.

'Crabs are well adapted to survive the hazard of having legs trapped under stones rolled on them during storms. Unless it can escape from this trap, the crab will soon starve. The trapped leg (or legs) can be broken off across a groove in its second joint by a specialised muscular contraction. In the residual stump are two membranous flaps which unfold as the leg is sheared and so staunch the flow of blood, the first drops of which, quickly coagulate and so totally seal the outlet. Then a complete new limb develops so fast within the stump that, a few weeks later, at the next change of shell, the leg emerges almost full size. Several legs can be replaced at this speed, at the same time.

'The ability to replace damaged parts, characteristic particularly of crustacea and starfish, reaches its climax with self-evisceration by sea-cucumbers. At the critical moment of attack by a predator, by a convulsive body contraction, the sea-cucumber causes its own gut to rupture and its viscera, genital organs and respiratory tissue are squirted out through its anus. This mass is strangely elastic and sticky and, at once, swells out into a white ball of 'cotton'. (Hence the vernacular name Cotton-spinners for sea-cucumbers.) The predator is distracted from the remaining body within which a new set of guts grows within ten days.'

As our search progressed we noticed that a number of seaweeds were peppered with little white dots which on inspection through a handlens turned out to be spirals. What were these?

'They are tubes within which worms live. There are not many worms on a rocky shore; they cannot burrow into rocks for shelter. However, two are easy to find. Both are able to extract molecules of calcium carbonate from the seawater from which they build stone-hard white tubes, within which they live in safety. The one we are looking at now is often on Bladder and Saw Wrack. Inside each spiral is a worm called *Spirorbis*. It is hermaphrodite and so fertilizes its own eggs, leading to larvae which swim away into the plankton. When they settle back as minute adults, no bigger than a pin head, they save themselves from at once being washed away, by seeking the shelter under the ridge of the midrib of these wracks. None that settles actually on the midrib, survives.

'The other white tube worm you will find is *Pomatoceros*. Its tube is much bigger than *Spirorbis*. Although built in the same way, it

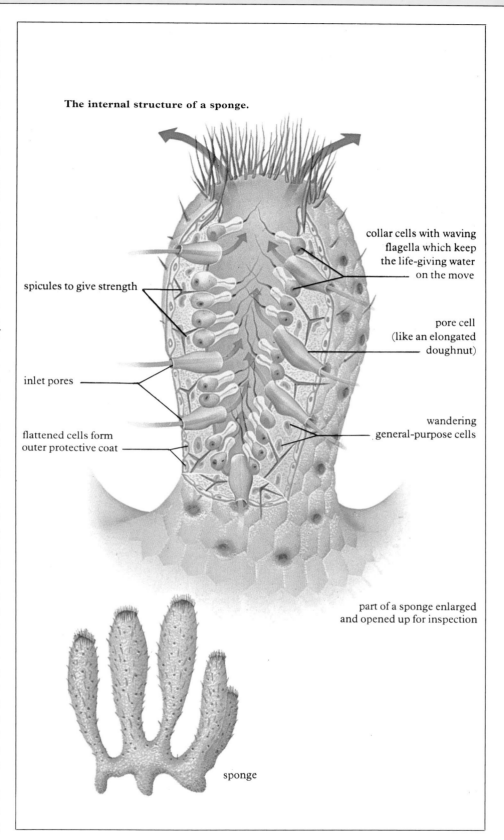

The internal structure of a sponge.

collar cells with waving flagella which keep the life-giving water on the move

spicules to give strength

pore cell (like an elongated doughnut)

inlet pores

wandering general-purpose cells

flattened cells form outer protective coat

part of a sponge enlarged and opened up for inspection

sponge

Sponges are considered to be amongst the most simple of animals. They have bodies made up of many cells, but although they are numerous these cells occur in only a few types. The bodies are generally encrusting, growing over rocks and organisms, or erect and flask- or goblet-shaped. They have evolved to be good pumpers. Their internal structures (shown here) range from simple ducts and chambers to complex layouts.

The orange globular colonies of a sea-squirt low down on a rocky shore. Within each colony are ten to fifteen individual animals. Sea-squirts (*tunicates*) have tadpole-like larvae whose bodies are stiffened by a carti-laginous thread which is lost when they change into adults and which echo the evolu-tionary appearance of a backbone some 420 million years ago. In the middle of the picture, the open crown of tentacles of

is triangular in cross-section. At the open end of the tube a tiny needle growth point indicates that an animal is alive within. *Pomatoceros* is often found on small flat stones, usually several together.

'You may also find some scale worms under stones. These have interlocking pairs of scales protecting their backs. They progress by sideways wriggling.'

We just had time left before the tide turned to go still lower down into gullies between the rocks. They abounded with red seaweeds and the large oarweeds, *Laminaria* species.

'Down here, particularly under the rock overhangs, you will easily find lovely patches of bright colours – often orange or green. These are sponges. Thirty species of these primitive animals flourish on our rocky shores. Through a lens you can some-times make out the tiny hole through which the animal draws in seawater – once again, for oxygen and food. Their waste is expelled through communal 'drains' which look like miniature volcanoes. These outlets are particularly prominent on a lump of Bread-crumb sponge, *Halichondria panicea*, less so on the other very common species, *Hymeni-*

acidon sanguinea. (Anybody who grows Chrysanthemum, Alstromeria or Antirrhinum in his garden has no reason to shy at the name *Hymeniacidon*!)

'If you look at the stalks of the oarweeds and many of the Saw Wracks at this level, you will see that they are wrapped round by a grey encrustation. On the oarweed fronds are irregular patches of the same kind of material. Through a hand lens you will see that each is made up of a fine honeycomb of tiny cells, regularly shaped. In each of these cells lives an animal, a Sea Mat. The two scientific names for the phylum, which contains them, suggests something of their character – Polyzoa, many animals, and Bryozoa, moss animals.

'Besides being so common, Sea Mats are complicated. They have a mouth leading into a digestive tract which curls up to an anus situated outside the circlet of tentacles on which fine hairs beat a stream of water into the central mouth. Each animal within its cell is a single entity. The corporate colony spreads and fuses where two edges of it meet. However, no fusion follows the meeting of separate colonies of the same species.

a tube-worm is extended for feeding beyond the grey end of its tube.

Left **Tubes of the worm,** *Pomatoceros triqueter*; **the needle-sharp points over the open end of the left-hand three indicate the worm inside each is alive.**

Below **Common sponges: the green form of the Bread-crumb Sponge** (*Halichondria panicea*), **mixed with orange pieces of** *Hymeniacidon sanguinea.*

Right **A sandhopper of the kind that lives in untold numbers among pebbles and seaweeds thrown ashore along the high-tide line. Other species live in equally large numbers under stones, all the way down the shore.**

'Commonly growing on these Sea Mat colonies, or on the seaweeds or the rocks, are little straw-coloured stalks, half an inch (12 millimetres) or more long. Through your lens you find that some have stubby pairs of lateral branches and some diaphanous divisions of the stem. These are colonies of sea-firs (hydroids), related to sea anemones and jellyfish. Within each cup, spaced along the branches, is a living animal surmounted by tentacles round its central mouth/anus. The beauty of the rhythmical beating of these tentacles has to be seen to be believed.'

There were so many other things to see but we had no time left. The competition for a place to live low down on rocky shores excludes all but fragmentary views of the underlying rock. Plants and animals are one on another – *Spirorbis*, hydroids, Sea Mats and other red seaweeds all cling on to Saw Wrack; barnacles and seaweeds are growing on limpets. Every nook and cranny is occupied. The variety of species and the beauty of their colours, patterns and movements will bring joy to any naturalist, and above all, to those with a seeing eye.

Now the flood tide was pushing us inexorably upwards. We had hardly covered more than a hundred yards since we started and had, even so, no more than glimpsed the riches that were before us on this length of rocky shore in Pembrokeshire.

The open network of thread 'rootlets' supporting a colony of the sea-fir (hydroid) *Dynamena pumila*, **with cups in closely opposite pairs, in each of which lives a minute sea-anemone-like animal.**

Sand Dunes

A supply of readily erodible rock out to sea and an onshore wind means that the coast will be fringed and protected by a belt of sand dunes. The dunes themselves owe their continued existence to a whole group of hardy plants, the most important being two grasses: Marram and Sea Couch Grass. This environment is highly unstable and a strong gale can change the whole appearance of a mobile dune system overnight. Yet these support a complex web of life which has adapted to exploit the full potential of this transient and exciting landscape.

What better person than Ted Smith, whose inspiration helped found the county trust movement, which is now under the 'umbrella' of the Royal Society for Nature Conservation, to show us around the dunes at Gibraltar Point in Lincolnshire.

Lyme Grass (*Elymus arenarius*), **a distinctive plant of the open sand dunes of our coasts.**

Sand Dunes
with Ted Smith

A gently sloping beach backed by a rolling belt of dunes is many people's idea of the perfect place to be on a warm summer's day. I can always remember the feeling of excitement when, as a boy, we would set off through the dunes towards the sea, especially when we mounted that final crest and the wide sandy beach would suddenly open out before us. The waves would be breaking down by the water's edge and small flocks of gulls would be drifting along between the distant knots of sunbathers. Tremendous. But for a naturalist the walk through the dunes themselves is as exciting as the beach, as we found out during our visit to Gibraltar Point Nature Reserve. Our guide through the ups and downs of this unstable environment was Ted Smith, who is Chairman of the Lincolnshire and South Humberside Trust for Nature Conservation and also, until recently, was the General Secretary of the RSNC (then the Society for the Promotion of Nature Conservation). Ted has known the dunes at Gibraltar Point for many years and is all too aware of the changes they have undergone since the war, in terms of both public pressures and physical change. We started our walk down by the strand line and whilst we picked our way between the flotsam and jetsam Ted introduced us to the site.

'We are here on the Lincolnshire coast at the Gibraltar Point Nature Reserve which consists of a large area of sand dunes and saltmarsh with both sandy and muddy beaches. It is at the north-west corner of the Wash and on a clear day you can see the coast of Norfolk, 13 miles away. The reserve covers about 1 000 acres and has been established since 1949, making it one of the earliest post-war nature reserves. It is managed by the Lincolnshire and South Humberside Trust for Nature Conservation on behalf of the owners who are the Lincolnshire County Council and the East Lindsey District Council.

'Any walk among the sand dunes ought to start out on the beach and that is where we are now, looking out to sea on a beautiful summer day with the waves tumbling lazily on shore. But if we were to visit this coast at a time of a big storm or when a high spring tide was flowing, we would see that the waves would be driving the sand and shingle up the beach. Quite a lot of this material is washed back into the sea but some of it remains on the upper part of the beach. On some parts of the coast the waves

come in at a right angle to the shore but often they come in at an oblique angle carrying sand and shingle in that direction. Some of this material is then dragged back into the sea at a right angle to the waterline with the backwash, and in this way the sand and pebbles are gradually carried along the shore. This process is known as "beach drifting". Here, you can see long ridges being built up southwards indicating the direction in which the beach material is moving at this particular point.

'As the tides return to a succession of neaps, leaving much of the shore exposed for long periods, the sand will dry out and the wind then comes into play and blows it further inland. Anything that traps this moving sand will serve to build up the beach. The first thing that does this is the tide wrack along the strand line, which is at our feet. This includes all sorts of human rubbish but most of it is natural material – either dead plant remains from saltmarshes or remains that have been washed up from the seabed. On rocky coasts a great deal of this would be seaweeds but here a lot of the wrack is made up of this brown stuff that looks for all the world like dried-up brown seaweed but is, in fact, of animal origin. It is called Seamat or Hornwrack and it was once growing on the seabed, attached by little pads, then spreading out, like the fingers of a hand. If we look at this specimen under a lens you will see that it looks rather like a honeycomb pitted with tiny cells. Each cell, when it is alive, contains a minute animal that lives by drawing in tiny morsels from the sea. It is a colony of animals and belongs to a group called Polyzoa, meaning "many animals". These dried remnants which resemble tiny, tufted trees are called Sea Firs. They housed colonies of hydroids.

'There is a lot of other material here. It is all very dry at this time of year as some of it has been here since last winter's gales. These are whelks' egg-cases, the familiar papery brown clusters of little balls; and these shiny black objects with horns at each corner are skates' egg-cases – "mermaids' purses". From our point of view all this dead material is important because it is the first thing that traps the blowing sand. It will also eventually rot down, like garden compost, to provide nutrients for the first land plants to grow. Incidentally, it is also the home for many small animals, particularly sandhoppers, which live in burrows under the wrack and come out at night to

The strandline – the first stage in the accumulation of the sand. This photograph shows a typical collection of flotsam and jetsam – whelk egg-cases, 'mermaids' purses' (skates' eggs), hornwrack, sea firs and human debris.

239

Above the strandline one of the first flowering plants to colonise the dunes is Sea Rocket (*Cakile maritima*). This sprawling crucifer provides a bright splash of colour amongst all the sand. Behind it is a clump of Lyme Grass (*Elymus arenarius*), one of the important dune forming grasses.

feed. If we were to disturb this wrack in the cool of the evening they would go jumping away in their thousands. You might be lucky enough in autumn or winter to see a Sanderling, one of the smallest and most agile of our shorebirds, chasing these sandhoppers, or better still, the more ponderous Turnstone snapping them up after pulling over the wrack.

'Quite often the first plants found growing along the strand line on the upper beach deriving nourishment from the buried debris, are fungi. One of them, the fairy-cup, *Geopyxis ammophila*, appears as a pale brown sphere which gradually opens into a cup with its rim at the level of the sand. But it is the first of the flowering plants which catches our attention and here is a marvellous carpet of Sea Rocket, *Cakile maritima*, just to the landward side of the wrack. This

large sprawling plant has pretty wallflower-like mauve flowers and, in fact, it belongs to the same family – the crucifers. It is an annual and, as you can see, by this time in the summer, it has really built up into quite a substantial clump. Its sprawling branches lying flat on the ground manage to collect quite a lot of sand and it has formed little dunes all along the beach here. It produces very abundant seed pods which are shaped rather like urns. They get washed out into the tide wrack and will be carried along the beach by the waves until they find a suitable niche where, next spring, the seeds can begin to grow. This is obviously a very chancy sort of existence and some summers there is very little Sea Rocket to be seen. This year, though, it is particularly abundant. It is a favourite plant for insects and you can see there are many bumblebees feeding on it. Another insect which you can find here is the Silver-Y Moth, which is a very pretty brown, black and purplish moth with a little silver "Y" on the forewing. The British population of this moth is entirely dependent on immigrants from the Continent in early summer which then breed here but do not overwinter.

'There is another early plant colonist on these dunes – here it is, this spiny-leaved plant, Prickly Saltwort, *Salsola kali*, which, like the Sea Rocket, you will find all around our coasts. It is also an annual and develops into a big rather sprawling bush by the end of the summer, helping to collect and consolidate its quota of sand. Typically these two plants grow together forming a zone along the upper strand line, as they do here. Obviously they must be able to tolerate quite a lot of salt because they are occasionally swamped by high tides and frequently subjected to spray drift. Saltwort like Glasswort, which we will meet later on, absorbs so much salt that it used to be burnt to provide soda for making soap and glass.

'Perhaps, at this point, we ought to ask ourselves a few more questions about the conditions in which some of these plants have to grow. It really is a most inhospitable habitat at first glance. For one thing, they don't have much soil to grow in, although they do derive some humus from the rotting debris on the strand line. But the main problem is one of insuring that they have enough water. As we can see, the surface layers of the sand are extremely dry. The rain falls and disappears almost immediately, but if we dig down a little way it begins to be moist, so that if the plant has developed a fairly deep and extensive rooting system it can draw on moisture. But that is not the only moisture problem, because on a very dry, breezy and sunny day like this, the plant is drawing up moisture and losing it by evaporation from its leaves. We know that on a day like this in the garden, very often a plant will wilt simply because its supply of water at the roots is not keeping pace with the loss of moisture through its leaves. The plants here on the exposed shore, have had to adapt themselves in various ways to avoid losing too much moisture. Sea Rocket has fleshy leaves which contain a large amount of water. Prickly Saltwort has a narrow spine-like leaf, so it has a relatively small surface area through which moisture can be lost. Both of the plants here are also low-growing, forming a mat of branches and leaves near the surface. This means that less of the plant is exposed to the desiccating effect of the wind so a certain amount of moisture is conserved under the mass of leaves. Most of the dune plants we will be looking at have some kind of device for making sure that they don't lose too much water.

'In addition to the Sea Rocket and Prickly Saltwort there are a number of other plants that are able to grow in these very early stages of dune formation. This is one of them. It is a species of Orache, the Halberd-leaved Orache, *Atriplex hastata*, and there is another, the Grass-leaved Orache, *Atriplex littoralis*. They are rather undistinguished plants with small green flowers in spikes. Another plant which grows successfully out here is the Sea Sandwort, *Honkenya peploides*. It has glossy green, fleshy leaves which are arranged along the stem in opposite pairs, making it very pleasing to look at. Although only a very small plant, growing two or three inches high, you can see that it has managed to collect a very considerable mound of sand around it. Furthermore, it has the ability to continue to grow up after being covered, and here you can see these new shoots coming through the wind-blown sand.

'Although these plants are important in their own way, the real builders of the sand dunes are the grasses and, if we walk along the front of the dunes here, we will be able to see the three main species.'

We made our way along to an area where the dunes were rising steeply out from the beach, where the grasses were obviously the dominant plants. Ted described them.

'The first grass to build up these fore-dunes is the Sand Couch Grass, *Agropyron junceiforme*. It is a relative of the Couch or Twitch which is such a pest in some of our gardens. This grass has a very extensive rooting system, running by underground stems or rhizomes, and then pushing up aerial shoots at frequent intervals. Like many of the plants here, it has the ability to grow up through the sand when it has been covered over. But its ability to grow upwards is limited and so we have to look for more powerful grasses to increase the height of the dune, and two that do that pre-eminently are the Marram Grass, *Ammophila arenaria*, and the Lyme Grass, *Elymus arenarius*.

'The Lyme Grass is not such an abundant grass around the coast of Britain as the

This sand dune which has been 'cliffed' back by last winter's tides clearly shows the extensive rooting system of Marram Grass (*Ammophila arenaria*). This grass is instrumental in building great ridges of sand around our coasts, some of which reach over thirty metres in height.

Marram. It is very striking, having a very distinctive colour – a blue-green on the upper side of the leaves, where it has these very prominent ribs and grooves. I spoke earlier about the devices for checking transpiration and, in these grasses, the stomata – the pores on the leaf through which moisture is lost – are mostly situated down in the grooves. Moreover, the grass ensures that they are further protected because in dry weather the leaf rolls up into a tube. This is especially noticeable in the Marram. Its appearance on a wet day, after rain, is quite different from that which we can see today, as the leaves would be open and flat.

'Along here the dune has been cliffed back by last winter's tides and it has exposed the rooting system of the Marram. Look at this tremendous mat of roots which not only helps to collect the sand but also binds and consolidates it. This little cliff shows that the Marram roots go down well over a metre or so and I have seen dunes with sections cut away to over two metres and the roots still go right down. Even at the bottom where they are dead, they are still performing the function of holding the sand together. Marram dunes in this country grow to about 20–25 metres (60–70 feet), but on the Continent they can go much higher, reaching over 33 metres (100 feet) on the Baltic coasts. As long as mobile sand is available Marram will go on building dunes almost indefinitely, but to flourish it does need a constant supply of new sand. It was widely used, incidentally, in coastal areas in the past for weaving mats – hence the old name of mat grass – and also for thatching stacks and buildings. Its importance for consolidating dunes as a sea defence was also clearly recognised and in many places – as on the Lincolnshire coast here – it was forbidden to cut it as long ago as the Fourteenth Century.'

We then headed inland, making our way between the handsome flower spikes of Marram and Lyme Grass. As we climbed up onto the ridge of the first dunes, Ted pointed out some of the smaller plants that were colonising the bare patches of sand between the clumps of grass.

'The first of the smaller grasses to come into the Marram community is the Sand Fescue, *Festuca rubra* var. *arenaria*, a variety of the Red Fescue. And here is a sedge, the Sand Sedge, *Carex arenaria*. This has long creeping roots which often extend in straight lines and, as you can see, send up shoots at quite regular intervals. It occurs through much of the dune succession and frequently colonises areas in the later fixed dunes, where vegetation has been removed and the sand laid bare.

'It would be appropriate here to reflect on the subject of plant succession. Vegetation never stands still, it moves from one stage to another, as you can see if you neglect your garden for any length of time. This succession happens for a number of reasons, but the most important one is that the plants, in the early stages of colonisation, create conditions which will eventually be suitable for other plants but unsuitable for themselves. So in a sense they are signing their own death warrants by creating these new conditions. You can see the processes of succession on sand dunes more clearly than in almost any other habitat. We started on the outer dunes and we have already seen the way the dunes are being built up, although here they are still mobile with open areas. Gradually as we move further inland we shall find that the dunes are completely stable and that some of the plants of these early stages, even the powerful Marram Grass, have died out or become very reduced in vigour. Eventually we shall reach the climax of the succession, the position of greatest stability, which at Gibraltar Point is the Sea Buckthorn scrub, which we can see on the dunes further inland.

'If we look at some of the plants in the open patches around here, we can see that many of them are plants which do well on bare ground inland – field and garden weeds. We've seen Creeping Thistle, for example, and along there is a large patch of Corn Sowthistle. There are some docks and the very tall plants are Great Prickly Lettuce. At our feet is a little succulent plant with yellow flowers carpeting the ground – the Biting Stonecrop. Further inland we have a lot of Ragwort and various hawkweeds and hawkbits. People often find their presence here surprising, but these are, after all, the conditions in which they flourish – open ground and lack of competition. Dunes must have been one of the few naturally disturbed habitats when most of the land was clothed in a dense cover of forest and other vegetation before the arrival of man with his axes and ploughs. Here, then, is probably one of the original homes of these weed species which were no doubt rarer in prehistoric times, than they are now.

'There is one plant here that is rather special and is highly characteristic of these mobile dunes. It is the Sea Holly, *Eryngium maritimum*. The first thing you notice about it are these handsome bluish-green leaves with their very attractive veining. The leaves are quite tough and leathery. They have a waxy cuticle over the surface which reduces the loss of moisture. In addition, the leaf surface is reduced by having spiny points, like a holly leaf – hence the name. The flowers are over now but they are rather like those of Teasel – a very handsome bluish-purple. This is a perennial plant but it dies right down to the base in the autumn and the seeds are usually spread by the remains of the plant blowing away. It has an enor-

mously long tap root which can be over a metre long. Every winter it tends to be covered by the sand and in the spring it grows up through this. Here, erosion has exposed part of the root and you can see each year's growth and can measure how much sand was deposited during the winter.

'I had hoped to show you the beautiful Sea Bindweed, but the dune where it used to grow has been eroded away by winter storms; an indication of the very unstable conditions in these early mobile dunes. The Sea Bindweed copes with the changing surface by producing an extensive creeping mat of roots which help to stabilise its imme-

Unlike its countryside and urban cousins, the Sea Bindweed (*Calystegia soldanella*) **does not climb but crawls and creeps about, binding the shingle.**

A Red-tailed Bumble-bee (*Bombus lapidarius*) feeding on a Sea Rocket flower.

The sand dunes are rich in calcium and provide a home for many snails which need the calcium to build their shells. These snails provide a welcome source of food for hungry thrushes. But how do they break into the shells? This rusting tin can provided a handy anvil on which the thrush can smash the snails' shells.

Opposite **Sea Holly** (*Eryngium maritimum*) is one of the most striking seaside plants, with its teasel-like flower head and boldly veined holly-like leaves. A banded snail is hiding from the heat of the midday sun under one of its thick leaves.

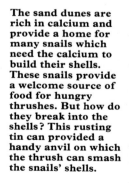

diate environment. However, it is helpless against the ravages of a powerful winter's gale.

'On the underside of one of the leaves of this Sea Holly you can see a very nice banded snail. There are a lot of snails on these dunes and you may well ask where they get the calcium with which to build up their shells. The dunes are, in fact, quite rich in calcium – the sand itself has a certain amount of it and a lot of calcium is also derived from the shells of molluscs that have been washed up from the sea. In fact, a number of the plants growing here are lime-loving plants, calcicoles. When we look at the older dunes we will find a number of plants that frequently grow on chalk downs.

'The other day I spotted a thrush's anvil –

in this case, an old piece of tin where it could crack open the snail shells. You could see that the thrush had done very well – most of the shells were from the handsome banded snails. It is obviously difficult for a thrush to find somewhere hard where he can break the shells, so the rusty tin had been quite heavily used.

'Another interesting thing amongst the Marram Grass are these heaps of seeds. These are the remains of the meal of a Long-tailed Field Mouse, a common mammal in these dunes. And almost certainly the Kestrels which we can see hovering overhead are looking for these mice. There are also Short-tailed Voles around and these are the favourite prey of Short-eared Owls. These large day-flying owls can often be seen quartering the marsh. While we are out here on these fore-dunes it is worth looking for the Robber Fly. He is rather sinister-looking and stays absolutely stationary, crouching on the sand until another insect comes within range. When this happens he darts up and catches it in his strong front legs. He will then puncture his victim with his proboscis, which possibly contains a toxic substance as the victim collapses almost immediately. He then sucks it dry. Occasionally Robber Flies kill too many insects and then you will find that they impale some of their dead victims on the sharply pointed ends of Marram leaves.'

We had now arrived on the landward side of the first ridge of dunes where there was a

tidal lagoon. We found some more of the strand line wrack but here there was less Prickly Saltwort and only the occasional clump of Sea Rocket. Ted described the scene.

'The majority of the plants here obviously prefer quieter more stabilised conditions, although they have to be just as salt tolerant as those out on the fore-dunes. Even more so, in fact, because the tide flows into this lagoon. One of the most noticeable plants here is the Shrubby Seablite, a shrub which occurs along the edges of shingle beaches and sand dunes. It reaches a height of up to a metre and eventually forms a wide bush with many branches springing up from the stem. Its centre of distribution is the Mediterranean and it reaches its northern limit in the British Isles. In fact, the bushes here may possibly be the most northerly specimens in Europe!

'Looking inland from here we can see something very different from the sandy dune landscape we have just walked across. And to explain it we have to consider how these parallel ridges of dunes are formed. Out at sea you will often notice that the larger waves are breaking in shallow water and they are building up ridges of sand and shingle some distance from the main beach. If a ridge of this kind becomes high enough it may stabilise and become an outer beach or offshore bar on which dunes can eventually develop. Between it and the shore the sea will still be able to flood in, forming a sheltered lagoon in which fine silts and mud will be deposited and on which saltmarsh will in time develop. This is what has happened here, which means that the dunes further inland, on the other side of this lagoon, were at one time the fore-shore. In fact, if we looked at old maps of this coastline we would see that it has been changing constantly in this way.

'We can walk down just a few feet from these sand dunes and have a look at the saltmarsh vegetation. We do not find the clear zonation that you have on a frontal saltmarsh directly open to the sea, but we can observe the early stages of colonisation. Saltmarsh plants have to live in a very difficult habitat, even more harsh, in a way, than the sand dunes, because although there is plenty of water, it is saltwater. The ways in which they have overcome this salt problem are fairly complex but to put it very simply, plants derive their water from the soil by exerting a form of suction pressure (called "osmotic pressure") in the roots which draws the water in. Now, if you put a garden plant into saltmarsh it would wilt and die in next to no time but these plants have adapted to growing in saltmarshes by, amongst other things, exerting a much greater suction pressure to overcome the effect of the salt in the soil. It is, perhaps, not surprising that few plants have managed to adapt to this terrain and it is therefore a very simple habitat in terms of plant composition. However, when you get to the edges of the marsh the conditions are not so extreme and if we walk along we will be able to see quite a variety of plants of the dune saltmarsh edge.

'Let's look at a conspicuous one first of all. This low shrubby plant with these grey spoon-shaped leaves and small yellow flowers is called Sea Purslane, *Halimione portulacoides*. It likes to grow in fairly well-drained places on the saltmarsh, hence it is on the edge here and you will also find it commonly on the banks of the creeks. It is a very good silt collector with its sprawling habit. It has an extraordinary leathery texture and if you look at it through a hand lens you can see that it is covered with a dense coat of fine hairs – another adaptation to prevent too much water loss.

'Then there is this rather pretty little plant with star-like pinkish flowers. This is the Greater Sea Spurrey which is quite abundant along saltmarsh edges.

'Further along here are two more plants of this saltmarsh fringe – Sea Milkwort and Sea Heath. The little prostrate plant with the oval leaves crowded along the stems radiating from a central rootstock, is the Sea Milkwort, *Glaux maritima*. It has pretty pink flowers in the axils of the leaves in May and June and occurs all round the coast of Britain. Sea Heath, *Frankenia laevis*, on the other hand, is much more localised; it occurs only on the south and east coasts of England and is at the very northern limit of its range here. It is a little shrubby plant which grows quite flat against the ground, sending out these long trailing stems, which eventually root down and extend the mat. The stems are an attractive reddish colour and it has small pink flowers.

Moving out now onto more open saltmarsh we have a lovely plant – the sea lavender. The species that grows just here – rather inappropriately named for this situation – is the Rock Sea Lavender, *Limonium binervosum*. It grows here on the slightly drier edges of the saltmarsh and is a

more slender plant with smaller leaves than the Common Sea Lavender, *Limonium vulgare*, which carpets large areas of saltmarsh.

'If we walk further out into the muddy areas we cross over a zone of almost pure Sea Meadow Grass, *Puccinellia maritima* – a low growing plant with prostrate stems which spread out to form a great mat. It forms a fine springy turf and where it is abundant it forms extensive grazing marshes. Here it is heavily grazed by rabbits.

'Here is a little bit of a creek that has left a bare expanse of mud and this is where we can see the two first colonists of saltmarshes apart from the vigorous cordgrasses which dominate the early zones of some marshes. This one is called Marsh Samphire or Glasswort, *Salicornia europaea*, along these coasts and it used to be regarded as quite an attractive dish, either boiled or pickled in vinegar. It is not to be confused with the Rock Samphire which belongs to quite a different family of plants, the Umbelliferae, and grows on cliffs. There is a passage in Shakespeare's *King Lear* where Edmund describes an imaginary view down a cliff face to the blind King Lear:

"The crows and choughs that wing the
    midway air
Show scarce so gross as beetles; half
    way down
Hangs one that gathers sampire,
    dreadful trade!
Methinks he seems no bigger than his
    head."

People who come here and see this samphire are very puzzled by that reference, but that is, of course, the Rock Samphire which is also gathered for food. Perhaps, it is best to call it by its other name, Glasswort, which refers to its use, like the Prickly Saltwort, as providing soda for making glass.

'The important point about Glasswort is its role in colonising bare mud. You can see if I pull up a plant, that it has a surprisingly long root with which to anchor itself in the mobile mud. It has probably been covered by several fresh layers of silt and has continued to come up through them. The plant consists mainly of jointed sections of stem with tiny scale-like leaves at the base of the joints from which numerous branches arise. The flowers have these tiny yellow anthers but they produce vast quantities of seeds which when it has died off are found all the way up the stem. These seeds provide an important winter source of food for large numbers of finches and other seed-eating birds, such as the handsome Snow Buntings which spend the winter here. The remaining seed is washed out by the tides, distributing the plant along the coast.

Here is the other of these early annual

Behind the first ridge of dunes is a salt-marsh lagoon. This is a plant which is typical of saltmarsh edges – Sea Purslane (*Halimone portulacoides*). 247

The masses of delicate pink flowers of the sea lavenders are one of the most impressive sites on our late-summer saltmarshes. These plants are Rock Sea Lavender (*Limonium binervosum*), but the most common sea lavender is *L. vulgare*.

colonists. This is the Annual Sea Blite, *Suaeda maritima*, which like the Glasswort is a succulent type of plant. It is usually prostrate, but where it grows in a dense sward with the Glasswort it tends to be more upright. It too has tiny flowers and produces abundant seed. Like Glasswort it plays an important role in arresting silt and mud and so building up the level of the marsh until the Sea Meadow Grass and plants like the

Sea Aster and the Common Sea Lavender can get going.'

From this saltmarsh lagoon and the fore-dunes we wound our way inland towards the older more stable dunes. The vegetation on these was markedly different, as Ted explained.

'We have moved inland now onto an older dune ridge where the vegetation cover is complete. Below us are mosses which are

some of the most efficient plants in fixing the surface of the sand once it is sufficiently stabilised for them to grow. There are several species characteristic of the early fixed dune stage, the most universal of which is *Tortula ruraliformis*. Another important moss is *Camptothecium lutescens*. Both have folded leaves with rolled-back margins, which are protective devices that help them to survive in dry periods. On dunes such as this, lichens also play an important part in covering the surface and they too, although becoming considerably shrivelled, are able to survive long dry spells. The two main types that grow here are *Cladonia* and *Peltigera* species, both of which are common on sand dunes. Where they grow thickly they give a grey colouring to the dunes and these are often then referred to as "grey dunes" as distinct from the younger, mobile "yellow dunes" where bare sand is still conspicuous.

'These fixed dunes have a greater variety of plants and some of the early colonists still survive here – we can see small non-flowering clumps of Marram Grass and Sand Sedge, which is rejuvenated as soon as a patch of sand is laid bare. However, most of the plants are now no longer exclusively seaside species. Over there are the stems of ragwort. They have been stripped of their leaves by the caterpillars of the Cinnabar Moth, which have bright black and yellow bands around their bodies, rather like a football jersey. The moth itself is scarlet and black and rather weak flying. Both the moth and the caterpillar are distasteful to birds and they use this bright warning coloration to make sure the birds don't forget once they have tasted one.

'Growing low to the ground we have the familiar Scarlet Pimpernel and here is Black Nightshade. Another common plant here is Hound's Tongue, which at this time of year has masses of seeds with little hooked spines that stick to your clothes.

'Covering the surface of a great deal of the dune is this creeping relative of the Blackberry – Dewberry, *Rubus caesius*. It sends out long stems which root down and has these distinctive fruits with a rather plum-like bloom to them. In the sheltered hollows in these stable dunes you can find a lot of interesting small plants such as the little Mouse-eared Chickweed, Thyme-leaved Sandwort, Early Forget-me-not, Rue-leaved Saxifrage as well as various tares and vetches.

They make miniature gardens when they are at their best in April and May. One of the more striking plants that you can find here is the Viper's Bugloss with its tall spikes of blue flowers; this is a typical plant also of the chalklands.

'If the vegetation here is not restricted by grazing or mowing it will "climax" into scrub. All around us we can see this climax vegetation in the form of a handsome shrub called Sea Buckthorn, *Hippophae rhamnoides*. It is native along the east coast of England, but has been planted in many dune areas in the south and west. It has silvery-grey leaves and is protected by wickedly sharp spines which effectively deter rabbits from eating all but the youngest shoots. The undersides of the leaves, incidentally, have a dense covering of silvery-white scales, which is yet another development to check transpiration. Sea Buckthorn has separate male and female plants and, since it spreads mainly by means of powerful underground runners, plants of the same sex occur together. This is most clear when the bright orange berries ripen on the female bushes, which they are just beginning to do now. They are at their best in October and

Above **A view across from the Sea Buckthorn covered dunes to the 'yellow' dunes of the foreshore with areas of saltmarsh in-between. The succession from the open sandy beach to the high scrub-covered dunes can be seen all around our coast where suitable conditions prevail. So pick your way with care next time you cross a landscape like this – you will be amazed what you will discover.**

The bright orange berries of Sea Buckthorn (*Hippophae rhamnoides*) amongst the distinctive silvery-grey leaves. These berries provide a feast for visiting winter thrushes in the late autumn and provide an eye-catching show of colour during an autumn stroll in the sand dunes.

November and during this time they form a very important food supply for migrant thrushes, particularly Fieldfares from Scandinavia. As you can see it forms a dense thicket up to three metres high.

There are other shrubs in this zone and by the path here is a venerable old Elder covered with lichens. There is also Hawthorn and Wild Privet, and Dog Rose. All this dense scrub provides a marvellous area for nesting birds. Whitethroats, Sedge Warblers, Linnets, Dunnocks and Yellowhammers are all common here. Later in the year on a favourable day in late summer or autumn the bushes are often alive with

migratory birds, moving south along the coast.

'The sheltered open areas in the scrub are also good places for quite a variety of butterflies such as the Meadow Brown and the Hedge Brown, the Small Heath and the Small Copper, as well as immigrants such as the Red Admiral and the Painted Lady.'

Before we made our way home Ted pointed out some of the ways in which sand dunes have been developed and some of the pressures that are threatening them.

'Where there are woodlands near the coast, sand dunes have often been invaded by tree species and many dune areas have

been planted with Scots and other pines. Because they have the right kinds of contours and are well drained with a fine short turf some sand dunes are much sought after as golf-courses, which incidentally, are often very good places for flowers, especially in the "roughs". The dunes are also, of course, very popular with seaside holidaymakers and on some parts of the coast this has led to serious erosion problems as the dunes are very unstable, as we have seen, and will not withstand a lot of trampling.'

At Gibraltar Point the paths through the dunes were clearly marked and often laid with old railway sleepers, keeping erosion

by the visitors to a minimum. It had been a real pleasure out walking with Ted Smith and we had seen a vast spectrum of seaside plants and animals, yet we had only scratched the surface. How different it must all be in depths of winter when the Marram has turned a delicate straw colour and the dunes are white with snow, and flocks of Snow Buntings are feeding out on the dunes. Or in spring when a whole range of different plants are in flower and the warblers are singing from the Sea Buckthorn thicket. It had certainly been shown to us that there is a fascinating world to discover amongst the dunes.

A Small Copper Butterfly (*Lycaena phlaeas*), **feeding on Ragwort in a sunny dune hollow. During a good summer this butterfly may produce three generations and can be seen on the wing from April right through to October.**

Wildlife organisations to join

Amateur Entomologists Society (AES)
355 Hounslow Road, Hanworth, Feltham, Middx. TW13 5JH.
Holds meetings, study groups and passes on information about
entomology via a quarterly bulletin. It is particularly interested in
the encouragement of young people and novices.

Botanical Society of the British Isles (BSBI)
c/o Department of Botany, British Museum (Natural History),
Cromwell Road, London SW7 5BD.
This Society promotes all aspects of plant conservation but is
particularly interested in British flowering plants and ferns.
Organises surveys of British plants and communicates information
via its regular Journal, Newsletter and other publications.
Members can be amateur or professional botanists.

British Butterfly Conservation Society
Sternes, York Road, Beverley, East Yorkshire, HU17 7AN.
Encourages interest in butterflies through meetings and
exhibitions, and via its members publication 'The News'. Its aims
are to protect British butterflies both by field conservation and
captive breeding and release.

British Trust for Conservation Volunteers (BCTV)
26 St. Mary's Street, Wallingford, Oxon OX10 0EU.
Young people over 16, undertake practical conservation work on
nature reserves and other wildlife sites. The Trust co-operates
closely with the RSNC, local authorities and other wildlife
organisations. It produces a quarterly magazine 'Conserver' and
produces handbooks on conservation techniques.

British Trust for Ornithology (BTO)
Beech Grove, Station Road, Tring, Herts' HP23 5NR
Appeals especially to the serious amateur ornithologist. Undertakes
ambitious surveys and research programmes and is involved in the
Bird Ringing Scheme with a team of professional biologists. The
Trust produces a quarterly journal 'Bird Study' and a newsletter
'BTO News'.

Council for the Protection of Rural England (CPRE)
4 Hobart Place, London SW7W 0HY
Promotes the improvement, protection and preservation of the
English countryside. Publishes a magazine 'Countryside Campaign'
three times each year.

**Council for the Protection of Rural Wales (Cymdeithas
Diogelu Harddwch Cymru) (CPRW)**
31 High Street, Welshpool, Powys SY21 7JP
Activities and aims similar to CPRE. Produces a newsletter three
times each year.

Ramblers' Association
105 Wandsworth Road, London SW8
Protects the public's rights of access to the 120,000 miles of public
footpath through England and Wales. It also encourages the care
and preservation of the countryside as a whole. It produces a
members' magazine 'Rucksack' three times a year.

Royal Society for Nature Conservation (RSNC)
22, The Green, Nettleham, Lincoln LN2 2NR
This is the United Kingdom's largest voluntary organisation
concerned with all aspects of wildlife conservation. It runs nature
reserves and coordinates the activities of 46 county Nature
Conservation Trusts. It produces an illustrated quarterly magazine
'Natural World', free to members, which is a forum for all those
interested or involved in the whole range of conservation work.
Watch: The Watch Trust for Environmental Education is
sponsored by the RSNC and *The Sunday Times*. It is a national
club for 8 to 18 year-olds, with more than 15,000 members and
250 area groups.

Royal Society for the Protection of Birds (RSPB)
The Lodge, Sandy, Bedfordshire, SG19 2DL
The largest organisation concerned with the conservation of birds
and their habitats. It has over 360,000 members kept in touch
through their magazine 'Birds'. It has been the major driving force
in persuading Parliament to pass legislation to protect birds and is
actively involved in enforcing these laws. The Society runs its own
reserves.

Royal Entomological Society (RES)
41 Queens Gate, London SW7 5HU
Society for amateur and professional entomologists which
encourages the study of insects. It holds meetings and symposia
and publishes a number of journals and a series of identification
guides.

Scottish Wildlife Trust
25 Johnston Terrace, Edinburgh EH1 2NH
The national organisation of Scotland concerned with all aspects of
wildlife conservation. It liaises with the government and
landowners on wildlife issues and arranges lectures for public
information. It runs over 40 nature reserves and produces a journal
'Scottish Wildlife' three times a year.

Wildfowl Trust
Slimbridge, Gloucester GL2 7BT.
Sir Peter Scott set up the Trust in 1946 to study and conserve
wildfowl. It now runs seven reserves throughout the country and
has the most comprehensive collection of wildfowl to be found
anywhere in the world.

The Woodland Trust
Westgate, Grantham, Lincs NG31 6iL
A registered charity which buys up areas of broadleaved woodland
to protect them.

World Wildlife Fund (WWF – UK)
11–13 Ockford Road, Godalming, Surrey GU7 1QU
Is an international charitable organisation which, in the United
Kingdom, concerns itself with the relationship between
agricultural policy and habitat loss, badgers and bovine
tuberculosis, and the problems of grey seals and fisheries amongst
many others. It also works on international issues such as trade in
endangered species and the exploitation of resources in Antarctica.

Index